Sex Bomb

First published in the USA as *Great Big Beautiful Doll* by
Barricade Books Inc., Fort Lee, New Jersey

ISBN 978-1-903854-68-6

Typset by e-type

Printed and bound in Great Britain by CPD

MILO BOOKS
The Old Weighbridge
Station Road
Wrea Green
Lancs
PR4 2PH

Sex Bomb

The Life and Death of Anna Nicole Smith

Eric & D'eva Redding

Milo Books Ltd

About the Authors

Eric Redding has been a photographer in Houston, Texas, for the past twenty-five years. His clients include Elizabeth Taylor, Kirk Douglas, Ursula Andress and Beyonce Knowles. D'eva Redding is a hairstylist and makeup artist who works with Eric in their photography studio and salon. The Reddings live in Houston and Las Vegas.

Dedication

We would like to convey our sympathies to Anna Nicole's family and loved ones. We are especially saddened that Anna's baby, Dannielynn, will never know her mother except from photos, writings, and her film and TV work. She will also have her mother's last movie, *Illegal Aliens*, which Anna did not live to see released.

Additionally, we want to extend our condolences to the family of E. Pierce Marshall, whose death was certainly a surprise considering his father, J. Howard Marshall II's living until ninety.

And lastly, D'eva and I would like to thank you, our readers. We appreciate your patronage and hope we've given you one side of the life of Anna Nicole Smith, our Great Big Beautiful Doll.

Foreword

ON 8 FEBRUARY 2007, a police operator called for urgent paramedic assistance for a woman who had collapsed in room 607 of the Seminole Hard Rock Hotel, in Hollywood, Florida.

Her voice calm, the female operator gave no indication of the frenzy about to be unleashed. "She's not breathing, and she's not responsive," said the operator, before pausing and adding…."She's um, actually, Anna Nicole Smith."

The call lasted precisely thirty-one seconds. Six minutes later a desperate fight to save her life began. An hour later, Anna Nicole Smith was pronounced dead at the age of thirty-nine.

"I can confirm that she is deceased. It's as shocking to me as to you guys," Ronald Rale, her lawyer, said. "Poor Anna Nicole."

It was about ten years earlier that D'eva and I turned on the television and found ourselves watching a horror show. It wasn't Freddy Krueger or hockey-masked Jason – we wished it had been. No, what we saw was much more real and certainly more scary. We saw a friend in total self-destruct.

A once-stunning girl, still young at twenty-eight, was a caricature of the beauty she had been. Her moment in the spotlight was continuing, but it had become a harsh glare illuminating dissipation, not happiness.

We were watching a rerun of *The Howard Stern Show*. We were no fans of his, but that night, Anna Nicole Smith was sitting across from the self-proclaimed "King of All Media" in his small studio, and at one time, we had been among her biggest fans.

Stern was being particularly smutty. His commentary was lascivious, his so-called humor characteristically straight out of the gutter. Yet there was something *un*characteristic about Stern that night, something unsettling.

Howard Stern, who usually didn't create a blip on the Sensitivity Scale, was trying to be kind to Anna.

It was apparent to anyone watching the show that she was higher than a kite on something, maybe heroin – which we had been told was her new drug of choice – or maybe cocaine, an old favorite. Her speech was slurred, her eyes barely open. Stern knew it, too, and made, for him, gentle comments on her condition. She gave, in political parlance, a "nondenial denial" about her physical state, but her flat, dull tone belied the words. She spoke just above a whisper.

While Stern would never stop the interview – he makes his living out of pandering to the ugly side of the world – he did wear kid gloves for a while. It wasn't like him. He was showing pity. Can you imagine being pitied by Howard Stern?

In only a few years, Anna Nicole Smith had gone from waitress in a fried-chicken restaurant to international-media princess, from *Playboy* centrefold to professed grieving widow of a billionaire, from a reed-thin high-school dropout to a symbol of overripe voluptuousness.

The journey had been recorded on front pages around the world, on talk shows, the big screen, and in courtrooms. What the world saw had more than a few heads shaking in disbelief. What we saw had our heads shaking in sorrow.

They say fame is a harsh taskmaster, and that has never been more true than with Anna Nicole Smith. But fame alone didn't bring her to the chair across from Howard Stern. Like us all, she had some control of her own fate. It was her drive, her lust for power, money, and sex that brought her into that studio.

D'eva and I were eyewitnesses to that bizarre passage. We met Anna in 1991 and contributed to her early successes. I took the Polaroids that led her to a *Playboy* centrefold. D'eva held her hand, assuring her she didn't have to be frightened about showing that remarkable body of hers. I watched as my talented wife, a hair and makeup stylist, transformed an unsophisticated girl into a glittering jewel right there in the studio. I was the lucky guy who got to tell Anna her dreams were about to come true after getting a call from Playboy Enterprises.

And as she became famous, we witnessed the dark side – drinking, drug abuse, reckless sex. We watched her as she turned on old friends and relatives, and disregarded her own safety and that of her son.

In 1996, we wrote a book about her life, called *Great Big Beautiful Doll*. In the years that followed, much happened in the world of Anna Nicole Smith – fascinating and foul.

We thought it was time for an update.

Eric Redding
March 2007

Chapter 1

TEXAS IS A giant state of contradictions and contrasts as big as its map. It is Black Lexuses and valet parking in Dallas and rifle racks and six-packs in El Paso. It is Silicon Valley in Austin and cotton picking in Lubbock.

It embraces the sprawl of Houston, with its 1,630,000 inhabitants, and the backwater of Mexia, with the little more than 6,300 people within its boundaries.

So it is little wonder that Anna Nicole Smith sprang from Texas – Houston and Mexia in particular. For she, too, was a mix of contradictions, contrasts, and was big, like the state. Her overboard flamboyance, outrageous ambition, and unbounded self-indulgence was quintessentially Texas. Which isn't to say that everyone and everything there comport themselves in such fashion. However, it would be hard to imagine Anna Nicole Smith as a product of Missouri or Massachusetts. It had to be Texas, and Texas it was.

Despite Anna Nicole Smith living at the tail end of the twentieth century, when record-keeping has reached a near–art form, one of the few things that is agreed upon about her background is that she was born on 28 November 1967, in Houston, as Vickie Lynn Hogan. From that point on, details get a little murky and change depending on who's doing the telling.

Her mother, born Virgie Mae Tabers, already had a son from a previous marriage. She had wed a David Luther Tacker in 1966, at the age of just fourteen – in Texas, girls can marry as young as thirteen and boys at fourteen with parental consent – and had a son,

David Junior, soon after. Their marriage lasted just a few months and next Virgie, whose disastrous relationships with men would be mirrored by her daughter, hooked up with Donald Hogan, a laidback carpenter who dressed like a cowpoke and bore a passing resemblance to the country singer Carl Perkins. Donald and Virgie were married in February 1967 in Harris County, Texas. He was nineteen years old and she was still only fifteen.

Nine months later, little Vickie Lynn was born. And a couple of years after that, Donald walked out. Why he abandoned his young wife and child is unclear but it would have a profound effect on his daughter. She would grow up without a natural father, and although he left too soon for her to have any memories of him, she would later pine for his affection. "I always wanted a father," she said. "I used to try to find him by looking him up in the phone book."

Virgie didn't stay single for long. In February 1971 she married Donald Ray Hart, who already had a daughter, Shauna, and a year later they would have a son, also called Donald.

Donald Ray and Virgie raised their four children – David from her first marriage, Vickie Lynn from her second, Donald from her third, and Shauna – in Houston, where Virgie was a cop. Little is know about David, now in his early forties, except that he became an FBI agent. Shauna later worked as a bus driver, ferrying handicapped children between different schools, before marrying a businessman and having two children. According to his mother, Donald junior suffered a brain injury when he was three years old, which crippled his whole left side. He would later serve time in Huntsville Prison, Texas, for kidnapping.

"Growing up we were always very poor," remembered Vickie. "My family life was disrupted when my parents got divorced. I moved back and forth between aunts and uncles and my mother. I have lots of cousins." Vickie seems to have been starved of attention, which would explain why she grew to crave it so much. In later life – admittedly while under the influence of drink or drugs – she would mark dark allegations of childhood mistreatment and beatings, even sexual assaults. 'You want to hear all the things she did to me?" she slurred. "You want to hear all the things she let my father do to me, or my brother do to me? Or my sister? All the beatings and the whippin's and the rape? That's my mother. That's my mom!" None of these allegations have ever been substantiated.

And after their childhood, Vickie cut all three half siblings out of her life, along with her mother.

Virgie said later: "I have three other children. And she was raised with all of them. And all of them love her. And, you know, it wasn't just me that she cut out, not cut out, but refused to see, it was all her brothers and sisters. And she was close to all of them."

Virgie would marry three more times, to Joe D. Thompson, James T. Sanders and finally James H. Arthur. Unsurprisingly, from the mess of various wrecked relationships, a brood of half brothers and sisters also emerge, with many only too willing to share their stories of Anna Nicole, even though they barely knew her.

From the age of fifteen, Vickie had little to do with her natural mother. Occasionally, she has even insisted that Virgie is not her mother, telling more than one person that Virgie's younger sister, Kay Beall, was really her mother and not her aunt. Vickie would under-score this contention by calling Kay "Mother" or "Mama Two."

This wishful thinking probably arose from the tension between Vickie and Virgie, who never got along well. Vickie would make claims of abuse such as being handcuffed to her bed so she couldn't sneak out at night. This story has some plausibility given that Virgie Hart has been a deputy sheriff in Harris County – which takes in Houston – for the past twenty years. But family members don't give the allegations much credence.

"Virgie was a good mother," Kay Beall says. "But you can't talk to her about anything. All my kids can talk to me no matter what. Even if it was about sex or what. If they need something, they can talk to me about it. I wasn't just their mother, I was their friend."

Kay Beall has another, somewhat stranger, explanation for Vickie's contention she was Kay's child. When Kay was ten, she lived with her sister and Donald Hogan, and she claims that Hogan raped her. "That's why Vickie always thought that maybe I got pregnant.

I couldn't get pregnant. I was still a child. But she would always try to make herself believe…that I was her mother. That I gave up the baby to Virgie."

In later years, as Anna Nicole Smith, Vickie would tell people there was a chance she was Marilyn Monroe's baby, conveniently ignoring the fact that Monroe died in 1962, five years before she was born. "Was she spaced out?" Kay Beall asked when she heard this story. "Someone's messing with her head. I saw Virgie have that baby. That's Virgie's baby."

Vickie Lynn was a student at Durkee Elementary School and Aldine Intermediate School in Houston, before moving to Mexia to attend high school and live with Kay Beall full time, although she had been a frequent visitor when she was younger. Virgie would later give a version of why her daughter moved in with her aunt. "She got hooked up with the wrong crowd in school, and I was just trying to get away from that crap, so we let her go live with her aunt, who lived in Mexia, Texas, for that semester."

Aunt Kay said, "The house she used to live in had no heat and Vickie would huddle under the thin blankets on her narrow bed. She just never had enough food or enough love and that's the reason why she became so absolutely ruthless."

According to her step-father, Donald Hart, in the TV documentary *Dark Roots: The Anna Nicole Smith Story*, "She snuck out of the house and met an older man and went off with him and got caught by her mother and brought back home. Then her mother took her to Mexia to live with her aunt Kay."

Kay, who worked as an attendant at a state school for mentally ill children, told *People* magazine, "She used to come over and stay with me and clean my house. I'd give her five dollars of my food stamps to let her go to the store and buy some candy." As part of Anna Nicole Smith's dirt-poor persona, stories are told of her stealing toilet paper from a local restaurant because Kay couldn't afford to buy any.

Her aunt converted the front porch into a third, tiny bedroom for her niece. Vickie could look out of her bedroom window at a rubbish tip framed against a skyline of disused oil cranes. Her schoolfriends used to make fun of the street she lived in – Nigger Creek Road. In truth, there wasn't much to smile about.

Mexia, pronounced *Ma-hay-a*, isn't much of a town. "Dusty" is the adjective used most to describe it. Set in flat farmland, its main street is usually empty, and its movie theatre has been converted into one of the town's twenty churches. If you're employed, it's most likely at the state home for the retarded.

Mexia, situated halfway between Interstates 35 and 45, some ninety miles south of Dallas, did have a brush with prosperity. It was once a boom town, after a natural gas discovery in 1920 saw the population swell to 35,000, almost overnight. Unable to cope with the influx, the town's elders declared martial law. It was also the site of the largest World War II internment camp in Texas, where prisoners from Rommel's Afrika Corps sweltered in the sun behind twin rows of barbed wire.

That was long ago. The annual star-spangled quilt show is about as exciting as it gets now. Mexia's older neighbourhoods are now a mix of clapboard houses and trailer-trash mobile homes. A few years ago, the average income for a family was less than $30,000, compared to nearly $46,000 statewide, and one of every five families still lived below the poverty line. About half the population is white.

Mexia's other claim to fame comes in the form of Ray Rhodes, former defensive coach of the Super Bowl champions the San Francisco Forty-niners, and later head coach of the Philadelphia Eagles. In the mid-Sixties, Rhodes was one of the outstanding athletes in southeast Texas, enough to make him popular in any small Texas town. He was great on the football field, the basketball court, and running track at Dunbar, an all-black high school in Mexia.

To come in compliance with federal desegregation rulings, Texas set up a "Freedom of choice" plan. Students, black or white, could choose which schools they wished to attend. Interesting concept, but in practice it meant the white kids stayed in the white schools, and the black kids in the black schools,

The head football coach at the white Mexia High School persuaded Rhodes's father to transfer his son. Because Ray Rhodes went to Mexia High School, other black students followed. The integration of Mexia High was one of the trouble-free exceptions in the Deep south. Ray Rhodes as town celebrity would be a hard act to follow for anyone. Vickie Lynn/Anna Nicole would never come close to filling the town with similar pride. Nevertheless, she deemed Mexia her "hometown," despite having lived there only a few years.

Being nationally associated with Anna Nicole Smith today would seem to be an honour many residents of Mexia could live without. As Bob Wright, the editor of the *Mexia Daily News*, has put it with admirable diplomacy, "She's definitely adopted the town more than the town adopted her."

At Mexia high school, where she arrived to join the ninth grade but failed to finish the tenth, Vickie went by the name of Nikki and Cricket and was not in the running for Miss Popularity. "She was just so common," a former classmate sniffed. "I'll tell you one thing," another Mexia resident said, "she's not home grown." Long after she'd packed up and gone, the citizens of Mexia took to wearing T-shirts bearing the logo: "There's more to Mexia than Anna Nicole Smith."

"A nerd" was how her cousin Melinda described Vickie in high school. (Vickie/Anna sometimes refers to Melinda as her "niece", further confusing her family tree.) Certainly, she was never going to win any gold stars for academic achievement.

"I remember her but she went by Nikki Hart then," said maths teacher Glenn McGuire. "I really remember her more as the girl who worked at the fried chicken restaurant in town. It's not like we're proud. You don't see signs when you come into town saying: 'This is the home of Anna Nicole Smith'. There are better things to be known for. It is not a path that I would recommend to our students."

On a video later recorded for *Playboy*, Vickie admitted that "I wasn't very popular in high school." However, she attributed that to her being flat-chested. She stares out of Mexia High School's 1985 yearbook, an attractive but unsmiling young woman with a sullen look.

Others in the town have a grudging respect for the self-made sex bomb. "Some people have it that she disgraced this town," said Alan Campbell, a burly trucker in the local natural gas industry. "But I don't think that she did. She had a goal and she did it."

Her advanced education ended in a fistfight with another student and expulsion. At seventeen, she went to work at Jim's Krispy Fried Chicken, a single-storey restaurant with a parking lot out front that, since her death, has become a tourist attraction. "She used to serve me chicken," said Don O'Brian, a retired steel mill mechanic. "She was a little skinny girl with brown hair. She wasn't beautiful, but she wasn't ugly – everyone liked her."

James Buchanan, who used to own a rival fast food outlet, admitted: "People have a soft spot for her. She went from being a nobody to a somebody."

For all the fame that was later to come her way, she claimed that serving fried chicken for a few dollars a week was the happiest time of her life. Despite her insecurities about the small size of her breasts, Vickie quickly realised that she was popular with the boys. "Working at Jim's Krispy Chicken was the best, best, best time of my life," she later said. "I was happier then than I've ever been. There was me and my friend serving tables and the guys would come from miles around to see us."

When Vickie wasn't taking orders from customers or lugging platefuls of food, she had eyes for baby-faced Billy Smith, who worked in the kitchen. A year younger than her, he had been a fellow pupil at Mexia High and was slim, fair and quiet. He paid her no mind, which drove her nuts with frustration.

"I could see men kind of liked me but there was one boy, a short order cook called Billy Wayne Smith, who paid me no attention," she recalled. "He drove me crazy. I chased him and chased him the way young girls do until I finally got him and married him. By then, of course, I wasn't interested."

They married on 4 April 1985, in Limestone County, two

teenagers who were simply not mature enough for adult life.

"Oh God, he was such an asshole. He was sixteen, I was seventeen, and it was a disaster," said Vickie. "For our wedding I wore a short dress – he had on jeans. We got married and had Chinese food then went home and went to bed. That night there was no sex, nothing, it was like I was waiting on him to make a move, but nothing happened. Until I did *Playboy* magazine, no man had ever seen me naked, not even my husband. I was very coy in those days."

Married life in Mexia turned out to be even duller than being single. "He was really nice to me when we were dating but when we got married I wasn't allowed to go out of the house or go to the store. He was so jealous." His jealousy, according to Vickie, was punctuated by his fists. Years later, Billy denied the abuse, claiming that only once did he lose his temper. "I kicked her and she fell out of bed. I didn't hit her. I guess she was looking for an excuse to get out of the marriage."

Vickie said she thought having a baby might save the marriage or at least make things better, but the arrival of their son, Daniel, didn't improve matters, which were not helped by living in a cramped mobile home. "It was not a particularly sexual relationship and I knew there had to be more to life than that. I stayed with him for two years – I was so naive."

"She was all excited about having a baby," recalled her aunt Elaine Tabers. "It was like, this is mine, nobody can take him away. It ended up in divorce and a lot of bitterness, there was a lot of battles between the two of them, and it didn't turn out, it was ugly."

The marriage collapsed after two years, although papers show it was not officially ended until 1993.

In another interview, with *LA Magazine*, Anna Nicole was scathing about life in Mexia. "I grew up in a small town, where there was totally nothing to do. All the kids would go up and down the drag and talk and drink beer. I did it, too – me and my friend Jo Lynn. Everyone in Texas drinks beer. I drink it when I go home. I think Mexia is a place to grow up in and then retire. I don't think there's a middle.

Chapter 1

"You should get out during the middle part 'cause all women do is get pregnant. Real young girls get pregnant and have babies. I got pregnant there and had a baby. But I wanted to get pregnant. Luckily, I got out when I did or I'd probably have five kids now. I got married at 17. But my husband was really physically abusive and jealous and would never let me go out. And I thought, well, if I was to have a baby, I would never be lonely – because he was at work all day. So I just kind of flushed my pills down the toilet. And then I got pregnant and had Daniel."

She was to recall later that at least one positive thing came out of the doomed relationship with Billy Smith. "I'd always been a skinny, anaemic thing with no chest but then I got pregnant with my son Daniel and I went from 8st 13lb to 15st 11lb and my boobs were like, phew! Jeez, they were like melons, almost as big as my mom's, which were a double-D. Then I had my son and they went all the way back down again. I hated it, I had skin hanging down and it was disgusting. I made the decision to have implants after that."

Packing the few belongings she had, Vickie Lynn, her six-month-old baby, and her ambitions slipped out of the squalid caravan and set off for the Big Time.

Chapter 2

HOUSTON. 1987. A great place for a great big beautiful doll with ambitions that went beyond frying chicken.

Dallas was a town of pretensions, a banking city where no one jaywalks. Houston was wide open, a boom-or-bust oil town, where each new skyscraper tried to outdo that last one. It was a place, as writer Mimi Swartz put it, of "big deals and big deeds, where self-invention has achieved the status of religion."

Vickie Lynn Hogan Smith was ready and more than willing to reinvent herself. Having dumped her husband and with a six-month-old baby in tow, Vickie did what any good red-blooded American girl would do — she moved in with Mama. Why either Vickie or Virgie, based on their acrimonious history, would think they could spend quality time together is anyone's guess. The room-mating didn't last long and was highlighted by constant arguing. Vickie then packed up again, leaving baby Daniel with Virgie, and moved into a trailer park with Deborah Hopkins, a hairdresser she knew. Hopkins was the one friend that Vickie would stick with through the years. She was the one who changed Vickie's hair color from the unremarkable shade of mouse-brown to traffic-stopping platinum. (Although as Anna Nicole, Vickie would often insist that was the colour that sprang from her gene pool.)

There was still the problem of putting food on the table and clothes on her back. Vickie tried waitressing at Red Lobster and worked at the local Wal-Mart store, but it didn't take a rocket scientist — of which Houston has many — to figure out that minimum wages and minimum tips would not finance the good times and excitement that she was craving.

What was a girl with little education and few marketable skills to do? If she was good-looking, which Vickie undeniably was, and willing, which Vickie proved unquestionably to be, you hit the topless bar circuit.

In Houston there exists a world that could send the Christian Coalition's Ralph Reed into a perpetual hissy fit. It is what the locals call "titty bars." Some are dark, sleazy, and only a cut above a truck stop. They are the kind of place that might make you send your clothes to be fumigated after spending a couple of minutes in them. The dancers who gyrate near-nude on the stage or practically in the customers' laps are often hard looking, as if from too much drugs, booze, and boyfriend abuse.

In 1987, at the other end of the titty bar spectrum was Rick's Cabaret. It boasted a faux-mansion décor with chandeliers and carpeting, good food and liquor, and dancers who were truly beautiful. But more than that, the women had that *Playboy* aura – the girl next door, that is if the girl next door was gorgeous and willing to drop her clothes for a room full of ogling men. These women exuded enough of a wholesome image that when it was reported that some showed up with their college course schedule to coordinate it with their dancing schedule, the story actually sounded plausible.

Rick's was the brainchild of Dallas Fontenot, who had operated run-of-the mill topless joints around Houston for years. He took over the lease of a disco that had hung on after Gloria Gaynor stopped getting air time, and he sought to fill a void. He wanted to create a "gentleman's club," a place for guys with Volvos in the driveways and nice dividend cheques at the end of the quarter, guys who wanted to be *in* topless bars but not be seen entering or leaving them.

Fontenot succeeded. Rick's rose above being a mere titty bar. It boasted a business clientele, a stage with a wind machine, lifetime VIP memberships and beer at seven bucks a bottle. There' was a no-tattoo rule for the girls. It was a place where celebrities – men primarily – flocked when they were in town or wanted a night on the town. One was country and western star George Strait, a native Texan known for his honky tonk sound and sometimes referred to as the "King of Country." Warren Moon, the former Houston Oiler quarterback and the only player ever to be enshrined by both the Pro Football Hall of Fame and Canadian Football Hall of Fame, was another visitor. British actor Michael Caine also dropped by, along with Orenthal James (O.J.) Simpson, in his pre-pariah days. Considered one of the greatest running backs of all time, Simpson swapped pro football for acting but became infamous for having been tried for the murder of ex-wife Nicole Brown Simpson and her friend Ronald Goldman in 1994.

If an object of the paparazzi's attention didn't want to draw any, there were private rooms from which the customer could watch the dancers. Corporate memberships were sold with the promise that "We'll do everything in our power to make your next business deal your best business deal."

Vickie Lynn Smith started out a club somewhere in the middle of the topless hierarchy, a place called the Executive Suites, which had no connection, corporate or otherwise, to the hotel chain of the same name.

The now-defunct Executive Suites was on the city's north side, conveniently near Houston International Airport. It catered to out-of-town businessmen and even provided limo service to the airport and nearby hotels.

Its manager, Terry Allen, remembers Vickie Lynn as being "fresh-looking" without the tough edge of a veteran. "I could tell she had a lot of potential…as she certainly was a pretty girl."

She was pretty enough that the club used her in one of its brochures. What Vickie wasn't enough of was endowed. She was a big girl at five feet eleven inches and between 160 and 180 pounds, big everywhere except where it counted in the topless bars. Which was one reason she worked the day shift, the time relegated for those were not so pretty or were flat chested, or overweight.

Vickie once told an interviewer that she initially thought stripping was sinful. Then someone told her that God loved her naked body, and after that she thought stripping might not be a bad way to get to heaven. All she knew about heaven was that it had golden floors.

"When Anna first started, she was very naïve," Ritchie Avantez, a former manager at Rick's, told the documentary *Dark Roots*. "She caught on fast. She really had a good look, she had a sweet personality, down-home Texas style. Anna was born for the business."

She certainly wasn't going to let any physical shortcomings hold her back. Soon after being hired, she approached another dancer, Terri Cobble, a brunette with long straight hair who favoured guys with leather jackets and motorcycles. She wanted Terri to teach her "how to dance seductively and give the men what they wanted," Terri recalls. "Vickie was a very quick learner and really became quite a seductive dancer in a hurry."

It wasn't long before Vickie had a following of regulars and was making more than $200 a day. Not being much of a money manager, she asked Terry Allen to set aside some of her earnings. Vickie had realized the truth of the topless business – the bigger the breasts, the bigger the tips – and she was saving for plastic surgery.

Despite the money she was bringing in, Vickie's nest egg didn't grow much. She kept asking for withdrawals from Terry Allen, with different excuses for why she needed the money. The real reason was probably that having a good time was becoming more expensive as Vickie was discovering new ways to have one. At some point, she added pills and drugs to her intake of alcohol. Wally Rodriguez, the hairstylist-makeup artist at Rick's Cabaret, says that "while Vickie would go do her dances and talk to her customers, I would have to hold her drugs for her, so she would not lose them. Her favourite drug or pill that she liked to take was Xanax [a popular prescription tranquilizer]…and boy, did she devour those…she lived on them. She used to keep them all in a Baggie and carry them around in…whatever."

According to Wally, Vickie was embarrassed by the size of her feet and would buy shoes that were too small. She would then turn to Wally for ministrations. "A lot of times when I was massaging her feet, she had taken so many Xanax and drank so much alcohol, that she would just pass out … right there with her feet in my hand." He had seen Vickie many times so "messed up," she could barely hold up her head.

"Kind of a dingbat" is how one dancer at Rick's bluntly remembers Smith. "She just wasn't brainy," she recalled. "She hustled, she worked a lot of tables," but management confined her to the day shift because she was too large for the busier night hours. The dancer noticed that Smith had an alcohol problem, even grabbing customers' drinks rather than waiting to be served by the bartender. Indeed, between July 1989 and January 1990, Smith was charged three times with drunk driving. She eventually pleaded guilty to one charge and was put on two years' probation. Smith always said she wanted to be a star, but in the twilight world of topless dancing, that dream still seemed a long way off.

Vickie's good time didn't stop with drugs and alcohol. Sex was added to the mixture, uninhibited, unrestrained, almost out-of-control sex. It might be argued that working where she did led to the wild behaviour. Or Vickie Lynn might have been attracted to the topless bars because she could get away with it there. In either case, people began to take note that Vickie's erotic exhibitionism was not confined to the stage.

One such person was the deejay at Executive Suites, Randy Default. While it's true, a dancer needs to stay in the good graces of the guy who plays the music – what he chooses can make her look bad or good – Vickie carried it a step further. Default called Vickie a "carpet muncher" because she would drop to her knees in the deejay booth, the tune saloon, to perform oral sex on him.

She didn't seem to mind if other people were around. Mitchell White, an ex-manager of Executive Suites, says that he was witness to Vickie on her knees in the tune saloon. He also has said that Vickie would take her clients to dark corners of the club if she thought it might help to get more money from them. She loved to talk "baby talk" to well-paying regulars, he said.

The topless bars were a circuit. Women didn't dance exclusively at one club. By 1988 Vickie – who went by the stage names of either

Robyn and Nikki – had gotten good enough to get a day gig at Rick's. Her weight and size-A bra precluded working the more lucrative night shift. Still, she was beautiful enough for Dallas Fontenot to choose her for Rick's 1989 calendar.

The shoots were set up in the woods of East Texas. Fontenot had a long Lincoln Continental "loaded with a bar with champagne and booze and cameras and the works" so that the models could get "all fired up" on the way. It was on the drives that Fontenot noticed Vicki's interest in the other women. "She never did, at that time, any kind of sexual deals with the girls on film," Fontenot recalls, "just in the car…hugging and kissing and things like that."

He also remembers that despite the drinking, Vickie could still perform for the camera. She was a natural. "I always told her that she was great. She would make it in *Penthouse* and *Playboy* big time."

Because of her breast size, Fontenot shot her full length from the back, wearing nothing but boots and a dimple. He though enough of the pictures that he sent them to Penthouse, but nothing came of it. "They weren't looking for big-boned women. Tall, big women. Especially tall, big women with no tits."

The breast size was a definite job liability. However, Houston was the right place to be if you wanted implants; it was practically the birthplace of silicone surgery.

Women through the ages have sought ways to enlarge their breasts and have allowed such varied substances as ivory and paraffin to be shoved into their bodies. The Japanese were the first to use silicone when women there wanted to be more attractive to American servicemen after World War II. The method used in this early silicone surgery was straight injection. It was not terribly successful. Even if the patient didn't' get sick, the silicone had a tendency to wander or even harden, and the eventual results were less than aesthetically pleasing.

In the early sixties, two doctors at Houston's Baylor University College of Medicine, where Michael de Bakey did his pioneer work in heart surgery, wanted to create their own medical history by developing a successful, safe breast augmentation procedure. One was Thomas Cronin, a Baylor professor of plastic surgery who had established a reputation by working with burn victims and hand injuries. The other was his resident, Frank Gerow.

It was Gerow who came up with the breakthrough idea one day at a blood bank. It was there that he saw blood being stored in plastic bags instead of the standard glass bottle. Why not put silicone into pliant plastic bags and implant them subcutaneously into a woman's breasts? In that way, the silicone wouldn't set out for destinations unwanted and would feel natural to the touch. Hence, the silicone-gel implant was born.

The doctors wrote at the time, "For some years now, at least in the United States, women have been bosom conscious. Perhaps this is due in large measure to the tremendous amount of publicity which has been given to some movie actresses blessed with generous-sized breasts. Many women with limited development of the breasts are extremely sensitive about it, apparently feeling that they are less womanly and therefore, less attractive. While most such women are satisfied, or at least put up with 'falsies,' probably all of them would be happier if, somehow, they could have a pleasing enlargement from within."

The implants were touted as absolutely safe and would last as long as the rest of the woman's body did. "They're as harmless as water," Gerow would say more than once.

Breast jobs became the fashion for Houston ladies. And not only for those who lived in the ultra-trendy River Oaks section of town. Secretaries and housewives were saving their pennies until they, too, could afford to increase their bra size by one or two cups – C and D being the most requested.

According to other dancers, one way Vickie was adding to her income was by accompanying clients to their cars and giving them blowjobs in the backseat for $25 or $50. Kimberleigh Graham, who knew her from Rick's, said she witnessed Vickie's second career on several occasions. When Beth Douglas was waitressing at a club where Vickie danced, she would always refer her clients to Vickie because Vickie was known as a "party girl" who was willing to party in the parking lots.

Chapter 2

Through whatever means, Vickie put together enough money for her first breast augmentation. Of course, according to her version of history – as it has been repeated in numerous periodicals – her remarkable breast size was an act of god. Forgetting her earlier words about how her breasts sagged after he was born, she was later to claim that she lost the weight everywhere except in her chest.

Vickie didn't stop at one operation, however. Unhappy with the first one, she had a second, but there were complications and an infection. One of her breasts had to be drained which left her temporarily lopsided. Nicole Alexander met Vickie in 1989 after the first rounds of surgery. Alexander feels the original augmentations "looked better than the one she has now. Because they didn't screw up her nipples and all that. They [the breasts] weren't as big."

But Vickie, apparently wasn't satisfied. She wanted her breasts even larger and her nipples smaller. Alexander suggested she see Dr Gerald Johnson, something of a legend even in a community of many plastic surgeon legends. In 1986 Dr Johnson held what he called "Grand Teton Days." "The most surgeries we did in one day was seventeen," he told *Texas Monthly* Magazine. In tribute to the many millions of dollars he earned from that particular part of the female anatomy, Dr Johnson had a swimming pool built in the shape of a breast. The hot tub served as the nipple.

Accordring to Suzy Pfardresher, a Houston pharmaceutical and medical supply saleswoman, Vickie's augmentation was unusual in that Dr Johnson implanted not one but two 450cc silicone sacks in each breast, one on top of the other. The result was a size 42DD bust, practically putting her breasts in a different zip code from the rest of her body.

Now this, Vickie liked. When Guadalupe Castellano met her, she remembers being "…in awe of her beauty." She was also in awe of the size of Vickie's breasts. Lupe was thinking of getting her own implants and finally asked Vickie if she could feel hers.

"Feel them babies all you want," Vickie told her. "You're looking at fourteen thousand dollars worth of work here. Hell, I could have bought myself a truck for what these damn things cost."

Actually it was a car, according to Nicole Alexander. "Some guy she was dating put out eight thousand for the boob job, because he was going to buy her a car. Instead, she had him pay for the tits."

Vickie continued to date her married benefactor, Alexander said, "until the money ran out."

"That's when she started making the big bucks," recalled former Rick's manager Ritchie Avantez. "Men loved the fact that here was this big ol' Texas girl with that big ol' blonde Texas hair, and she milked it. Many girls will put on a persona once they hit the door and they will hold onto that throughout the night. Anna changed her name, she was going by Robyn at that point."

On one visit home to Mexia she wowed her friend Jo Lynn. "When she came back, she was absolutely gorgeous," Jo Lynn said. 'She had coloured her hair champagne blonde. Her body was perfect. She had filled out.' As the Eighties ended. Vickie made the rounds of other north-side clubs, places with pseudo-glamorous names like Chez Paris, Puzzles, and Gigi's. Her good-girl looks made her a natural for club ads – she posed in fake furs and rhinestones or lounging across a Porsche.

Vickie and her new breasts made their way through the topless circuit. She worked intermittently at Rick's, although the day manager took exception to her drinking. Dallas Fontenot says she was " a real roller…a party type girl. She'd get drunk and drink, raise hell."

"Anna [Vickie] was a voracious party-er," said Ritchie Avantez. "I remember the day that she fell off the runway. She was so smashed, and her name was called to go onstage and she came rolling out and just fell right off the front of the stage, right into a customer's table, drinks in his lap. We fired her after that. It became a running rule that we would hire her back and within twenty-one days, if not sooner, we'd ask her to leave again."

Her antics went down badly with her mother, who cared for Daniel while her daughter worked but who was not happy about her being a stripper. "Vickie wasn't raised that way," said step-father Donald Hart. "She wasn't supposed to be doing it and her momma let her know it. And her momma being a police officer, she went in a couple of these places and dragged Vickie out by the hair of the head."

Vickie worked the Landing Stop, Legg's, Baby O's, but Gigi's Cabaret would end up being the most important club for Vickie's future. Gigi's was a dark and grungy club complete with a pole for the dancers to entwine themselves around and slide seductively up and down. The main action was downstairs, but customers could request private table dancing in an upstairs room.

Donna Scanlin was a dancer whose career ended after three days at Gigi's. She was asked to table dance upstairs by a man she didn't know. "At Gigi's it's known that the upstairs is pretty risky compared to doing a table dance downstairs...I could kind of tell that he really wanted a lot more than I wanted to give."

When Donna turned him down, the guy wanted to know who would go upstairs with him. Being new at the club, Donna wasn't sure but when she asked around, she was told to get Vickie. "So later on I ended up going upstairs...to do a table dance for someone I knew, and Vickie was up there dancing for that man...Her G-string was pulled over to the side, and he was fondling her. I actually hurried up and finished my table dance and went downstairs. I never went back to Gigi's and danced again. That's the last time I ever danced."

Gigi's is where Vickie became close friends with April Story Richardson, although they had met earlier. The first time April "laid eyes on her, she was on her back with her legs spread on stage" at the Landing Strip.

The women danced together at Gigi's. "The management really liked us, and the owners, too. We got to come and go as we please. Nobody ever told us no and we knew we could never get fired." This was lucky for Vickie since her drinking and drugging and sexual forays were stretching the limits of even the no-holds-barred world of the topless clubs. The woman was out of control, even when it came to those she considered friends.

Take the time she asked April and her husband to drive her to the airport. A customer Vickie had met only three hours earlier wanted her in Dallas. April thought the rendezvous was a bad idea, especially since Vickie was drunk and getting drunker in the backseat with something she'd bought for the road. That's when the ride went from bad to bizarre. "Before we go to the airport," April says, "she had leaned over the driver's seat and taken her right hand and grasped my husband between the legs as I sat in the passenger seat. Of course, my eyes are bulging out at this time. I couldn't believe this. I didn't know to be mad or laugh. It was just one of those situations." April's husband didn't say anything. "He just kind of stares into space." When they pulled up at departures, Vickie hopped out as if nothing untoward had taken place.

That was the beginning of the end of April's marriage. After April split with her husband, Vickie moved in along with two cats, two toy poodles, and Gizmo, the cockatiel. It was only then that April began to notice what half of Houston already knew – Vickie liked more than just guys. "She made comments to me about former lovers she had and they were girls." One even had had a likeness of Vickie tattooed on her back.

If anything, Vickie preferred women. In paying a high compliment to a male boyfriend, Clay Spires, she said he used his mouth like a woman in lovemaking.

Nicole Alexander said, "She was more partial to women, because she would get money from men and buy stuff for her girlfriends." According to Nicole, Vickie mostly dated dancers, but she also went regularly to a Houston lesbian bar, Bacchus.

Lupe Castellano said she had heard through the club scene that Vickie mostly "just preferred women," although that didn't preclude her from bringing men home or "even couples." Most of the women she'd seen Anna with were surprisingly unattractive and very butch. Vickie needed the spotlight, and she didn't' want competition.

Another dancer, Nikki Mizzell, had seen pictures of Vickie with a lover – a woman who had been with both Nikki and Vickie. The photographs showed two women in the nude with Vickie snorting a line of cocaine from the other's stomach.

Cocaine. Xanax. Alcohol. Downers like Ecstasy. Gifts for girlfriends. Not even the side trips to Vegas with three other dancers and four wealthy businessmen – especially when the men lost their mortgage cheques at the tables and stiffed the women – could cover Vickie's appetites. So it was a very lucky day when the octogenarian multimillionaire decided to have lunch at Gigi's Cabaret. Had he chosen a more posh dining setting, Tony's or the River Oaks Country club, J. Howard Marshall II might have never met Vickie Lynn Smith, which would have left a lot of future tabloid pages to be filled.

Chapter 3

J. HOWARD MARSHALL II was as much a product of Texas as Vickie Lynn Hogan, although their beginnings were far apart in time, distance and social standing. Like all very wealthy men, his story was as much mythic as real, a self-serving portrayal of an honest, hard-working individualist driven by the frontier spirit:

> J. Howard's autobiography, *Done in Oil*, harkens back to a nostalgic period in American history of allegedly self-made entrepreneurs who shaped our country. It recalls a time when the saying "go west young man" was the siren song for men and women of our country who left humble beginnings and crossed the rivers and plains to settle huge expanses of the nation. These ruggedly honest individuals walked the Oregon Trail, settled the Oklahoma territories, worked the California gold fields and inspired phrases like "Remember the Alamo," which needs no explanation to Americans. The myths and the reality of these individuals of character and vision survive and now form a large part of our country's history and folklore. J. Howard set himself in the context of these enterprising pioneers.[1]

J. Howard came from a prominent Quaker family that could boast of having in its tree John Marshall, the preeminent fourth chief

---

[1] Judge David O. Carter, Findings of the US District Court for the Central District of California, *E. Pierce Marshall vs. Vickie Lynn Marshall*, March 2002.

justice of the Supreme Court, who established the power of that court through his interpretations of the constitution. J. Howard's grandfather was in the steel business. In 1902, three years before J. Howard was born in Philadelphia, the grandfather sold his company to Andrew Carnegie for the then-staggering sum of $18 million.

As a boy, J. Howard was educated at a succession of exclusive private schools and followed the Quaker tradition of addressing adults as thee and thou. But by the time he was ready to enter college, the family fortune had been dissipated. J. Howard, as determined in his way as Vickie Lynn was in hers, did not let diversity stand in his way. He had already proven an inner strength when the doctors said he would never walk again after a bout with typhoid fever when he was twelve. His mother burned his crutches and he eventually walked – although a limp stayed with him for the rest of his life.

Marshall worked his way through both Haverford College, an elite Quaker school on the prestigious Main Line outside of Philadelphia, and then Yale Law School, where he graduated *magnum cum laude*. While working on the *Yale Law Review* in 1931, he took an assignment that determined the direction of the rest of his life. He went to research an article in the Oklahoma oil fields. The article must have been impressive because two years later Secretary of the Interior Harold Ickes asked him to investigate the rising acrimony between regulators of the Texas Railroad Commission and oil producers accused of exceeding extraction allowances.

Marshall had to dodge a few bullets while in Texas, but it was worth it for the contacts he made there. During World War II, he was appointed chief counsel of the Petroleum Administration for the War. In 1944, he left public service and set out to make money. A consummate dealmaker, he moved to Ashland, Kentucky, and helped Ashland Oil become a major player. Later it was instrumental in the expansion of Signal Oil and Gas, for which Howard worked in the mid-1950s. In 1954, he was one of the founders of the great Northern Oil and Gas Company, the business that would eventually make him the richest man in Texas.

By then he was married, to Eleanor Pierce, a refined, gentle and religious woman who later became a minister. They had two sons, J. Howard III and Pierce, who were raised largely by Eleanor, as her husband was so often away pursuing his business ventures. Howard III was a scholarly young man who graduated top of his class at Cal Tech and took up residence in southern California. Pierce attended military college and served in the Navy before working as an invest-ment banker.

Despite their father's success, it wasn't until 1961, at an age when many men would have been planning for retirement, that this small man with big ears and a bigger voice found his true home, a place where someone who had written the regulations in Washington could make them work for his and his partners' profit. Marshall moved to Houston, Texas. There, after a stint with Allied Chemical, he merged his resources with Fred Koch's huge energy firm in what he called in his autobiography, *Done in Oil*, "the best deal I ever made." That best deal, with him eventually controlling eight percent of Koch Industries, would land him on *Forbes* magazine's 1991 list of the 400 richest people in the United States, with an estimated net worth of $400 million. There were those who scoffed at the esti-mate, saying Marshall's true worth was closer to three billion.

Koch Industries, a huge petroleum and chemical conglomerate headquartered in Wichita, Kansas, was an unqualified success. It became the second largest privately held company in the United States, based on revenues of approximately $35 billion. Its history can be traced back to Great Northern Oil and Gas company, which formed in 1954 with J. Howard owning 16 percent. Subsequently, Fred Koch bought a 40% stake. When Union Oil sought to take over Great Northern and make it a publicly traded company, Marshall and the Koch family prevented the takeover. Fred Koch and Marshall shared the same ideas about business. They believed that earnings should be reinvested in the company to create sus-tained growth, and that their company should be privately held. To them, the management advantages of a private company out-weighed short-term benefits of going public and making a quick profit in the public market. They wanted to be able to make quick business decisions without being encumbered with the need for shareholder approval, which was time consuming and often divisive. They also did not want to be subject to yearly shareholder demands for high dividends. This private business philosophy was steadfastly adhered to, and the business changed its name to Koch Industries.

The move to Houston also brought on domestic changes for Marshall. He ditched his wife of thirty years, Eleanor Pierce, writing in his autobiography that "she never really understood my driving passion for the oil business." The divorce didn't sit well with his younger son, Pierce, but maintaining warm relationships with his family never seemed to be a major concern of Marshall's. Having gotten rid of wife number one, Marshall married number two a few months later, in December 1961.

He had known Bettye Bohannon since the mid-1930s, indeed he may have been conducting a long-term affair with her during his marriage to Eleanor. Bettye, nicknamed "Tiger," was later described (in a court battle over Marshall's will) as "strong, intelligent, street smart, astute in business, and a good match for J. Howard." From all outward appearances, their union was a happy one, though they would have no children. Tiger worked with Marshall in the oil business for some twenty years until she developed Alzheimer's disease in the early 1980s.

While Marshall was making his millions, trouble was looming. On his death, Fred Koch left equal shares of his voting stock in Koch Industries to his four sons, Charles, David, Bill, and Freddie. Meanwhile Marshall had given his two sons four percent each of the voting common stock. "Boys, these are the Crown Jewels," he said. "Take care of them."

Which would have been fine. But in 1980, a feud erupted between the Koch siblings about the future of Koch Industries. Bill and Freddie Koch believed that the best approach was to go public. Charles and David Koch knew that their father would want the company to stay private. A fight for control of the family business ensued. Freddie and Bill and their allies could count 48 per cent ownership in the company, just short of the majority that they would need to install a new board that would approve a public offering.

To find the extra votes, they looked outside the family. Freddie and Bill approached Pierce Marshall and asked him to vote his four percent with them, but he declined. However, when Bill and Freddie approached Pierce's older bother, J. Howard III agreed, giving them the votes needed to oust the old board – and his own father.

Marshall, not surprisingly, felt betrayed by his eldest son. He flew to California to try to change his son's position, but was unable to convince him. "I asked Howard to stand with me," he later wrote. "He flatly refused." So instead he offered to buy back the crucial four percent stock he had given him – as a wedding gift – at the vastly inflated price of $8 million. Marshall had honored his commitment to his friend, the late Fred Koch, but at the cost of his relationship with Howard III. The old man flew back to Houston and disinherited his eldest son. He considered the $8 million payment an early inheritance and planned to give him nothing more – ever.

It was a bruising time, and with Tiger suffering from Alzheimer's, Marshall found himself virtually a widower although his wife was still alive. Then, in 1982, according to *Texas Monthly*, he "…landed at the Houston Hobby Airport and driving home, I thought, well, maybe if I had a drink I'd feel better, so I stopped at some little place that I didn't' realize what I was getting into. It was a strip joint – or as the boys call it now – a titty bar. And I walked in and Lady was there. She was one of the strippers."

JAWELL DIANNE Walker, bosomy, tall, leggy, had only been in Houston two years when Marshall spotted her. She had barely arrived in 1980 when her fourth husband returned to Georgia, leaving Lady with three kids. She went through a series of low-paying jobs – receptionist, waitress, whatever she could get

– until, at the age of forty-tow, she took to the stage at the Chic Lounge, dancing topless. To say that Lady Walker was a character would be a gross understatement. She had panache, Southern charm, and amusing tales of affairs with the likes of Elvis Presley and Pete Rose.

Marshall liked what he saw that first night and asked for a private dance. He must have been even more impressed for within days he bought Lady a Cadillac El Dorado, a new house – complete with furniture – a diamond ring, and the list got longer and longer. By all evidence, he was genuinely smitten with Lady. He sent her love notes along with the gifts. One read, "To love and be loved – to a man who has dedicated his life to his work, this is truly life's great experience."

The one glitch in the romance, however, was Bettye, his ill wife. Marshall wrote Lady's mother that "I would marry her this afternoon…if I were free and she would have me. I cannot leave an ill wife to whom I have been married. I think it might kill her and I would feel guilty for the rest of my life. Perhaps a time will come."

Because of Bettye, Marshall and Lady entered into an accommodating arrangement. The mores of Houston society deemed it improper to be seen with your mistress in the evening, but taking her to lunch was no problem. So three days a week for ten years, Marshall and Lady lunched in the best places in Houston. Lady made the most of it. She dressed with such flair, it was impossible not to notice her – hats, scarves, and plenty of jewels. She and Marshall practically held court at their tables, with him telling amusing stories of his Washington days and her just being flat-out charming.

According to California judge David O. Carter, who would later conduct a hearing into Marshall's legacy:

J. Howard wanted Lady Walker to be his exclusive mistress and he often professed his desire and commitment to marry her if Betty died. Money was immediately bestowed upon her. The intensity of his pursuit is set forth in his letters to her. These letters contain repetitive and aggressive protestations of his love, always coupled with a reference to money. "Jungle Money"and "Pin" are code words for money that J. Howard gave to Lady Walker. "Pin" was a regular payment made on a consistent and timely basis, "Jungle money" was a payment for her own pleasure, and "big kills" were larger sums given sporadically to Lady Walker. J. Howard also gave Lady Walker enormous amounts of jewelry, including more than $1 million purchased from Harry Winston and Nieman Marcus, the same stores at which he would subsequently buy jewelry for Vickie.

At one point, J. Howard sent Lady Walker the Koch Industries prospectus in an apparent attempt to impress her with his wealth. The front of the first page reads, "For Lady-/The Crown jewels/ J. Howard." This pattern of giving money, and even the terms that J. Howard used, is the same pattern that Vickie describes of J. Howard's pursuit of her a decade later. Lavish jewelry, regular payments of money, and sporadic gifts ushered these bar dancers into J. Howard's life. Apparently, it was extremely lucrative to have an affair with J. Howard. J. Howard spent approximately $2 million a year on Lady Walker, which is approximately the same amount of money he spent each year on Vickie when he pursued her a decade later.

Marshall often would unobtrusively pass blank cheques to Lady at the table. (It was later alleged by Marshall's son Pierce that she was spending $100,000 a month.) Once he made the mistake of giving them to her openly for all to see. "Put it in my purse. Don't just hand it across the table," she instructed him. She didn't' get the nickname Lady for nothing.

By Marshall's account the sexual part of their relationship was over, by mutual consent, when he was eighty-three. According to *Texas Monthly* writer Mimi Swartz, Lady "intended to get on with her life as long as Marshall remained married," but that she did plan to marry him one day. "He may have been old," Swartz wrote, 'but he was more than willing to share his knowledge with her."

Marshall continued to indulge her expensive tastes – she was said to have had a jeweler on retainer who was paid $25,000 a month. One house wasn't enough for her. Marshall bought her a second, larger one. It was extravagantly furnished and appointed. Lady's swimming pool, with her name in tiles on the bottom, was designed by the man who had created Liberace's, famous for its piano shape. One thing the house was lacking was Marshall. Lady ruled that "When I can set foot in his house as Mrs Marshall, he can set foot in mine."

Lady filled the void in her household with a bodyguard-lover named Dale Clem, whom she showered with cars and diamonds and money. It is clear that Marshall knew of Clem's existence, but what later became a matter of legal contention was whether he was aware of their intimate relationship. Marshall did write a letter to his son Pierce about this time instructing that in the event of his death, Pierce should "take care of [Lady] in any way she may need, financially and in all ways...I'm completely obligated to take care of her!"

Then Lady and Marshall started having tiffs over money – including her liability for taxes on the gifts that Marshall had given her over the years without reporting them to the IRS. He went so far as to close an account without telling her. To her mortification, she bounced cheques all over town, but he eventually covered them.

It wasn't only Marshall Lady was fighting with. There were fallings-out with friends and family. Lady was not living up to her nickname. Some of her ill-temper may have been due to reaching that iffy age for mistresses. Even when your paramour has thirty years on you, turning fifty can be an awkward passage. So Lady did what many women in a similar position do. In 1991, at the age of fifty-one, she signed up for cosmetic surgery.

The night before the operation, Lady updated her will. Her $5.8 million estate consisted of what Marshall had given her, and she was leaving that to her children. Except for a truck, a diamond bracelet, and a poodle named Fancy that were to go to Clem.

Lady died on the operating table. The cause of death was listed as a congenital brain defect, although later rumors swirled around about Lady's morphine pump having been tampered with. Marshall gave her a grand burial complete with a copper casket. But not long afterwards, he found out about Lady's will and over lunch with Clem, he found out about Lady's sex life. To add to Marshall's emotional trauma, in September, Betty died.

In early 1992, Having learned that Lady had been living with another, much younger, man during most of their affair, Marshall sued her heirs and some of her friends in an attempt to retrieve every dime he'd ever spent on his mistress – to the tune of $15 million. He had given those gifts to her, he contended, not her kids and certainly not to Dale Clem. He even claiming she received kickbacks from merchants after the items were purchased and the merchants charged his account.

Marshall was to testify that, "I was blinded by love. I did more or less what she asked me to do, and I don't make any bones about it, I was a damn fool. But men in love do stupid things, and I was sure guilty." (Although it's been suggested that what he really was a damn fool about was transferring one million dollars worth of stock into Lady's name, a transaction which the Securities and Exchange Commission definitely frowned upon.)

Marshall claimed that Lady had given the appearance of loving him exclusively while all the time she was carrying on affairs with other men. He said that the gifts he had given her had been in trust only – Lady wasn't supposed to own them until his death. In fact, he claimed, she'd swindled him out of his fortune. All this, even though Lady was heard saying to him many times that as long as he was married, she would continue to see other men. It was a particularly juicy legal brouhaha, which kept Houston amused for awhile. It was settled a year and half later with Marshall getting the lion's share of the estate. Lady's family didn't have the resources to keep on fighting.

After Lady Walker and Betty died in 1991, Marshall entered a period of deep despondency. He appeared to his family and friends to have lost his zest for life. Though an immensely successful man who still served on the boards of numerous corporations and banks and went into the office every day, he told his eldest son that "he enjoyed having pretty women on his arm when he entered the River Oaks Country Club in Houston and that a great light had gone out of his life."

That light switched on again when Marshall, apparently a man of consistency, ventured into another topless bar in October 1991 and had another tall, busty dancer catch his eye. This time it was no Lady, it was Vickie Lynn Smith. According to not only Vickie, but others as well, this momentous encounter took place while Lady was still alive, making Marshall's cries of betrayal more than a bit hypocritical.

Dan Manning, Marshall's driver, remembers that day at Gigi's Cabaret. Manning frequented the bursleque bar and had talked to his boss about going there "to cheer him up." Because of Howard's age (he was then 86) and physical condition, he did not go out at night, so they arrived for lunch during the day-shift. Marshall spotted Vickie and was intrigued by her. He sent Manning to bring her over to the table so he could get a better look. He apparently liked what he saw, and tried to grab her post-implant breast while she danced.

Vickie, for her part, thought "he looked terrible, he looked like he had lost the will to live." But as Dallas Fontenot says, Vickie was "the kind of girl you can sit down and talk to and she would sit down and talk to you for hours. She wasn't a hard hustler like some of the girls. They got their three-minute drinks, [and then it was] I got to be back up there dancing. She wasn't that kind of girl. She'd spend time with you. Especially if she thought her career could go places."

Talk she did. She told Marshall how she didn't really like to dance, but she had to in order to support her young son. This must have been *déjà vu* to Marshall, still he wanted to help her out, Dan Manning recalls. Thus began Howard's aggressive pursuit of Vickie's affection. He asked to her to have lunch with him the next day.

Howard took Vickie to a restaurant hotel and ordered room service. He told Vickie about Betty and Lady Walker and funny stories about himself. When she became concerned about her job, he gave her an envelope with $1,000 in cash and told her not to go to work. The following day they had lunch at River Oaks Country Club, where once again she was given cash. On each occasion, money was given to her ranging in amounts of $1,000 to $5,000 in cash. Vickie "stopped dancing right after Howard met me that day." Howard was soon paying all of Vickie's bills. Shortly after they met, J. Howard purchased a white Toyota Celica as a gift for her after her own car had been repossessed.

The geriatric oilman would melt when Vickie would start in with her baby talk, a ploy she used with many of her older customers. Manning says initially his employer would hand Vickie an envelope filled with money at those lunches, perhaps heeding Lady's admonition on etiquette, but that ritual soon ended when Vickie stopped all pretense and just removed the bills from Marshall's wallet.

According to some of those who were around at the time, there was a quid pro quo involved. April Richardson, for one, remembers one afternoon Vickie told her that Marshall had given her some money and expected a blow job in return. She had to hurry up and do it, so she could get more money. "[Marshall] was very old," April said. "Sometimes he was very rude, very abrupt. We all put up with him because he was so rich. [Vickie] didn't seem to mind going out to him. She liked him. And he sure liked her."

She started receiving $2,000 cheques twice a month. These cheques were

recorded by Howard's assistant Eyvonne Scurlock for consulting, just as his previous "pins" to Lady Walker had been. Within a week of their meeting, Howard told Vickie that he was going to marry her. He had been reinvigorated by Vickie. While he had fallen into a state of deep despair after the deaths of Lady Walker and Betty, his relationship with Vickie brought him back to life. He called her "the light of his life."

Chapter 3

But at this point in Vickie's life, Marshall was just another guy giving her money, albeit a staggeringly rich one. She had more important things on her agenda.

Chapter 4

VICKIE LYNN SMITH had ambitions beyond shaking her assets on the stage of Gigi's Cabaret and picking up extra income in the parking lot. She, after all, had written on her April page of Rick's calendar, "My one ambition and goal in life is to be a high-fashion model."

With that in mind, Vickie went to the Intermediate Modeling Agency/Page Parkes School of Modeling. Vickie was advised to darken her hair, lost weight, change her image, and then she might be accepted into the modelling school – for a fee, of course. Vickie didn't have the money.

Her new boyfriend, a bodybuilder named Clay Spires, suggested she follow up on an ad they had spotted in the Houston edition of *Health and Fitness* magazine. It was an ad we ran. We were recruiters for Playboy Enterprises and were looking for potential Playmates of the Month. When we found young women with potential, we'd have then fill out a standard one-page biography. Eric would take Polaroid test shots of them au naturel – in the nude and without makeup. We'd send the pictures to the *Playboy* photography editors for evaluation.

Vickie called us in September, 1991, to ask for an appointment. She gave the impression she was only contacting us because Clay Spires insisted. Eric had to practically cajole her into making an appointment. He pointed out that the potential rewards were great, the risks were few, so why not take a chance? Once she was convinced that the appointment would simply be an honest evaluation followed by some quick test shots, she set a time. It took three cancellations before she actually made it to the studio late in the afternoon of Saturday, September 7.

The first thing you noticed about Vickie Lynn Smith was invariably her size. There was a lot of her to notice, the five feet eleven inches, the 160 pounds, those outrageous 42DD-cup breasts. It was somewhat overwhelming. But once Eric got past the initial impression and really took a look at her, he realized he was looking at a truly beautiful woman.

Vickie had perfect skin and a stunning heart-shaped face with large eyes and a generous mouth. If you wanted to nitpick, there was a flaw, a small crease below her right eye that became marked when she smiled. But that's why airbrushing was invented. She was a complete stunner, even without a drop of makeup.

She talked about Clay and Daniel, her son. Eric was surprised to learn she had made them wait downstairs in the car instead of bringing them to the studio. But he thought their presence might make her even more nervous. As it was, even the easiest topics seemed to fluster her, and finally she admitted she was afraid of posing nude. "You can see everything so clearly!"

With a straight face, she said she never let any of her boyfriends see her naked. Lovemaking was strictly a lights-off affair. Eric had to play diplomat/psychiatrist, reassuring her that the session would go quickly and she would be nude only for a few minutes. Still she sat shaking in her chair. Eric felt sorry for her, there was something so childlike about her. She acted and sounded as if she had just gotten off the bus from a small town that hadn't had the benefit of a grammar teacher.

To get her mind off the shoot, Eric had her fill out the requisite one-page biography. It usually took a few minutes to answer the questions, but Vickie didn't understand several of them and asked more than once for clarification. Finally, after a half hour, she was done.

Under occupation, Vickie first wrote dancing, scratched it out, and then put modelling. However, she neglected to alter the phone

Sex Bomb

To Playboy Enterprises, Inc. ("PLAYBOY"), 680 North Lake Shore Drive, Chicago, Illinois 60611: In consideration of my being considered as a candidate for the PLAYBOY Magazine "Playmate of the Month" and for other good and valuable consideration, receipt of which I acknowledge, and with knowledge that you intend to act in reliance hereon I irrevocably give you, your subsidiaries, affiliates, agents, successors, assigns and licensees all right, title and interest, including all copyright and other literary property, commercial and publication rights in and to, and the absolute right and permission to copyright, use, publish and distribute in whole or in part, all photographs (whether photographs as stills, motion pictures or on video tape) in which I may be included, and my name (whether real or fictitious), my voice and any biographical material pertaining to me, for editorial, advertising, art or promotion, or for any lawful purpose whatsoever in any and all media in perpetuity worldwide and without restrictions. I am posing for the photographs as an independent contractor and not as an employee, and I release you from the responsibility of unemployment reporting and other employment associated duties.

I hereby waive any right to inspect or object to the finished product and the printed material that may be used in conjunction therewith and the use to which it may be applied.

I hereby certify that I have not posed for any nude or semi-nude photographs except those now being submitted to PLAYBOY, with exceptions as noted. (The term "semi-nude" is defined as any pose in attire more revealing than that usually seen on a public beach in the United States.) I further certify that I have not been guilty of any illegal action (other than such things as minor traffic offenses) which might damage the PLAYBOY image or lessen my promotional value to PLAYBOY.

I further agree that I will do no posing in the nude or semi-nude for still photography, motion pictures, or for any commercial purposes whatsoever (such as night clubs) until you advise me whether or not I have been accepted as a Playmate of the Month, and if I am so accepted, until two years after the cover date of the issue in which I appear as Playmate. Exception to this rule can only be made by written permission from PLAYBOY.

I hereby release, discharge and agree to save PLAYBOY harmless from any liability by virtue of any blurring, distortion, alteration, optical illusion or use in composite form, whether intentional or otherwise, that may occur or be produced in taking or reproducing said pictures. I AM 18 YEARS* OF AGE OR OVER OR HAVE HAD THIS FORM SIGNED BY MY PARENT OR GUARDIAN.

Signed _Vickie Smith_ Date _10/2/91_

Permanent State of Residence _Texas_

I, as parent or guardian of the minor who signed the above release, consent to the signing of such release, and agree to defend and hold the beneficiaries of the release harmless against any claim that the minor may make (before or after reaching the age of Majority) because of the use of the photographs in any manner permitted by such release. I fully understand that the beneficiaries of the release are and will be relying upon my agreement and signature which are intended to induce them to accept the release.

Signed_____

(Parent or Guardian)

Name_____ Date_____

(Please Print)

Address_____

No.   Street   City   State   Zip Code

* 19 years in Alabama and 21 years in Mississippi, Nebraska, Pennsylvania and Puerto Rico.

PHOTOGRAPHER'S AGREEMENT

I hereby certify that I am submitting to PLAYBOY all nude or semi-nude photographs, negatives and transparencies that I have already taken of this Playmate candidate. In the event that she is accepted as a Playmate of the Month, I further certify (in consideration for value received, receipt whereof is acknowledged) that I will submit all photographs, negatives and transparencies of her which I must take to fulfill PLAYBOY requirements. I agree that, upon completion of this Playmate shooting, I will not take any further nude or semi-nude photographs of this model, except when specifically assigned to do so by PLAYBOY, for a period of two years from this date or the date when I have completed these shootings, whichever date is later. I certify that I have no knowledge or any reason to believe that this model is guilty of any illegal action (other than such things as minor traffic offenses) which might damage the PLAYBOY image or lessen her promotional value to PLAYBOY. I further agree that all nude or semi-nude photographs I have taken of this model shall become the sole property of PLAYBOY. (The term "semi-nude" is defined as any pose in attire more revealing than that usually seen on a public beach in the United States.) In the event PLAYBOY elects to photograph, on motion picture film, video tape or otherwise, one or more photographic sessions with this Playmate candidate, and in the event I am included in said photography as a subject, I hereby grant to PLAYBOY the right to use said photography of me, plus my name, voice and biographical material, for any lawful purpose whatsoever in any and all media in perpetuity worldwide and without restrictions.

Photographer _____ Date _10/2/91_

Witness_____

ANY ALTERATION OR ADDITION TO THIS RELEASE IS NOT VALID UNLESS ACCEPTED IN WRITING BY PLAYBOY ENTERPRISES, INC.

44

number she gave for the original answer, that number being the direct line to Gigi's Cabaret. This oversight would come back to haunt her.

She wrote that her hobby was "Watching scary movies." That "horse back riding" was her sport or special activity. Under likes, she put, "Gentlemen who no [sic] how to treat a lady." Dislikes: "Cigeret [sic] smoke, bums with no jobs." Ambition: "To be in *Playboy* + model, actress."

In retrospect, the most incongruous response she gave was to About Men (Likes or Dislikes): "I don't like men who always talk about how much money they have." (Although in her defence, she probably didn't want to hear about the money, she merely wanted to get it.) Under Other Interesting Remarks About Yourself or Family, she wrote "I have a 5 yr old son we been raising by myself and my mom is a very big help to me." Parent's Occupation(s): "mother is a deputy Sheriff."

And finally, she filled in these statistics: Height 5"11 [sic], Weight 140, Bust/Cup 42, DD, Waist 26, Hips 38, Hair Blonde, Eyes Hazel, Shoe Size 10.

With the excruciating process of completing the form over, Vickie went to the dressing room, where she was to remove all her clothes, put on a robe, and wait until the marks from her bra straps had disappeared.

This meant more time for talk and confidences. Vickie had a dream, a big one, she told Eric. And she was convinced that making the pages of *Playboy* would be the first big step toward that dream. She wanted to become the next Marilyn Monroe. Vickie was not the first blonde to wish that, nor would she be the last, but sitting across from her wrapped in a terry-cloth robe, with her perfect face and her lush curves, Eric could almost believe she had a shot.

Finally, it was show time. No more hesitation. If Vickie wanted to grace the pages of *Playboy*, the robe was going to have to come off. When it did. Eric could see she was an exceptional girl. His eyes went first to her breasts. And little wonder, they looked even larger in the nude. As a photographer for *Playboy*, Eric had seen many busty girls in his studio, but Vickie had outdone them all. However, on closer inspection, he was shocked to see that her breasts were scarred quite badly around the nipples and aureoles and that she had deep, long stretch marks that were going to be tough to hide with makeup.

Her breasts weren't the only thing that were out of the ordinary, especially for a woman who wanted to be a centrefold. She was big boned, with very large hands, arms, thighs, and an especially large derriere.

Most of the women that come in for Playboy photographs are thin, with toned bodies that are small and tight, even if the woman is tall. Not Vickie. She was a Rubens painting, zaftig, full, and exuberant. She was unlike anyone Eric had seen before.

What came next was standard procedure. First, Eric took about a dozen Polaroids that included a closeup of her face, a beside-the-swimming-pool pose, full-length shots, front and back. The photographs were taken against a plain background without any props. Her hair and makeup were not professionally done, and there was no effort to mask flaws. The *Playboy* editors want to get a good look at the girls at this stage. No distractions.

When the session ended, Vickie was heading back to the dressing room when D'eva got her first glimpse of her. She studied Vickie with an artist's eye. "God, you have a beautiful face," she said. "That face is going to make you a lot of money."

Of course, Vickie was thrilled to hear this. She thanked D'eva and went to change into her street clothes. D'eva repeated her assessment to Eric. That face was going to make Vickie a fortune. Her skin was clear and beautiful, there was a youthful look about her. Very lovely, very innocent. The illusion was spoiled somewhat when Vickie returned encased in a Spandex minidress and spiked heels.

Vickie, naturally, wanted to know when she might hear something from *Playboy*. Eric told her it usually took a week or so. She thanked us and left.

Chapter 4

Eric sent the Polaroids to Playboy photo editor Linda Kenney, and her boss, Marilyn Grabowski. It took only three days for Linda Kenney to call back with instructions to do a *Playboy* Playmate Test on Vickie. The Polaroids are the first step in the screening process. They whet the editors' interest to see what the model can do on 35mm film, if she can come alive before the camera and project the look they want.

A *Playboy* Playmate Test (PMT) is usually a day photo shoot. The model is asked to show up with no makeup, clean hair, and loose-fitting clothes. Tight garments could mean lost time waiting for body marks to fade. The model's hair is then styled and makeup applied, usually by a licensed cosmetologist, which D'eva is, so Vickie agreed to use her for the session.

The PMT was scheduled for Monday, September 17. Only one day would be needed to do both the studio and outdoor shots. However, that Monday morning Vickie called to report that she'd had a boating accident the day before and that she had cuts and bruises all over her body.

Cuts and bruises are virtually impossible to cover up with makeup, and it was agreed that the session would be postponed until she'd healed somewhat. Linda Kenney was not happy on being informed of the delay. She'd seen something in those first Polaroids, and she wanted the PMT done as quickly as possible.

Vickie finally came in for her PMT on Tuesday morning, October 2, 1991, alone, freshly scrubbed, and without makeup. D'eva took her into the salon area of the studio, where they quickly got into a discussion about skin types, hair styles, colours, and an overall approach to enhancing Vickie's beauty.

It was clear Vickie didn't know much about style. This was the second time we'd seen her, and once again she was wearing a skin-tight Spandex dress and five-inch heels.

At that time, we were unfamiliar with the topless dancing sub-culture and assumed that Vickie was dressed in what she naively thought was glamour garb. Being from that tiny town in Texas, it made sense that she wasn't sophisticated and that she would go over-

47

board on makeup and overall flash. It was only later that we realized she wasn't the innocent flower she claimed to be. Her style was titty-bar chic, and she did everything she could to advertise her body, especially her breasts.

D'eva had other plans for her, however. She trimmed Vickie's hair and gave it a much softer look. As for makeup, D'eva astonished Vickie with her sill. It's quite possible that Vickie hadn't realized, until she looked at herself in that mirror, just how beautiful she really was. It was as if she'd been granted a wish by a fairy godmother. She was Cinderella. She was touched by D'eva's magic.

Our destination was Sugar Land, an upscale subdivision on the southwest side of Houston. There was a small lake on the outskirts, one Eric had used as a backdrop before. Although not on a main thoroughfare, it wasn't isolated, and he cautioned Vickie that someone might see him taking the photographs. She would be nude, of course, and he asked her if that would be a problem. She assured him it would not.

Once there, we carried the equipment down to the lake, and Eric set up for the first shots. When it was time for her to disrobe, Vickie, instead of being shy as we expected, ducked under a tree and whipped off her dress. It was clear she was excited, and she wanted to be in front of the camera. Quite a change form the first session, when she'd literally trembled at the thought of being nude.

After D'eva touched her up and applied some body makeup, Vickie was ready. What Eric saw through that lens was something he'd never forget.

Vickie Lynn Smith *loved* the camera, and the camera loved her right back. She blossomed out there in Sugar Land. D'eva stood to the side, coaxing Vickie into different poses, but the student soon outpaced the teacher. She was a natural, a goddess. Eric had never seen anything quite like it. Vickie was a photographer's dream come true, and we knew this girl was going to make it.

All the reticence from the first session had disappeared, and

Vickie showed herself to be quick, supple, clever. She surprised us over and over again with her verve and willingness to experiment.

The three of us were stoked by the time she got dressed. It was a thrilling day, filled with untold promise. When we drove to the net location, Vickie had buried all vestiges of shyness. She talked on and on about her dreams, about how she'd always wanted to be a *Playboy* centrefold, and how that was going to be her steppingstone to acting. She was like a kid on Christmas, and we felt a little like Santa Claus.

The next set was our attorney's house where Vickie posed in front of his elegant brick fireplace. The shoot moved quickly, with no wrong turns. By the time we were through, we all felt the need to celebrate, and Eric made a quick trip to the liquor store. When he got back, D'eva and Vickie were more than ready to party, and the champagne cork popped to a chorus of cheers. We toasted the future, the fame, the money, the sheer excitement of it all.

Vickie really put away the bubbly. D'eva didn't think much of it at the time and certainly didn't realize that this was not the exception, but the rule. She just thought Vickie was a sweet kid from Mexia who was about to set the world on fire.

How were we to know that she'd lied on the biography? That the boating accident which had delayed the PMT had been a car accident, one that got her sued for personal injury because she rear-ended another vehicle while allegedly under the influence of alcohol? Or that the fresh-faced beauty with such endearing naivete had been a topless dancer and selling her favors for the past four years?

.8

TENTATIVE FEATURE: _____
PHOTOGRAPHER: _____
EXACT DATE(S) AND LOCATION OF PHOTOGRAPHY: _____
_____

BIOGRAPHICAL INFORMATION

Legal Name: Vickie Smith
Home Address: 300 Woerner #2117
Phone #: 5375670   Social Security #: _____
Place of Birth: Houston   Date of Birth: 11-28-67
Education: Mexia High
Current School Address & Phone # (If Applicable) _____
modeling
Occupation: ~~unemployed~~   Business Phone #: 6863401
Hobbies: watching scary movies
Sports or Special Activities: Horse back riding
Likes: Gentlemen who no how to treat a lady
Dislikes: Cigeret smoke, Bums with no jobs
Ambition: to be in Playboy + model, Actress
About Men (Likes or Dislikes): I Don't like men who always talk about how much money they ha
Other Interesting Remarks About Yourself or Family: I have a 5 yr old son we been raising by myself and my mom is a very big help to me
Parent's Occupation(s): mother is a Deputy Sheriff

Height	Weight	Bust/Cup	Waist	Hips	Hair	Eyes	Shoe Size
5"11	140	42.DD	26	38	Blonde	Hazel	10

CLOSE FRIEND OR RELATIVE WHO CAN ALWAYS FIND YOU

Name: Virgie Hart   Phone #: _____ Area Code
Address: 8106   No. Street City State Zip Code
How Related: mother

Chapter 4

PLAYMATE DATA SHEET AND MODEL RELEASE

In the event you are selected as a Playmate of the Month for PLAYBOY Magazine, the information provided below will be essential for our story. All questions should be answered as fully and truthfully as possible, in your own handwriting.

LEGAL NAME __VICKIE LYNN SMITH__ AGE __23__

ADDRESS(Street) __300 WOERNER__ (City) __HOUSTON__ (State) __TX.__

PHONE (Home) __713-537-5670__ (Business) _____ ZIP CODE __77090__

NATIONAL EXTRACTION __UNITED STATES__

HEIGHT __6FT 3"__ WEIGHT __140 150__ EYE COLOR __HAZEL__ HAIR COLOR __BLONDE__

BUST __42 DD__ WAIST __26__ HIPS __38__

SWEATER SIZE __MEDIUM__ SKIRT SIZE __9__ DRESS SIZE __9__

BIRTH DATE __11-28-67__ PLACE OF BIRTH __HOUSTON__ MARITAL STATUS __S__

NUMBER OF CHILDREN, IF ANY __1__ AGES __5__

S.S.# _____ SHOE SIZE __10__

OTHER CITIES AND COUNTRIES IN WHICH YOU'VE RESIDED:

__MEXIA, TEXAS__ From 19 __82__ until 19 __86__

__(MY MOM + GRANDPARENTS ARE FROM__ From 19 ___ until 19 ___

__MEXIA - SO I HAVE LIVED THERE ON + OFF)__ From 19 ___ until 19 ___

FATHER'S NAME __DONALD HART__ OCCUPATION _____

MOTHER'S NAME __VIRGIE HART__ OCCUPATION __DEPUTY ~~SUPERVISA~~ SHERIFF__

CITY AND STATE IN WHICH PARENTS RESIDE __HOUSTON, TX.__

IF UNMARRIED, DO YOU LIVE AT HOME? ___ ALONE? __✓__ WITH ROOMMATE(S) ___

HOW MANY BROTHERS __2__ AGES __18, 24__ SISTERS __1__ AGES __27__

IS THERE ANYTHING PARTICULARLY INTERESTING OR UNUSUAL ABOUT ANY MEMBERS OF YOUR FAMILY? __MY MOTHER IS A POLICE OFFICER + HAS BEEN FOR 16 YEARS.__

51

GRAMMAR SCHOOL(S) DURKEE ELEM. City, State Hou, TX 1977 to 1982

+ ~~HOUSE~~ ALDINE INT. City, State Hou, TX. 1982 to 1984

HIGH SCHOOL(S) MEXIA City, State MEXIA, TX 1984 to 1986

_____ City, State _____ 19__ to 19__

COLLEGE(S) NA City, State _____ 19__ to 19__

_____ City, State _____ 19__ to 19__

COLLEGE MAJORS NA DEGREES _____

OTHER SCHOOLS ATTENDED PAGE PARKES City, State HOUSTON 19? to 19?

MODELING SCHOOL City, State _____ 19__ to 19__

PLANS FOR CONTINUING YOUR EDUCATION _____ WHERE? _____
?

CURRENT OCCUPATION MODELING / MOTHER

NAME OF CURRENT EMPLOYER (Firm) VARIOUS (City) HOUSTON

NATURE OF BUSINESS MODELING EMPLOYED SINCE ?

PREVIOUS EMPLOYERS (Firm name, city & state, how long employed and position):

(1) BREAKFAST COOK ?

_____

(2) _____

CAREER AMBITIONS TELEVISION + VIDEO MODELING —
LIKE MTV FOR INSTANCE

PREVIOUS MODELING EXPERIENCE: Pin-up___ Nudes___ Fashion✓ Artist___ Other ADVERTISING

THEATRICAL EXPERIENCE: Stage___ Movies___ TV___ Nightclubs___ Other_____

TITLES OF PLAYS, MOVIES, TV SHOWS, NAMES OF NIGHTCLUBS NA

HAVE NUDE OF SEMI-NUDE PHOTOGRAPHS OF YOU EVER BEEN PUBLISHED IN A MAGAZINE?___

IF SO, GIVE NAME OF MAGAZINES(S) AND DATES(S) PUBLISHED NA

HAVE YOU EVER POSED FOR NUDE OR SEMI-NUDE PHOTOGRAPHS OTHER THAN THE TEST SHOTS NOW
BEING TAKEN FOR PLAYBOY? NO IF SO, WHEN AND FOR WHOM? _____

DID YOU SIGN A MODEL RELEASE FOR THE PICTURES?_____ WERE YOU PAID?_____

The questions below will be most important in determining your picture story. Please give each question some thought before answering and give as much detail as possible.

DO YOU PLAN TO DO ANYTHING IN PARTICULAR WITH THE MONEY EARNED AS A PLAYMATE?

I WOULD LIKE TO TAKE MY AUNT WHO RAISED ME, ON A CRUISE — ESPECIALLY SINCE SHE IS IN ILL-HEALTH. ALSO, I WOULD GET A CAR.

IF YOU COULD CHOOSE ONE PLACE IN THE WORLD TO VISIT, WHERE WOULD IT BE AND WHY?

I WOULD LOVE TO VISIT PARIS BECAUSE OF THE FASHIONS, BUT ALSO, I WOULD LOVE TO GO TO THE CAYMAN ISLANDS, BECAUSE I LOVE THE SUN

IF YOU COULD CHOOSE A CAREER FOR YOURSELF, WHAT WOULD IT BE AND WHY?

AN ACTRESS, BECAUSE I WOULD LIKE TO BE SEEN IN THE MOVIES.

IF YOU WERE TO DECIDE WHAT KIND OF A PICTURE STORY IS DONE ON YOU, HOW WOULD THE STORY GO? IN THE COUNTRY, WITH LOTS OF HORSES, HAY, AND COWBOYS — I LOVE COWBOYS.

WHO, IN THE ENTIRE WORLD, WOULD YOU LIKE TO MEET AND GET TO KNOW? WHY?

HULK HOGAN — BECAUSE HE'S FUNNY AND MAKES ME LAUGH.

PLEASE GIVE US AN EXAMPLE OF A TYPICAL DAY IN YOUR LIFE.

GET UP AND EAT BREAKFAST, TALK TO MY SON PREPARE FOR THE DAY, PHONE CALLS, ETC., WATCH TV.

WHAT DO YOU DO IN YOUR SPARE TIME? I LOVE TO RIDE HORSES AND WATCHING SCARY MOVIES!

WHAT WOULD YOU LIKE TO DO IF YOU HAD MORE TIME? I WOULD LIKE TO GO TO MEXICA AND SPEND MORE TIME WITH MY AUNT.

FAVORITE BOOKS I DON'T READ MUCH!

FAVORITE AUTHORS ———

FAVORITE MOVIES DRAMAS, SCARY MOVIES

FAVORITE TV SHOWS SIMPSONS

FAVORITE FOODS AND DRINKS I LOVE BIG RED + PASTA

FAVORITE KIND OF MUSIC COUNTRY

FAVORITE PERFORMERS GARTH BROOKS, KENNY ROGERS

FAMOUS MEN AND WOMEN YOU ADMIRE CHRISTIE BRINKLEY

WHY? BECAUSE SHE IS BEAUTIFUL + IS WHERE I WOULD LIKE TO BE.

YOUR PET PEEVES ARE I CANNOT STAND FOR A MAN TO ASK ME FOR PHONE CHANGE + NOT OPENING DOORS

YOU'RE PARTICULARLY WILD ABOUT COWBOYS

DESCRIBE YOUR IDEAL MAN (Age, Occupation, Character, etc.) SOMEONE VERY ROMANTIC, ABOUT 35, + WHO LOVES TO TRAVEL. ALSO, WHO HAS A FUNNY PERSONALITY.

DESCRIBE YOUR IDEAL EVENING COCKTAILS, ROMANTIC DINNER, + SLOW DANCING.

DESCRIBE YOURSELF (What kind of person are you?) I AM A VERY KIND-HEARTED PERSON WHO IS FUN TO BE AROUND, BUT CAN BE A SERIOUS PERSON WHEN I NEED TO BE.

IF YOU COULD CHANGE ONE CHARACTER TRAIT IN YOURSELF, IT WOULD BE I'M TOO KIND-HEARTED AT TIMES WHY? — BECAUSE PEOPLE TAKE ADVANTAGE OF ME.

AMBITIONS (What you want from life in general) TO STAY SINGLE + JUST HAVE FUN FOR A WHILE — LATER I'LL GET MARRIED + HOPEFULLY HAVE A DAUGHT

WHY DO YOU WANT TO BE A PLAYMATE? IT'S JUST BEEN ONE OF MY DREAMS! I'VE ALWAYS WONDERED IF I COULD BE A PLAYMATE + HOW I WOULD FEEL.

DESCRIBE THE CIRCUMSTANCES THAT LED TO YOUR APPLYING TO BE A PLAYMATE I'VE ALWAYS TCHED LOOKING IN THE MAGAZINES TO FIND AN ADDRESS, BUT COULDN'T. I SAW ERIC REDDING'S AD IN THE NEWSPAPER FROM YOU GUYS.

DID YOU SEND THE PICTURES IN YOURSELF? NO

DID A PHOTOGRAPHER OR TALENT SCOUT APPROACH YOU? ERIC REDDING

OTHER UNUSUAL BIOGRAPHICAL INFORMATION AT 5'11", I TOWER OVER A LOT OF MY DATES, AND HAVE TO LAUGH ABOUT IT SOMETIMES.

ADDITIONAL COMMENTS I WOULD LOVE TO BE A PLAYMATE, AND IF I DO, ONE OF MY DREAMS WOULD HAVE COME TRUE!

Chapter 5

WE DON'T KNOW if a record was set, but only three days after the film on Vickie arrived in the Los Angeles offices of *Playboy*, Linda Kenney called Eric. She wanted to speak to Vickie and then have her get out to Los Angeles as soon as it could be arranged.

It's always great to be the bearer of great news, and we wanted to deliver this in person to Vickie. Eric called and asked her to get over to the studio. Normally it took her about an hour to drive in from her apartment, but this time she made it in thirty minutes. When she walked in the front door, it was clear she had figured out something good was going on. Her smile lit up the room like a strobe.

"Guess what, darlin'," Eric said. "You're going to be a *Playboy* Playmate!"

The three of us hugged and laughed, then hugged again. It truly was a moment we would never forget. The sheer *promise* of it all was so palpable! When Vickie managed to regain her composure, Eric told her that she needed to talk to Linda and photo coordinator Stephanie Barnett. They would arrange for her to fly out the next weekend. Once there, they would talk to her, and she would be photographed some more.

We left Vickie alone for the twenty minutes she was on the phone with Linda Kenney and don't have any firsthand knowledge of what transpired. We do know that after Vickie hung up, she appeared confused and somewhat angry. Eric was naturally concerned. This was Big Break Time, Dream Come True Time, what could be bothering her?

"I'm mad at you," she said.

"Why?"

Chapter 5

"I thought you told me they were going to fly me to Los Angeles."

"They are," Eric said, growing more bewildered by the moment.

Vickie shook her head. "No, they're not. They said they're flying me to California!"

Eric just stood there for a minute with his mouth open. It was such a bizarre statement that he fully expected her to burst out laughing and tell him he was kidding. But no, she was serious.

It took a while before Eric was able to make her believe that Los Angeles was in California. Even with D'eva's help, Vickie thought he was trying to pull a fast one. She was under the almost unshakeable impression that Los Angeles was in New York. Finally Vickie got her coasts straightened out. American students have been shown to have a dismal knowledge of geography, but this wasn't Liechtenstein we were talking about.

The incident was more than a little unsettling. We knew from her difficulty in filling out a simple one-page biography that we weren't dealing with a candidate for a Nobel Prize in anything. Still, this was a bit much and more than a bit worrisome. Was this a case of a deficiency in the American educational system or a deficiency in her brain capacity? In either case, it was clear this girl needed management. Brighter, savvier women had crashed in the fast lanes of Los Angeles. Since we were the ones sending her there, we volunteered to help her navigate.

Getting ready for the trip to L.A. proved to be an adventure in itself. We told Vickie that if she had any questions or problems, she should call us anytime, day or night. She really had no idea what to do. This twenty-four-year-old girl/woman had yet to venture out of her home state (or at least that's what she told us), and from what we could ascertain, had done very little venturing within her home state. Now she was going to the Playboy mansion. It was heady, and exciting, and terrifying for her.

Vickie called every one of the next six days as she prepared for her adventure. Sometimes four or five times a day. Who else could she turn to? Virgie? Aunt Kay? They were less-seasoned travellers than she was.

Even luggage was a big issue. For starters, she had none and didn't want to borrow any. It was not until the day before her departure – no, the night before – that she went somewhere and bought three pieces of matching luggage. She was thrilled with them. It seemed as if those suitcases represented her bright new future: money, fame, success. And they were matching.

Her unsophisticated enthusiasm and nervous exhilaration was understandable. The kid had grown up with nothing. And suddenly she was invited into a world that represented the epitome of glamour to her, the world of Hugh Hefner and Playboy bunnies. It was the stuff her dreams were made of, and she had just been handed a first-class ticket. Actually, Playboy booked her in coach, but hey, Vickie was revved so high, she could have flown to L.A. on her own power.

Vickie's difficulty in getting her luggage act together was one of our smaller concerns. Some of her other worries had us worried. For instance there was the call the night before she was to leave. It was late, and we hadn't heard from Vickie all day. That in itself had us wondering since she'd been calling so often. But we dismissed it, figuring she was busy shopping and getting ready.

When she did call, she told Eric something had been bothering her all day. It was a rumour she'd heard. Was it really true that to even be considered for a centrefold, a girl had to sleep with Mr Hefner?

With someone else, Eric might have joked about the silliness of the rumour, but Vickie was clearly upset and taking it seriously. Instead, Eric said, "I honestly don't know firsthand, but since Mr Hefner is married now and just had a child, I kind of doubt it." He went on to assure her that the people of Playboy select the Playmates with great care and professionalism, and she really didn't have to worry about sleeping with Hugh Hefner.

She seemed satisfied with that response and said goodbye. She promised that her next call would be from the Playboy mansion.

About five minutes later, the phone rang again. It was Vickie.

"I have one more question," she said. "Do you have a minute?"

"Sure, what is it?" Eric asked.

"Well, uh, do you know if the girls have to run around naked the whole time they stay at the mansion, or when they're working at the studio?"

This time Eric had to laugh. "No, honey," he said. "These are all professional people. They'll treat you like a lady. I promise."

Her sigh came across the wires, and Eric could feel her relief. Who had been filling her head with this nonsense?

She said goodbye and hung up. Eric hadn't made it to the next room when the phone rang still another time.

"This is the last time I'll bother you guys, but I just remembered something."

"Yes?"

"They said that they're going to pick me up at the airport in a black-and-white limousine. I was wondering what they mean exactly. Do they mean a black-and-white chequered one like you find on the floors in restaurants, or what?"

Eric had to sit down. This was going from mildly amusing to seriously bizarre. Yet he knew she was earnestly confused. He explained that it would be either a white limo with a black console top, or a black limo with a white top. But she didn't have to worry – the driver would have a sign with her name on it. All she had to do was find the driver.

She thanked him again. Actually, it was pretty sweet, and they said their goodbyes – this time for real.

Vickie first checked in with us Monday night from the guest quarters of the Playboy Mansion. She'd arrived safely, but she did have a bit of trouble at the airport. She'd been surprised at how much luggage was at baggage claim and how much alike the suitcases were. It took her a long time to find hers, but when she did, the nice driver had carried them to the limousine (which, by the way, was black with a white console top).

She hadn't been in the mansion for more than thirty minutes when a phone call came from the airline. She had walked off with the wrong luggage, and what she had taken didn't even remotely resemble the set she had so lovingly and proudly chosen.

The nice driver had to return to the airport to make the switch. Vickie apologized to him, explaining, "Well, they all looked alike to me." What was never explained was how the airlines found Vickie at the Playboy mansion.

The next day, Linda Kenney reached Eric. He could tell things were working out well by the tone in her voice. She'd always been professional and courteous to him, but that afternoon she sounded giddy with enthusiasm. She wanted to tell him that he and West Coast photo editor Marilyn Grabowski were in love with Vickie, and that she was one of the best models to come along in ages. They just wanted to congratulate us on finding Vickie and having such good instincts about her.

We were thrilled that it was all turning out so well, and then came the topper – Marilyn had already decided to feature Vickie on the cover of the March 1992 issue of *Playboy*!

Playboy is in the business of selling magazines, and the staff there often go with their gut feelings on what the public wants to see. As far as they were concerned, a voluptuous blonde beauty by the name of Vickie Lynn Smith was what the public was waiting for.

Chapter 6

THE NEWS OUT of Los Angeles had been great, and we figured it was clear sailing for Vickie from then on. What we hadn't figured, however, was that LaLa Land got a bit LaLa-ier with her arrival.

Eric got the distress call. Vickie sounded more upset than usual. Before she could launch into what was bothering her, Eric interrupted. If what she had to say was confidential, she might want to find a pay phone somewhere. He had been told phone conversations from the guest quarters at the mansion were recorded. Vickie was silent for a moment and then she said she'd get back to him.

Eric made up a hundred scenarios while he was waiting. Things had been going so well that he couldn't imagine what had caused that alarm in Vickie's voice. Had he steered her wrong – *was* she really expected to sleep with Hefner? It seemed inconceivable, but what else could it be?

Finally, an hour later, Vickie got back to him. She had found a public phone, although Eric wasn't sure how or where.

"Eric." Vickie's voice was shaking. "Are there cameras in the guest rooms?"

"Cameras?"

"You know, security cameras."

He had no idea, of course, but Vickie seemed desperate to know, so he promised to find out what he could. His next question was why he cared. She answered, "Please, just find out and I'll tell you later."

Eric contacted Linda Kenney. Apparently this was not a question that arose very often, and she didn't have the answer but promised to check into it.

It did not take Linda long to get back to Eric. She had discovered that, yes, there were video cameras installed behind the air-conditioning vents in the guest rooms. For security purposes only, she said. Linda showed remarkable restraint and tact. She didn't ask why he needed to know about the cameras. Of course, Eric didn't know himself.

That evening, a panicky Vickie got through from a pay phone at the Playboy studios. Did Eric know? Were there cameras? When Eric confirmed that there were, she gasped and then was silent. After waiting a long time, it felt like several minutes, Eric asked her what was going on.

It seems Vickie had packed some toys in her matching set of luggage to keep her amused. Sex toys. To help her wile away those long, lonely hours at night.

"You mean you masturbated?" Eric asked. "Well, that's no big deal. I'm sure they couldn't see anything with the lights off."

"No," she said. "You don't understand. The lights were on. I was, um, at the mirror."

"What?"

"I was there for, like maybe two hours," she said, near tears. "All the lights were on and everything. Eric, I used all my stuff."

"Stuff?"

"You know, like um, dildos and shit."

"I see," he said, even though he was having trouble assimilating what she was telling him.

This "show" had evidently gone on every night for six nights. She hadn't thought a thing about it – until one of the other girls mentioned the cameras.

Eric tried his best to calm her. Of all the places she could have indulged in this pastime, the Playboy mansion was probably the safest. It didn't matter what he said, she was inconsolable and worried that this peccadillo would ruin her brand-new career. Of course, Eric had no way of knowing then that Vickie wasn't a stranger to masturbating for an audience. It was something she used to do at the topless clubs.

First thing the next morning, Eric was on the phone to Linda Kenney. Hearing the rundown of Vickie's confession, Linda kept repeating, "You're kidding!" Each time Eric assured her he wasn't, she went off again.

Finally when Linda could speak with a reasonable amount of control, she told him not to worry. The mansion staff was incredibly discreet, and no one would blow the whistle on Vickie.

Later Eric found out that the security crew at the mansion all got copies of the surveillance camera tapes. They're undoubtedly collector's items now.

There were no repercussions from the security camera escapade. If anything, *Playboy* loved Vickie. That same magic that had been evident in the PMT was alive and well in California. The pictures were stupendous, and Marilyn Grabowsky told Vickie, Linda, and many others that Vickie was the most beautiful woman she'd ever seen, even without makeup.

Ironically, the March 1992 cover they chose for Vickie's debut had a debutante theme. They dressed her in an emerald green gown, seated her on an ornate antique chair, and somehow made her look like a lush, full-figured Grace Kelly. This poor kid from nowhere, with no education, and no sophistication was chosen as a symbol of old-world money, class and elegance. It was probably an inside joke on *Playboy*'s part, but if anyone ever burned with the desire to be a sparkly deb, it was Vickie Lynn Smith.

It was about this time that Vickie's past rose up and bit her in the rear. The staff had examined her biography and noticed the word dancer had been scratched out and replaced by the word model. Stephanie called the number Vickie had provided and reached Gigi's Cabaret.

Playboy is an American institution. It sends out scouts to Ivy League campuses in search of Playmates. It courts schoolteachers and police officers. It will accept girls who work in upscale places like Rick's. It definitely does not want strippers, especially not ones who table-dance at Gigi's Cabaret.

When Linda Kenney came straight out and asked Eric if Vickie had been a stripper, he covered for her. He told Linda he didn't think so. He barely knew Vickie and although she had said she was a dancer, he wasn't sure at that point if it had been nude dancing or just topless dancing. Again, *Playboy* drew a line at baring or breasts and baring it all. David Davari, the owner of Gigi's at that time was also called, and he, too, covered for Vickie.

Vickie told Linda Kenney and Marilyn Grabowski that she had been a dancer for a very short time, only because she'd been forced into it to support her son.

For a while it seemed that *Playboy* was going to back away from Vickie. She wasn't coming across as its archetypal fresh and unspoiled girl next door. But instead of giving her a ticket back to Houston, Vickie was given a centrefold.

A cover pays $500, a centrefold a nice $20,000 plus promotional gigs that can really add up. Vickie was going to be Miss May 1992, bumping several other girls to later issues.

Ordinarily a model doesn't make the centrefold so quickly, but Vickie was strapped for money. Payment to the models is due upon publication, and Vickie didn't want to wait. The fact that *Playboy* was willing to accommodate her was a testament to how much she was liked there. When Vickie was named Playmate of the Year, she received another $100,000 and a Jaguar. All in all, it sure beat dancing at Gigi's – if you didn't count potential income from octogenarians who wandered in for lunch.

Anna Nicole had this and several similar photos, shot on top of her baby grand piano, blown up to 40" x 60" size as a Christmas present in 1992 for her future husband, eighty-seven-year-old J. Howard Marshall II.

Vickie Lynn (bottom right) with brothers Donald and David and sister Shauna.

Mother Virgie Hart, a Harris County (Texas) deputy sheriff.

Cousin Melinda Beall, Aunt Kay Beall's daughter.

Sophomore Anna, who was using the name Nikki Hart, pictured in the 1985 Mexia High school year book.

After dropping out of school, Anna Nicole worked at Jim's Krispy Fried Chicken.

Anna Nicole was Vickie Lynn Smith when this picture was taken with her baby son, Daniel.

Eric Redding's Polaroid test shots of the then Vickie Smith that caught the interest of *Playboy* magazine.

A different type of shot – a mug shot taken by the Houston Police Department after Vickie Lynn Smith was picked up for Driving While Intoxicated, 21st September 1989.

An ad for Gigi's Cabaret, where Anna danced topless as "Miss Houston's Hot Robyn".

Anna doing a publicity stint at the Silverado Club to preview her March 1992 *Playboy* cover.

Virgie Hart with Al Bolt at a benefit honouring the Houston Firemen Calendar Men. Virgie bought a dance with Bolt for $75, which greatly displeased her daughter.

With boyfriend/bodyguard Pierre DeJean.

J. Howard Marshall II and Anna Nicole on their "honeymoon" in Bali, April 1994, several weeks before their 27th June wedding.

Chapter 7

VICKIE'S COVER SHOT for March 1992 hit the newsstands at the end of January, transforming her into a minor Houston celebrity. One of the first fringe benefits to her new fame was a gorgeous firefighter named Al Bolt.

Al met Vickie in January at the Silverado Club, a country and western place outside of Houston. Every year as a fund-raiser to benefit burned and crippled children the Houston Fire Department issues a calendar featuring its best-looking guys. Al was one of them. He was at the Silverado signing the calendar, and Vickie was autographing her *Playboy* cover. We knew Al from photographing the calendar, so we introduced him to Vickie.

Al, a divorcee with three children, said, "I was attracted to her by the way she was being presented as a home-town girl from right here in Texas. Came up dirt poor, made it big, decided she was going to try out for the *Playboy* centrefold, and like within three days, they called her back and said, yes, you're the one we want."

As part of the fund-raising, the firemen were auctioned off for dances. Vickie was not happy when her mother Virgie won him with a $75 bid. Later, she gave Al an autographed cover of *Playboy* on which she had written: "To Al, I would have paid a whole lot more."

That was more than enough encouragement for Al. He didn't just give Vickie his phone number. He gave her his pager number, his office number, and his car phone number as well. However, Vickie didn't call them. It wasn't that she hadn't been attracted to the handsome, dark-haired fireman/paramedic, it was just that *Playboy* commitments were gobbling up her time.

She was somewhere nearly every night, signing photographs and layouts, hosting talent searches for *Playboy*, going to parties, spending her money. There were the trips to the Playboy mansion.

So it must have been kismet when Al, on an excursion with his kids at a park in Tomball, saw Virgie assisting some traffic accident victims. After things settled down, Al reintroduced himself to Virgie and asked her for Vickie's phone number.

Virgie obliged. When Al reached Vickie, he explained how he got her number and she indicated she didn't mind.

Their first date was in March 1992. It was casual, lunch, no pressure. Al brought along her centrefold, which Vickie autographed with a smiling hear above her name. Al was charmed at how shy she was, how innocent and sweet.

That isn't to say he wasn't knocked out by the lady's physique. And that face. But it was the whole picture that gave Al his mission. He wanted this girl; he wanted to take care of her, to protect her, to make sure she came to no harm.

It was all so clear for him at the beginning.

"It started out as a daytime thing," Al said. "Eventually, we started going to nightclubs like the Yucatan and Bayou Mama's. These weren't dinner dates, though. This was publicity. Being part of the *Playboy* crowd. At the time Vickie was representing *Playboy*, and she wanted me to be there with her. I kind of fell into being her boyfriend."

Put two healthy young people together, and things are bound to heat up. "When Vickie wants to win you over, she could pour on the charm," Al said. "Her idol was Marilyn Monroe, so she would come on with that soft, smooth kind of voice that told you…whatever she wanted, she could use that to lure you onto whatever she wanted you to do."

Soon, Al was invited to Vickie's house. Kay Beall, her boyfriend Floyd Harrison, and daughter Melinda were all staying with her at that time. Mostly to watch Daniel. But also to reap some of the rewards of Vickie's new financial status.

Chapter 7

Al was surprised by her relatives. "They were really country oriented," he said. "When I say country oriented, I mean there's country people that are poor but clean. Then you have country people that are poor, trashy, and lost.

"Her Aunty Kay was very large, very sloppy. Vickie invited her to come from Mexia to Houston to watch out for Daniel. So, the whole family just moved in. They were all living there and none of them worked. Vickie was the only breadwinner. Where she was getting her money, I don't know. Because she didn't have a job. She just had the centrefold."

It didn't take long, however, for Al to get an inkling of the source of Vickie's money. "The income was coming from a guy that I found out about after our relationship was going on. His name was Howard Marshall. He was supposed to have been an oil tycoon that lived in River Oaks."

Vickie told Al about meeting Marshall, although in her version, it was in a restaurant. "His driver had come over and asked her to go and talk to him. Vickie told me that she 'brought him back from the dead.' She told me he was really down because his wife had died. That he didn't have anybody to talk to and all that kind of stuff. So she went over and talked to him, and that's how they became good friends."

Of course, it wasn't just Marshall's wife who had passed away, but also Lady Walker, his mistress. And not many customers went to Gigi's for the food. And, of course, there was more to Vickie and Marshall's relationship than idle chit chat.

But Al didn't know any of that. He still saw Vickie as the sweet young thing from Mexia. Slowly, the truth started to come to light.

Visits with Vickie's relatives disabused him of any thoughts she was getting money from them. "They had no money. Nothing. [Their house] had bugs crawling on the furniture and things like that. It wasn't very clean."

Then he found the pay stub in Vickie's car. It was from J. Howard Marshall's company. "She went into a store one time and I happened to be driving the car. And on the side of the door, there's like this pocket thing. There was a check stub sticking up out of it. I picked it up. It had Howard Marshall's name on the top of it and his company. Down below it had Vickie's name as the recipient. So, I felt like maybe he was carrying her as an employee and just paying her, but she didn't do anything for him. At least not for the company."

Al began to suspect that Marshall was paying Vickie for sexual favours.

"She had a brand new Toyota Celica, I remember. White. And she got that before she did the *Playboy* layout. The money didn't come from her family. It all came from Howard Marshall. I heard later that the old man liked to watch. That he would like it when Vickie was with another girl. He'd pay 'em to watch the sex act. He was too old to do much for himself, but I know Vickie serviced him."

Then there was the matter of the phone calls. Al's relationship with Vickie only lasted nine months, but for a brief time, they lived together. "I might be in the bed laying right beside her, and we might be laughing and cutting up having a good time. All of a sudden the phone would ring. When she'd pick it up, she'd put her finger to her mouth and tell me to be quiet because it was Howard. She'd cover the phone and tell me to hush.

"She didn't want him to know that I was in her life. Howard was not to know about me at all. She felt like if he knew about me, her days of money would be over with…It would upset me. We would have arguments about it. I would tell her, hey…I'm a person, too. I'm a human being too. I don't have a lot of money, but the problem is, you say he's a businessman, well, I'm a businessman, too."

That argument didn't carry much weight with Vickie. According to Al, she was at Marshall's beck and call. If he wanted a platter of sandwiches, she would race out and get it for him. What Al resented was Vickie would elicit his help as well. "It kind of made me sick…I'm supposed to be her boyfriend, yet she's going with this old, antique rascal that I guess was her sugar daddy. He's given her a tennis bracelet that had multiple diamonds on it. He'd given her rings. Diamond earrings. I'm talking real big diamonds. A person on a fire department salary would never be able to maintain the lifestyle that she was hunting for."

As Al's relationship with Vickie continued, more and more of her wildness surfaced. Once when they were driving back from Mexia, Vickie decided it would be fun to flash truckers on the highway. She opened the car's moonroof, and when the car pulled close to a truck, she'd expose her breasts. "Those truckers would blow their horns and stuff," Al said. "She'd say 'Now speed up and get to the next one.' Well, you know that they've got CB radios. All of them knew she was coming. She flashed every truck from Mexia to Houston."

Al hung in, even though his friends were cluing him in on Vickie's past. He wasn't sure if they were jealous that he was dating her or were genuinely concerned for him. "What they didn't know was I was trying to change her from the inside. Being that I'm a Christian, I took that as a challenge. I was looking at a soul that was out of control and that maybe…I could get her to turn around."

Al had no idea what kind of challenge he had taken on.

Chapter 8

BECOMING A *Playboy* centrefold meant Vickie could leave her dancing days behind her, along with many of her friends who were told that *Playboy* didn't want her to associate with them anymore. Vickie represented the magazine now. She would continue to bare her body but with a degree of respectability that the titty bars could never attain. When it's for two hundreds bucks a night on a dark stage, it's dirty and sneered at. When it's for twenty thousand bucks in a national magazine – it's admired and applauded.

We had signed on as Vickie's managers, and a large part of that task turned out to be baby-sitting. Vickie was a wild girl, and as we got to know her better, we discovered that her taste for the fun life was quite catholic.

She liked partying, any kind, all kind. Sex, any sex. Drugs and alcohol, as long as it was in excess. It was a struggle keeping her sober enough for promotional events. Sobriety wasn't the only problem. There was her diet, her appearance, her propensity for picking up men or women or men *and* women for the night.

Whenever possible, we went with Vickie to her publicity events, and when that wasn't an option, we tried to line up chaperones.

We weren't always successful keeping her under rein.

In February 1992, Houston hosted the annual Livestock Show and Rodeo. Joe Healy, director of marketing and advertising for the Appletree Grocery Store chain, hired Vickie to represent his company. She was to ride a float, along with Ray Childress, defensive linebacker for the NFL's Houston Oilers. He was a big man with a big reputation – regarded as one of the greatest quarterbacks ever to play American football. Later he was to become a philanthropist. Along with his wife, Kara, Childress started the Childress Foundation in 1995 to help Houston's at-risk children get an education and become involved with community service. He now runs a major car dealership in Texas.

Childress made it clear he wasn't happy having to associate with Vickie, even to the limited extent of sitting next to her on the float. But she behaved well enough that Childress was able to remain civil.

As it turned out, Vickie was interested in him for more than his number of sacks on the field. It made no difference to her that he was married. She asked Eric if he thought Childress had a big "package." She'd noticed his large hands and to her that meant only one thing. She asked the linebacker if he wanted to take her dancing, but he, wisely, declined.

Later that week, Vickie's job was to mingle with clients in the skyboxes, shake a few hands, and act the gracious hostess. Apparently the open bar was too much temptation for her. It didn't take long before she was drunk, boisterous, and something far from gracious.

According to Deborah Keener, account executive for country radio station 92.9, the main topic of conversation that night was not the rodeo, but Vickie Lynn Smith. Seems they were expecting a more typical *Playboy* bunny – slim, attractive, classy. What they got was Vickie – big, inebriated, coarse.

Still, Joe Healy used her again later that year. In conjunction with East Texas Distributing, he hired her as the celebrity spokesperson for their booth at a New Orleans convention.

Two days before the event, Vickie let Eric know she was unhappy with the deal: five hundred a day for two days. Although she'd agreed to the fee because of the free time she'd have in New Orleans – it would be something of a paid vacation – she informed Eric that she wouldn't go unless she got more money. Her new rate was now two thousand a day for all public appearances.

Eric tried to reason with her, pointing out the contract had been on the books for seven or eight months. It fell on deaf ears and limited scruples. She wouldn't get on the plane unless her demands were met.

Eric called Ken Stilling, vice-president for East Texas Distributing, and told him the situation. Ken, ever the gentleman, offered to renegotiate the deal directly with Vickie. After all, his invitations had been sent out. He had his own reputation to consider.

Ken never told Eric the details of the agreement he and Vickie reached, but it was clear he bent to her money demands. However, her tantrum created a great deal of embarrassment and a professional rift between us and East Texas Distributing. More that that, it signaled the beginning of the end from the management relationship between Vickie and Britt Redding Associates.

The actual New Orleans event went well; Vickie signed autographs and did a standout job. It was after hours that things went to hell.

Vickie, had brought along a female friend who she had met at some promotional event. She also brought along her son, Daniel, who was six at the time.

"Working with Vickie at the convention was [an experience] of utter disbelief and disgust," Joe told Eric. "Vickie worked very well with the people all day at the booth signing autographs, mingling, you know. Things began to unravel at the end of the day when Vickie started to get bored. She wanted to start drinking."

Vickie became intoxicated but still managed to persuade her female friend, Ken Stillin, and Joe to hit Bourbon Street. Even poor little Daniel was to be included in the party.

Joe hesitated, wondering if he wasn't better to leave the boy behind, but Vickie was adamant. She wouldn't leave Daniel by himself in the hotel. Besides, she said, Daniel was "used to hanging out with his mom."

Again, Joe and Ken tried to discourage her, but Vickie refused to budge.

Daniel may have been accustomed to accompanying his mother,

but that didn't mean he liked it. He started to cry in protest. Vickie told him to hush, and the little boy was forced to go along.

Bourbon Street. It has bars, jazz clubs, stunning Spanish and French architecture, and of course, world-class cuisine. And it's also known for its wild side – porno shops, hookers of both sexes, muggers who prey on tourists.

It was clear immediately that Vickie wanted to concentrate on one aspect of that infamous district: the bars.

The group went from one to another. Joe and Ken attempted to keep things under control, but as the night progressed, and Vickie got more and more inebriated, they recognized that there was no stopping her.

The drunker she got, the wilder she got – at one point, she declared loudly enough to be heard in Biloxi that she didn't need to wear a top anymore. And, in front of her son and her bosses, Joe Healy and Ken Stilling, she whipped off her blouse to reveal Dr Johnson's efforts in pyramid building. Naturally there was no bra.

Vickie bounced to the centre of the street, where she could show off to the most people. Of course, tourists and locals went wild. According to Joe, Vickie nearly started a riot. Soon, onlookers wanted more, and Vickie didn't object. Strangers fondled her, both men and women. Mind you, Daniel was there, witnessing the entire bacchanal.

Eventually, the novelty of her impromptu titty dance wore thin, and Joe was hopeful that the horror of the evening was over. But no, there was still room left on Vickie's dance card.

Vickie spotted an adult toy store. She grabbed her friend's hand and led her inside. Between the two of them, they spent more than five hundred dollars on specialty merchandise. Dildos of all kinds: strap-on, double-headed, electric. Then there were the vibrators, lotions, masks, cuffs, and more. Daniel observed it all.

At this point, Joe and Ken had had enough. Daniel was clearly overtired and overstimulated, and the adults were drunk. They were able to persuade Vickie to head back to the hotel.

"You won't believe what happened next," Joe told Eric. "Once we were in the elevator, they started ripping each other's clothes off. In the damn *elevator*. In front of Ken and me and Daniel, for God's sake. They started kissing each other and groping each other." Joe paused, the very memory making his neck flush red.

"They then pulled out some of the sex toys that they had just bought and started to carry on with those…like inserting them in each other."

When the elevator reached the floor, he and Ken Bailed out. Neither one had ever seen anything like it. It was as if Vickie was from another world, a place where morals, standards, and propriety had no meaning.

The next morning, the whole group came together again for brunch. Nothing was said about the events of the night before. Vickie acted as if she didn't have a care in the world, except for the hangover, or course. Daniel wanted pancakes. Joe and Ken wanted to get the conference over with, deposit Vickie on the plane, and return to a semblance of sanity. Mostly, though, they thought about Daniel and the effect his mother's behaviour was having on such a young psyche.

Vickie had no such worries. When asked about the situation, she would say, "If I treat Daniel like an adult and keep him around in adult situations, he will mature quicker." Somehow, we never thought that she got that from Dr Spock.

Her attitude toward Daniel's education had shocked more than Joe and Ken. Al Bolt remembers many evenings when he, Vickie, and little Daniel would watch videos – Vickie's Playboy videos.

"Her son was right there in the room," he said. ""I would talk to her. Tell her it wasn't good for Daniel to see her all naked and sexy." She countered that Daniel knew what she did for a living and that she wasn't ashamed of anything.

Chapter 9

BACK HOME IN Texas, things were deteriorating between Vickie and Al Bolt. They'd been together since January 1992, and in March he moved into her house. At the time, Vickie's Aunt Kay Beall, boyfriend Floyd Harrison, and her niece Melinda were all living in the house, too. However, once Al settled himself in, the family moved back to Mexia.

Vickie still continued to meet Howard Marshall often, usually at the River Oaks Country Club. Al's position as man of the house mostly consisted of doing the housecleaning and laundry. He tried hard to be a good role model for Daniel, but it wasn't easy. The place was a mess, and the more Al tried to make it liveable, the less Vickie seemed to like him. Finally, she hired a maid – Maria Cerrato. Whatever she wanted from Al didn't include a feather duster and Windex.

Her drinking and drug taking were reaching new heights – or depths, depending on your perspective. Al told of a time when Vickie took him out to Mexia, and they stayed at the Drillin' Rig motel.

Vickie invited an old school friend, Tim, to the room for drinks. Lots of drinks, as it turned out. Eventually Tim staggered off, and Al put Vickie to bed. This was not the first time Al had to take care of her when she was beyond walking under her own power. "I would physically carry her to the bathroom. Then I would take her and put her in bed. It would get to the point where she would actually urinate in the bed.

"I would go to sleep and miss taking her to the bathroom, and she would just let it go in the bed. I don't think she really realized how much help I was trying to give her. She felt like I was trying to run her life. I wasn't. I was trying to help her get on a good track. There were times when we were at her house, she would talk about her old boyfriends. About how they weren't good for her or just wanted her money. Then she'd say that I was better for Daniel. A father figure."

But it was no use. Their fights became more frequent. And Al was never able to accept her relationship with Marshall. In August, they split up.

Vickie let go a lot quicker than Al. Even though he finally knew the truth about Vickie – that she wasn't the sweet young thing of her press kit but an ex-topless dancer with extracurricular tricks for adding to her income and a current mistress – he had fallen in love with her. He wanted to save her.

The only problem was Vickie had no desire to be saved.

The most devastating aspect of their relationship happened at the end. Al was and is a religious man. He attends church regularly and volunteers his time to charitable causes. His three children mean the world to him, so when he discovered Vickie was pregnant with his child, he naturally wanted to marry Vickie.

"Vickie and I would have had a beautiful kid together," he told Eric. "She was dying to have a baby girl. At least that's what she said. She had that hope chest in her bedroom. The one with dolls and girls clothes."

It was not to be. There would be no marriage and no child. At first Vickie told Al that she wasn't pregnant. However, she did confide to us that she was, indeed, carrying Al's child.

Then Vickie dropped a bombshell on Al. They were arguing again. It was the very end of the relationship, and things had grown bitter. But nothing could have prepared Al for the news Vickie gave him – in public. She told him, with bystanders taking in what could have been a scene on *The Young and the Restless*, that she had been pregnant with his child, but it was just too damn bad. She'd aborted the baby, and she was through with him.

Chapter 9

Al was crushed. Abortion was against everything he believed in. He had truly loved Vickie and had wanted another child. How could she have made that decision without consulting him?

After it was over, Al continued to call Vickie. Often enough for Vickie to start proceedings on a restraining order. Her attorney, Saul Gower, warned the fireman to keep his distance, and, with the threat of being arrested, Al did.

But he still carried a large wound. Even now, he can't talk about Vickie without getting upset, without wishing he'd done things differently, without shaking his head about Daniel.

As for Vickie? She was off and running.

By the time she and Al said goodbye for the last time, she had already made another *Playboy* video. She took the cameras to Mexia, where she pouted her way through a tour of her old haunts. There was a new man in her life – bodybuilder Alan Mielsch. Only thing wrong with that relationship was that Alan was married with two children at the time. But the affair only lasted a few months.

Vickie went on promotional tours and signed thousands of autographs. This wasn't easy for her. Spelling was not something she'd mastered – Fred could be spelled Fread, Andrew could be Andru.

We accompanied her to most of these sessions, having worked out a system. If Vickie needed assistance spelling someone's name, she gave us one look. If she needed help writing the personalized message, she had another signal, and there was a third one if the person asking for her autograph frightened or bothered her.

However, despite the worrisome spelling and occasional creep, Vickie was in heaven. Nothing pleased her more than being the centre stage. The centrefold put her there. She was a celebrity. Men wanted her. Women wanted her. Vickie had no intention of letting them down.

A typical night would include an appearance in at least one nightclub. Not necessarily to work, but definitely to be seen. Alcohol eased the way, softened the edges, turned her on.

One night, she'd gone to dinner with us and a lovely young blonde named Colleen Rafferty. Several bottles of champagne later, we left the Palm restaurant and went to a karaoke bar called The Sing-A-Long Club.

Of course, Vickie needed to get drunk to get up on the stage and alternated between beer and champagne. After an hour of steady consumption, she went to the stage to sing and took Colleen with her.

The remarkable thing about this was that Vickie and Colleen had decided earlier that day to dress in identical outfits. Pink-and-white-striped midriff tops and matching shorts. But they looked as much like twins as Danny DeVito and Arnold Schwarzenegger what with Vickie almost six feet tall and weighing about one hundred sixty-five pounds, and Colleen at five foot four in her highest heels and no more than one hundred ten.

Yet there they were, drunk and dressed like demented candy stripers, and neither one of them able to carry a tune. Of course, the song Vickie selected may have been the problem. She'd chosen "My Ding-A-Ling."

The ladies could barely stand, let alone sing. They did have a good time hugging and touching each other. The patrons in the bar hooted and clapped. It was a show they wouldn't soon forget. Mercifully, the song ended and somehow Vickie and Colleen made it back to the table.

It was after midnight, so the night was still young. Vickie decided to take Colleen to the back of the club where they had a photo booth, the kind that spits out four black-and-white shots in sixty seconds. Their laughter nearly drowned out the cowboy singing on stage.

Eric took the opportunity to call Clay Spires, who was back in Vickie's life as her boyfriend of record, and Colleen's boyfriend Jim, asking them to come for the inebriated pair. Which they did, but instead of taking the women home to sleep it off, as Eric had intended, Clay and Jim ordered up another round of drinks.

Just before we were about to leave, Vickie and Colleen went to the restroom. It took so long that Eric got worried. He figured one or both of them was sick given all they'd had to drink. He sent into the hallway leading to the restrooms but discovered sickness was not the source of the delay.

Vickie had Colleen's shirt down to her waist and was kissing her breasts. Neither seemed to mind Eric's intrusion. At one point, Vickie made eye contact with him, and it was very clear that the "audience" made the moment all the sweeter.

We left. After all, it was nothing more than another typical night with Vickie Lynn Smith. Just like the *Playboy* Playmate model search held at Bayou Mama's, a local Houston nightclub.

We hosted the ten-week event. Each girl who wanted to compete was interviewed and had the rules explained, including, of course, the understanding that nudity was involved. Each girl would have nude Polaroids taken of herself before she could compete in the finals.

Twenty-five women make it to the finals. Vickie was a judge, and it was her job to give the winner a trophy and a diamond bunny necklace in addition to the traditional roses.

Vickie had no real say about the winners – none of the judges did. The winner had been determined a week earlier, based on the nude Polaroids. The ceremony was for show.

After the contest, the partying began. As usual Vickie drank champagne as if it were Evian. She'd liked one of the girls, Tracy Johnson, and focused on her when the whole group moved to a place called Randy's for dancing.

Tracy didn't reciprocate Vickie's interest and when it came time to leave, Vickie was an unhappy camper. She didn't like it when things didn't go her way. She was hot, and she wanted action.

She wanted D'eva.

In the middle of the club, with most of the contestants close enough to hear, Vickie declared that she was in the mood and graphically expressed what she wished to do to D'eva.

D'eva was embarrassed, as was Eric and everyone within earshot. Eric hustled Vickie out of the club and drove her home. With great difficulty, he managed to put her to bed, alone, where she passed out as soon as her head hit the pillow.

D'eva took the incident in stride. She'd gotten to know Vickie, and so it wasn't too much of a shock. But from then on, she made it a point to avoid being alone with Vickie.

Chapter 10

IN AUGUST OF 1992, Vickie received a phone call that changed the direction of her life. It would offer something that she had dreamed of her entire life – financial security.

Paul Marciano, the president of Guess and the brother of fashion designer Georges Marciano, had been impressed with Vickie's *Playboy* spread. More than impressed. He wanted to meet this voluptuous woman, who looked nothing like the thin, waif-like models so in vogue at the time. He got in touch with *Playboy's* West Coast photo editor Marilyn Grabowski and asked her to arrange a meeting at an Italian restaurant in Houston – " oh, you know the name of it," Vickie told *Texas Monthly*. "It's got two names. Wait – it's called, uh, Something-Something."

Actually, the restaurant was Anthony's, a popular upscale bistro close to downtown. Once there, Marciano, a dapper man with exquisite taste in clothes and a European sensibility, told Vickie about his quest for the new Guess Girl. He was looking to replace Eva Herzigova, a Marilyn Monroe look-alike, who had come after Claudia Schiffer, a Brigitte Bardot look-alike.

Vickie had never heard of Guess Jeans. She did all her shopping at Kmart and Wal-Mart. And Guess Jeans weren't found hanging on the racks of those establishments. It didn't help that Vickie had trouble understanding Marciano's French accent and had to ask him to write the word "guess," which Marciano pronounced Gee-yess.

Guess may have been an unknown commodity to Vickie but not the rest of the world. It was a jeans company with an attitude and certainly could be categorized as a phenomenon in the clothing industry. It began with four brothers, the Moroccan-born sons of a rabbi who were raised in the south of France. Maurice was the financial man, Paul advertising, Armond operations and production, and Georges was the designer.

Guess arrived in the United States in 1981 just as the designer jeans fad was on the way out. As the story goes, Georges took the company's "Marilyn" jeans – faded denim and so supertight that zippers were needed at the ankles – to Bloomingdale's. The buyer didn't care that the Marilyn style was selling faster than hot crepes in Paris and wouldn't over order any. Georges was furious but had enough presence of mind to leave fifty pairs on consignment before he left the store in a huff.

Within three hours, all the jeans – with price tags of more than fifty dollars – had been sold and Guess was on its way to becoming a billion-dollar company.

There were some bumps in the road of success. Employees quit because they couldn't deal with the acrimony in the brothers' less than brotherly dealings with each other. And then there was the little problem with the Nakash brothers, owners of Jordache Enterprises.

The Nakashes bought half interest in Guess in 1983. This was not a deal made in heaven, and within a year the Marcianos took legal action to rescind it, basically claiming that Jordache was stealing Guess designs. After more than five years of nasty legal wrangling, a settlement was reached out of court.

During that time, Guess continued to grow in sales. Credit is given both to Georges's designs and Paul's approach to advertising. People talked about Guess ads and the models that were used. Besides Schiffer and Herzigova, there were Carrie Otis and Naomi Campbell.

That Vickie was ignorant of the Guess phenomenon did not seem to bother Paul Marciano that first night. After dinner he took her to the Galleria, the premiere shopping address in Houston, where he bought her Guess outfits. Her opinion? "Y'all make real nice clothes."

The next day, Vickie was flown in Marciano's private jet to San Antonio, where a Guess baby clothes layout was being shot. Despite his attention to Vickie, Marciano wasn't very optimistic about her potential as a Guess model. She was nothing like the sophisticated swans he was used to. This was a girl from the country. Uneducated, naïve, inexperienced. But as long as she was there, he decided to take a few photographs.

Marciano sent her off to get her makeup and hair done while he concentrated on the more important business of the baby clothes shoot. His concentration was broken when Vickie emerged from the trailer. Everything stopped.

"I could not believe what I was seeing," Marciano was to say later. "I had never seen such an extraordinary face. The temperature was 100 degrees, and she was still natural in front of the camera. She could have worked all day. She gave me a hundred different looks."

In a story as close to a fairy tale as you can get without a pumpkin, Marciano used the very first test shot as the centerpiece for his new campaign. Many consider the shot of Vickie – lying in a field, chewing on a piece of straw, wearing a red-and-whit shirt – the most beautiful of her career. Marciano was impressed enough to give her a three-year multimillion-dollar contract.

Vickie's involvement with Guess might have played out differently if, at that first meeting, she had told the truth. Marciano had a strict policy that everyone connected with his company have and maintain a spotless image – except for, maybe him, of course. It was something of an obsession with him. He asked her point blank if she had anything in her past that could hurt the Guess image. Vickie smiled. And finished her wine.

Things moved quickly after that. Marciano and Monique Pillard, an Elite Modeling agent in New York Vickie had signed with, hammered out a contract. But first, they decided Vickie Lynn Smith had to go. The name, that is.

It was Paul Marciano who came up with the new name. And so it was that Vickie Lynn Smith was laid to rest in August 1992, and

Anna Nicole Smith was born. From then on, there was no more Vickie, it would be Anna Nicole and nothing else.

Marciano didn't stop with a new name. Boxes of clothes began arriving at Anna's newly purchased house with instructions to "use what you will and disregard the rest." Anna did just that. Her rejects were sent to the Salvation Army. After she thanked her benefactor, she promptly asked if he could send some clothes for Daniel. Of course, he obliged.

The gifts weren't all so mundane. According to Al Bolt, who was still living with Anna, Marciano flew her to his yacht in Mexico for a three-day cruise. On board, he presented her with a pair of onyx-and-diamond earrings, worth about ten thousand dollars. It was the most extravagant gift she'd ever received from an admirer.

Their relationship continued for several months.

Chapter 11

ON CHRISTMAS EVE 1992, Anna Nicole had a party at her ranch house for friends and family. The million-dollar ranch was paid for by beau-in-abeyance J. Howard Marshall II. Fifteen acres of land, a barn, a workout area for horses, a swimming pool, a house, and guest quarters. Animals wandered freely – cattle, horses, pigs, chickens, sheep, dogs, cats, even peacocks. Anna Nicole had, she said, wanted a ranch "all my life" and she described it as a place where she could "chase the chickens and pigs and play in the mud and run the horses." It was also a place where she could give Daniel all the things her childhood had lacked.

The guest list that night consisted almost entirely of family. Virgie, Melinda, Kay, even Anna's brothers and sister in rare display of familial love. Only a few friends were invited – us, Debbie Hopkins, Anna's longtime pal and hairdresser, Debbie's husband Bill, Anna's then-boyfriend/bodyguard/personal trainer Alan Mielsch, and a few others.

The house had been decorated with care. There was a fourteen-foot white-flocked Christmas tree by the fireplace with gifts stacked all around it. There were tinsel, candles, poinsettias all over the spacious living room, and Anna's family was deeply impressed.

The food was not the run-of-the-mill Christmas party fare unless your family tradition us pimento-cheese-and-tuna-fish sandwiches, with the crusts cut off the white bread. Fritos and bean dip circulated along with the beer and orange soda. There was champagne, but that was hidden way from the family and only doled out to certain friends. Seems Anna was certain her kin would just guzzle the fine wine down. Blood ties only went so far.

When everyone had eaten, Anna Nicole brought out a case of Guess calendars and Guess notebooks, and asked her family to stand in line to received them. She autographed each one, reminding her family that from now on, she was Anna Nicole Smith – Vickie Lynn Smith was dead and buried.

Next came presents, and Anna outdid herself. For us and several relatives there were $400 snake-skin boots. For Virgie, a big-screen television. Daniel got a miniature motorcycle, complete with leather riding clothes, helmet, and boots. Alan Mielsch was gifted a full-sized Harley Davidson motorcycle. Anna's maid, and Aunt Kay received a Chrysler LaBaron; both cars were adorned with big red bows.

There was much whooping and hollering during the opening of the presents, but right after the last gift had been given, the family took off. Within fifteen minutes, the entire family had gone. Vanished.

Anna didn't seem concerned by this, but it felt to us that the quick departures were about as ungracious as it gets. Some guests didn't even bother to say goodbyes. They just took their booty and made tracks.

We stayed, as did Debbie and Bill and two gay friends of Anna's, Tim and Jeff. Elaine and Melvin Tabers lived in the guest quarters, and they retired for the night. Kay and Melinda Beall stayed at the main house, but they went up to bed moments after they'd received their gifts.

Once the relatives were gone, Anna brought out the champagne, vodka, and marijuana. Things heated up quickly, and Anna got weepy. She dragged all of us to her bedroom and kneeled next to an oak hope chest. She proceeded to haul out baby clothes, dolls, and accessories she hoped to give to a daughter.

That was when J. Howard Marshall II called. He'd called many times during the evening, but Anna refused to talk to him. This time she did but told him she wasn't feeling well and that she'd call him later. No mention of the party was made.

After hanging up, Anna led everyone outside, where Tim and Jeff had cranked up the Jacuzzi. It was clear Alan was going to stay for the night, which was odd, seeing as how it was Christmas Eve and the man was married with children.

The tone of the evening changed from innocent fun to the beginnings of another night of wild partying as Anna and her guests stripped off their clothes and clambered into the hot tub. That's when we left.

ANNA CONTINUED to gain popularity as a *Playboy* Playmate. She received an extraordinary amount of fan mail, which would be forwarded to her from the magazine.

Al Bolt remembers her sitting on the floor surrounded by her mail. It was like Christmas. She would tear open the big packages first. Men would send her pictures and ask for autographs. Sometimes they would send her taped messages to her.

Of course, she got letters from wackos, too. One guy thought she was an alien. But she tried hard to answer the letters, even though she continued to have trouble finding the words.

Things were not so rosy between Anna and us. She had changed considerably over the course of the year. Not only was she becoming famous, but she was becoming a *star*. At least, that's how she thought of herself.

Personal appearances were no longer the fun they'd once been. Anna was demanding, petulant, even rude. She wanted money, lots of it. She wanted to be the centre of attention and not just in Houston. The *Playboy* cover was just the beginning, and once she'd spoken to Paul Marciano, she figured this was it. Her time. Her chance.

She had stepped into the media spotlight just as Alice had stepped through the looking glass. Nothing would ever be the same.

She abruptly stopped calling us. When the contract-year expired, there was no discussion, no good-byes. Anna managed herself for a while, getting help from Melissa Byrum, the woman from the car show in Ohio who had taken part in that bizarre trip to New Orleans. And she had signed with Elite Modeling in New York at about the time of Guess breakthrough.

She was on her way out of Texas, and as long as someone, anyone, could tell her the difference between New York, and California, she was ready to circumvent the globe.

Chapter 12

ANNA NICOLE AND J. Howard Marshall II went public in the beginning of 1992. He took her to his favourite haunt, the River Oaks Country Club, often. Of Course, she was living in the house he bought for her, and each time she saw Howard, money exchanged hands.

It wasn't until 1993, however, that the big money on jewels started to come to light.

In March 1993, Marshall bought Anna over $100 worth of Godiva chocolates and more than $350,000 worth of jewellery from Neiman Marcus – or "Neiman Mark-up" as Anna sometimes called it. Only a month later, the couple went to New York City and made a stop at Harry Winston's. Marshall was in his wheelchair, and Anna was in heaven.

According to one salesperson, Anna was "allowed to pick out whatever she wanted." That included a two-carat diamond ring, a round diamond ring, a marquise diamond ring, a diamond necklace, a pearl-and-diamond necklace, a diamond bracelet, a pair of diamond ear clips, and a pair of pearl-and-diamond drops.

Texas Monthly, in its October 1993 issue, reported that all this shopping took place in under an hour. The tab? Two million dollars. Paid for with a platinum American Express card.

Beneath the extravagant trip to Harry Winston's lurked something more sinister. According to Betty Morgan, a nurse charged with looking after Marshall, Anna used drugs to get him in the mood to open the purse strings. Morgan would tell a court some years later that she specifically told Anna that Marshal could not take Valium, but that Anna fed him the drug during that shopping trip to sedate him. Morgan testified that Marshall was alert and aware of his surroundings when he entered the store, but left in a daze. "He was way down in his chair," she said, "drooping to one side and drooling,"

Of course, Marshall had a track record for being generous with his mistress – until death did them part.

$\mathcal{A}$NOTHER OLDER man re-entered Anna's life in 1993, though with far less of a financial impact: her long-lost father, Donald Ray Hogan. Vickie used her newfound wealth and self-confidence to track down the man who had deserted before her second birthday.

"When I was younger I used to look for his name in the phone book," she said. "When I was finally able, I contacted a company called Birthrights and within a week they found him."

"It started with a phone call," said Mr Hogan. "They called me and wanted to know my full name and everything, and I told them and they said they located missing persons and obviously I was the missing person. They asked me if I knew a Vickie Lynn Hogan and I hadn't saw her in twenty-four years and it kind of came as a shock, you know, but ten minutes later I was on the phone talking to her. A few days later I was out visiting her and I never expected it to happen that way, with so many years gone by."

Anna had her dad collected at LAX in a stretch limo, now her preferred mode of transport. They visited at her ranch and seemed to hit it off right away.

" I think she has really done great for herself," said Hogan. "She is beautiful and I love her."

"And I love you," said Anna, in a baby voice.

Chapter 13

THE PRESS WATCHED everything Anna Nicole did and reported it to the world. She was called a supermodel, a starlet, a phenomenon.

On 15 June 1993, she was Larry King's guest on his CNN television show. Dressed in a blue-and-white polka-dot halter-top dress, with her hair done a la Marilyn, she was stunning. It was clear Larry King thought so.

He would later recall that first meeting: "She is an extraordinary pretty girl. The unusual thing is she did a painting that we have here in the house. She is kind of an amateur painter. I have an oil painting she has done here. I think that she was a special person; she was an unusual person. She was genuine; she was funny; she had some class."

Anna told the story she'd rehearsed over and over again. How she's sent Polaroid pictures to *Playboy*, how she's been whisked out to California and onto magazine covers, how Paul Marciano had turned her into the Guess girl.

The questions didn't matter and neither did the answers. Anna Nicole was utterly charming. She called Larry "sir," and even after he asked her not to, she repeated the honorific several more times. She was nervous, that was easy to see, but that just added to the picture. He asked her about her weight, she told him that she's big but wouldn't tell him her size. It didn't matter. He was under her spell.

It was difficult to pose nude, she said. She didn't get to see her son often enough. She wanted to tone up, not lose weight. She'd always looked up top the *Playboy* models. Her grammar was awful, and that, too, added to her charm.

The first caller was a woman. She told Anna she was beautiful, earning a delicious smile. Then she said Anna was a role model for women who aren't thin. Anna Nicole got serious and told the caller that there were times she'd been depressed about being so large, but now she loved her weight.

The second caller was another woman, and she also praised Anna for being a full-figured woman. Anna told of the many modeling agencies who asked her to lose weight. Her smile grew a bit evil.

Larry asked about this reaction from women. Anna confessed that women had always been mean to her before.

It ended too quickly. Anna was on a roll. She looked like she could take on the world. The camera focused on that million-dollar face. She smiled.

Inside Edition did a story on "The hottest model in the world right now – Anna Nicole Smith." Open any magazine, the host said, and you'll see her.

Marilyn Grabowski from *Playboy* talked about her magic. Old schoolmates recalled that she was just a small-town gal, nothing much to look at. One old friend, Jo Ann Hughes, marvelled that one day Anna was living on peanut butter, the next on Dom Perignon.

They showed Anna with Hugh Hefner, getting her $100,000. They showed her with her new Jaguar. She told the camera that she's getting back at everyone who was ever mean to her. "I'll take all I can get."

E!Entertainment did a show on supermodels. Anna stood alongside Cindy Crawford, Lauren Hutton, Isabella Rossellini, Iman, Elle Macpherson, Christie Brinkley, and Kate Moss.

Anna talked about how hard the work is. Her number one tip? Be real bubbly and have fun.

Arsenio Hall had her on his show, which was to run until 1994. He was the son of a Baptist minister, whose programme was known for the audience's shouting "Woof, woof, woof" while pumping their fists. Hall later faded into obscurity but, at the time, was able to attract top guests, including Bill Clinton, who played saxophone on the show.

Anna Nicole wore a black jumpsuit and dwarfed the host. She told him how much she wanted to meet Brad Pitt. How she liked her newfound fame. How she preferred men who were not too big or too small and looked at his hands to see how he measured up.

It was Virgie's birthday, and Anna told her "I love you, Mommy," right there on camera. The audience ate it up.

Inside Edition reported that Anna Nicole nearly started a riot in Hong Kong. She's revered there as a goddess. But, she told the reporter, she would never appear nude in a movie – unless she had the starring role.

In 1993 she was crowned Playmate of the Year, declaring, "I want to be the new Marilyn Monroe and find my own Clark Gable." The same year, she modelled for the Swedish clothing company H&M. She was dressed in underwear and arranged in seductive poses.

And then the days of magic were over. It was just that fast. For a few brief moments, she was the golden girl basking in the golden rays of the media sun. It started to get overcast with the news that she'd been hospitalized for a drug overdose.

In February 1994, *People* magazine reported that she and a twenty-year-old male friend, Daniel Ross, were hospitalized in Los Angeles for what police described as an overdose of prescription drugs and alcohol. Anna's publicist said she went to Cedars-Sinai Medical Center suffering from a severe migraine. However, people close to her disclosed that security guards found Anna sprawled naked on the bed in a Beverly Hills Peninsula Hotel suite, along with Mr Ross. They also found smashed vases, overturned chairs, and torn photos. Anna was at the hotel, in the $1000-a-night suite, because her home, one previously owned by Marilyn Monroe, had been damaged by an earthquake.

According to *Globe* magazine, "Anna drank an entire bottle of tequila on her own. She also took eight tablets of Vicodin and seven Xanax."

A staff member of the hotel told one reporter that Anna and Daniel had been in the hotel lobby the night before, embroiled in a screaming match. They had been drinking Sex-on-the-Beach, a vodka-based concoction, and plenty of them.

"Then he ordered some cigarettes and Anna started nagging him bout his smoking," the hotel employee told the *Star*. "She was saying she didn't like the way it made her hair smell, and she wouldn't kiss him because he had bad breath."

Ross went to another part of the bar, and some other guy took the opportunity to make a move on Anna. That's when Ross started yelling. A shoving match almost turned into a fistfight, but Anna ran to her room with Ross in pursuit.

The *Star* article claims that Anna had a purse full of prescription drugs, including Imipramine, temazepam, Alsactazide, Decdron, Methocarbamol, Prilosec, Propulsid, Paxic, Seldane, Synthroid, and Vicodin.

It was Ross who alerted the front desk and asked for a cab to take him to a hospital. Paramedics were dispatched, but by that time, hotel security had found the unconscious Anna.

One witness said, "She sure didn't look like a supermodel," as Anna was wheeled out to the ambulance. "Her hair was sticking up straight like a broom, and her makeup was smeared all over her face."

Ross was reportedly in no better shape. He was taken to the Century City Hospital, and by the time he arrived, he was in convulsions. His heart rate was over 160, and he was listed as critical.

Both Anna and Daniel told police that the overdoses were accidental, that they didn't realize mixing drugs with alcohol could be so dangerous.

Chapter 14

ANNA WAS ALWAYS a woman driven by her appetites. Not just food, not just champagne, not just sex, but all of them, all the time.

Clay Spires, who had been her boyfriend beginning in January, 1990, then shortly thereafter her bodyguard, told the *Globe* that J. Howard Marshall II had called many times while he and Anna were making love. "She'd tell me to keep quiet while she talked to him."

That same story was told by Al Bolt, another ex-boyfriend. He was also told to "hush up" when "Paw-paw" called.

Clay Spires also came forward with stories of Anna's relationships with women. He talked about Sandra Powledge, whom he claimed was Anna's lesbian lover. Once, he told reporters, he witnessed Anna and Sandy, naked in bed together, painting each other's toenails.

Sandi Powledge was a mysterious figure in Anna's life, and would even be referred to in court documents as "The Potted Plant Lady." For years she kept their relationship quiet. They had met in 1991, about the time Anna – or Vickie as she was then – first met Howard. One night, Anna swayed into a gay and lesbian bar in Houston called the Hill. The place had seen nothing like it, remembered Sandi years later. "All these old butch dyke girls began going, 'Oh! oh! oh!' and even the gay guys were saying, 'Oh, I could change my ways.'"

After slugging tequila to get up some courage, Sandi fought her way through the crowd and asked Anna to dance. To her surprise, the answer was yes. They were an incongruous pair: Anna the voluptuous blonde sex bomb, Sandi short and plain in a baseball cap and sweatpants. Yet they had things in common. "Both had come of age in small towns," reported the *Houston Press*. "Anna had grown up on food stamps in a house without heat, stealing toilet paper from local restaurants. The experience had left Anna hungry, but Sandi was content making $6 an hour at the garden supply store. Sandi was warm and smart and funny and utterly without ambition.

When their dance ended, it was Anna who kept talking. Though Anna was the stunning beauty, it was she who pursued the plainer and less feminine Sandi, as men had pursued her. She sent Powledge a dozen roses at work and called repeatedly to ask her out. After awhile, she gave in. "I guess I was afraid she'd stop asking me," said Sandi.

For their first date, the 23-year-old Smith arrived at 30-year-old Powledge's house in a working-class area in a stretch limousine. She brought a change of clothes for Powledge to wear to the upscale Del Frisco's Steak House. "She wanted to take me somewhere nice, and I was just in jeans. Maybe she thought I didn't have anything nice to wear. She brought a dress, shoes, a bra and panties. Everything fit. I don't know how she knew my size."

Smith was little like her later TV persona. "She was quiet. She was shy. I was so nervous to see her, but then I'd see she was shaking. She would grin a lot. I think she was a little more insecure than I thought she would be," said Powledge. Anna was "just innocent. She just seemed like a kid to me. She was so young – very beautiful. She wore very little makeup, just natural. I think that's when she looked her best." She was also emotionally lost. "I don't know if she ever believed anyone really loved her," Powledge later told the *Houston Chronicle*. "She was just hungry for love, hungry for approval – just like a bucket with a hole in the bottom."

If there was any pattern to Anna's chaotic life, it was lunch with Howard at the River Oaks Country Club, and nights with Sandi at the Hill. Anna was fun. She would laugh uproariously at jokes and then lean over and whisper, "What did that mean?" She flirted with everyone. After writhing against a woman, Anna would ask, "How'd I do?" And Sandi would say, "Great! You crushed her!" Sandi grew secure with Anna, because at the end of the evening, they were always together. Owner Ann Kellas recalled finding them entwined in a bathroom cubicle. "It was nothing," said Kellas. "Everyone does it."

When Howard gave Anna a white Toyota Celica for her 24th birthday, she and Sandi would head off in it. One day in early 1992, Smith beckoned Powledge to the car. "I want to show you something," Smith told her. The blonde bombshell drove to a Stop N Go convenience store, where Anna laid a 12-pack on the counter and asked for the current issue of *Playboy*. "Do you know who I am?" she said to the clerk. When she held up the magazine to show him, he refused to believe her. She had often found prettier girlfriends than her brothers, but they were awestruck when they opened *Playboy*.

"I went grocery shopping in limousines. My lover was Playmate of the Year. I got my nails done every week. It was a different world," said Sandi. "All of a sudden, it's not your world – she just let me share hers for a little while." The Guess Jeans advertising campaign would soon catapult Anna's image before millions. "Look, look," she would nudge Powledge, as they drove by one of the many billboards featuring her face.

Their first year together was a happy one. According to Sandi, they exchanged vows of commitment on the diving board at Smith's home in Spring, and Smith gave Powledge a diamond ring. Smith avoided wearing a ring herself because of the questions it might raise. They shared some wild times, frequently going out on drinking binges and not knowing how to get home. Smith stopped her car and asked a passing jogger to drive them home after one booze-filled spree.

They also hit it off between the covers. "She was very considerate," giggled Powldege when asked about their sex life. "Very sweet. Very."

Powledge kept a photo album of their relationship. It included pictures of their days together in Houston, a shot of them kissing on a bed, shots of Smith posing topless on her baby grand piano and on horseback at her ranch in the Cypress-Rosehill area and scenes of Smith modeling that she mailed from exotic locations: Anna in a leopard-skin with a stuffed tigress; Anna as a mermaid, coming out of the waves; Anna in jewels, blowing a kiss. Usually, on the back of the postcards, she wrote only ''Dido,'' which was her way of spelling "ditto," the word a character in the movie *Ghost* used to express his love. "Hey girl," she wrote otherwise. "I do miss ya. Call you soon. Are you okay financially? Let me no [sic]. Your fairy God mother."

They also had "their" song: Whitney Houston's "Run to You," from the soundtrack of the movie *The Bodyguard*.

Anna's image began appearing in magazines and on billboards around the world. She became the most supercharged sex symbol of the day. When she asked if Sandi would come live with her in New York, she had her lover met at the airport by a makeover crew. They put Sandi her in a dress and a more feminine wig, and painted her face with cosmetics. Anna had just been named Playmate of the Year; she was a *heterosexual* sex symbol and could not be seen with a butch lesbian companion.

For several months, they stayed in an apartment with young Daniel. Sandi wore the wig and served officially as Anna's personal assistant. She paid bills, vetted calls, accompanied her to public appearances and watched her sign autographs. Finally, she left. Though she was fond of Daniel, with his innocence and curiosity, Sandi was living a lie in New York and could no longer pretend to be someone she wasn't. Anna, conversely, couldn't return to who she had been in Houston.

Anna came looking for her to get her back, arriving at the Hill with straight men in tow, making a scene, throwing drinks. She fell out of a chair, drunk. She danced naked and caused fights. The owner asked her to leave. "I could buy this fucking place!" retorted Anna. She was learning to play the self-obsessed star, telling *People* magazine during this time that she had given enough of herself, and "maybe it's my time to receive."

A lurid account of their remaining months together later appeared in the *Houston Chronicle*:

Howard had installed Anna in a large brick house outside of Tomball, behind an iron gate. Anna installed Sandi in a small tin-roofed bungalow nearby that had engine parts strewn across the front yard and the smell of garbage in the air. Whatever charm the interior possessed was owed directly to Anna, who blotted the walls with great pink impressions of her bosom.

They called this place the Love Shack, but no love was conducted there. Sandi always came to Anna, who was usually found in bed, topless, watching television. It was a king-size four-poster bed, and for the bliss Sandi initially experienced there, she referred to it as "the Pearly Gates." But now the bed was simply where they sat as they watched comedies through the night. It became Sandi's job to rub Anna's feet and to braid her hair. When Sandi nodded off, Anna would elbow her awake and give her a pill. There were pills to stay awake and pills to go to sleep. Anna rewound to the last joke, and life went on.

For servants, Anna had hired her aunt Elaine and uncle Melvin. At all hours of the night, she would call for them, and sometimes she wanted them to get drunk with her, but more often than not, she wanted food. Usually she craved something Elvis would have liked. Her favorite food was mashed potatoes and brown gravy, which she ate from the pot. She'd order pizza with everything, eat all the toppings and leave Sandi the crust. Anna liked pickles and salt, fried bologna with cheese and whole packages of biscuits. Her bedspread was covered with stains from Colossus burgers. After devouring one of these, she would crush the paper into a ball and say, "I gotta throw up now."

Her method of weight control was liposuction. Anna's faith in her sex appeal never wavered. In the same way a golfer might practice his swing, the model would throw off her shirt and strike a pose. She flopped her breasts down over the piano. She cradled them in her arms like fat chickens. As she lolled topless on the horse, Aunt Elaine snapped pictures, while Uncle Melvin held the reins and stared at the ground. Anna's breasts became larger and harder, the nipples moving from here to there. They were more pleasing to the eye than to the touch, said Sandi, but Anna felt she owed everything to her breasts, and everyone in the house was expected to pay their respects.

ONE EVENING in December 1993, Sandi and Anna were lying in bed when Anna rolled over and said, "Why don't you get my face tattooed on your back?"

"Okay," said Sandi. And off she went to have Anna's face and name tattooed on her shoulder blade.

"How big is it?" Anna asked from New York.

"Big," said Sandi. "Takes up the whole shoulder."

"Shoulder!" said Anna. "I wanted your whole back. Go do it again."

Sandi refused. Others in Anna's family didn't. Her Aunt Kay had an image of Anna on her back, and a niece got branded on the ankle. Uncle Floyd had a tattoo of his niece in the nude.

Tattoos were no asset for a model, but Anna wanted one anyway. She figured, there was one area of her body where she might be able to have one without it affecting her career – below her bikini line. On 27 February 1994, she drove to a small strip mall on Aldine-Westfield and walked into Bubba's Skin Pin Studio. Sandi stood over Bubba as he worked on Anna Nicole's shaved crotch, inking an S with a line descending from the lower loop, forming the initials SP. Then, beside a likeness of two cherries, he slowly etched the words "Pawpaw's heart."

Paw-paw was, of course, her pet name for Howard. He thought Sandi was no more than Anna's friend and once paid her way to Bali when he and Anna went on vacation there. Sandi, for her part, was never jealous of him. It seemed to Sandi that Anna didn't take Howard's constant proposals seriously until he began getting sick. Anna dangled him on a string.

Sandi and Anna would be lying in bed when the phone would ring and the answering machine would pick up.

"Precious?" came the croak. "This is your man."

Anna would ignore his messages, taking days to return his calls. When he persisted, she'd pick up the telephone and sooth him with baby talk.

Sometimes he would not be denied. A driver would wheel Howard into the house; Anna would wheel him into the bedroom and close the door behind them. After what seemed a long time, the door would open, and Anna would say with a sour face, "I don't want to talk about it. Get me a beer."

Then, shortly after she was tattooed, Anna turned to Sandi and asked if she should tie the knot with him. "I'll never be able to support you like Howard can," said Sandi, stating the blindingly obvious. Maybe, said Anna, Sandi could come and work as their maid? No, said Sandi, she would not be Anna's "damn maid."

Anna was incapable of monogamy. She was bisexual, not lesbian, and Powledge would soon discover evidence that she had been with others, finding photographs of her with men. Still, Anna expected monogamy from Powledge and gave her a pager and phone so they could remain in contact while Smith was out of town. "She told me, 'I'd better not hear music in the background when I call you.' She didn't want me at a club with my friends when she's going off doing her thing," Powledge said. "Here I am dating the Playmate of the Year – please! What in the world is there to be insecure about? She's gorgeous, I love her, she makes me laugh."

Clay Spires would claim in an issue of the *Globe* that Anna Nicole drugged J. Howard Marshall II to hide another lesbian lover. "In fact," Spires said, "when Mr Marshall came out to California…I think Anna Nicole tranquilized the old gentleman- because she put him to bed and locked the door to the bedroom she was sharing with [another lesbian lover] Susie."

Spires told us that there were many threesomes. Sometimes he would watch, sometimes he would participate. It was something that both he and Anna enjoyed, but Smith's infidelity caused fights with Sandi. Her aunt, Elaine Tabers, who along with her husband lived with their famous niece at the ranch in the Cypress-Rosehill area, would often persuade Sandi to make peace.

"Don't say anything," Elaine would tell Sandi. "If you love her, leave it as it is. Hang on and work this out."

As J. Howard became older and sicker, Smith began seriously considering his marriage proposals. She asked Powledge for her opinion. "I think she cared about him like a grandfather, like a dad. He was good to her, and he loved her. She loved him – I just don't know to what extent." Powledge recalls Anna showing off her bridal gown as she prepared for her 1994 nuptials, even while Powledge continued to wear the ring Anna had given her.

As Smith grew more famous and left town more often, their contact grew less frequent, and Powledge tired of waiting for her. She moved back to her hometown of Winnsboro, 100 miles east of Dallas, without telling Smith, sparking a fight. Smith angrily demanded that Powledge return to Houston to see her, and Powledge did, driving 260 miles through a rainstorm with her brother.

The final blow came before Smith married Marshall, when Powledge drove six hours down to Houston to see Smith in a hospital following surgery. In the hospital room was Smith's boyfriend, Clay Spires. Powledge demanded that Smith make one of them leave. Later in the weekend, back at Smith's home in Spring, Powledge discovered evidence that led her to believe Smith had slept with Spires. The two women fought and Powledge left. They never spoke again.

"It was just too much. I had a life up here; I had my painting business. I was tired of being at her beck and call," Powledge told the *Houston Chronicle*. "I'm there every time she says jump. You've got to step back at some point and say, 'Sandi, where's your dignity?'"

Anna's excessive taste for pills and alcohol had also come between them. "I'd say, 'Can't we just have a night without it?' She'd say, 'Yeah.' But as the night wore on, I could always tell by her slur or the look on her face," said Sandi, who would later struggle with drugs herself. "At the time, I didn't have a problem. I could drink or not drink."

"She got drunk just about every night I was with her," confirmed Clay Spires. "She also regularly abused drugs. She's really into painkillers and also likes an illegal amphetamine called Ecstasy." One time, he recalled, she got so spaced out on booze and drugs that she "thought she was getting sucked into a picture of Marilyn Monroe."

Food, an addiction Anna battled most of her life, was just another substance she abused. Clay talked about the whipped cream, waffles, burgers and fries, candy, ice cream, in never-ending supplies. Of course, after these excesses, Anna would throw up and take great quantities of laxatives. Just like so many bulimic women in this country, Anna was convinced that she had to be at her "fighting weight," which was quite large according to Hollywood standards, and that she would do anything to stay that way-except, perhaps, eat properly.

Anna had at least two liposuction procedures, each one causing her tremendous pain and discomfort, only to begin eating great quantities after the surgeries. Melinda Beall, Anna's young cousin, accompanied her to her first liposuction treatment and recalls that she was so bruised afterwards, she couldn't drive for two weeks.

"We had to wait on her hand and foot," Melinda said. "She thinks now that she got her liposuction, she can eat donuts and cakes. We bought her a cake – she ate the whole thing in less than twenty minutes. It had icing piled up high, it was a little teddy bear made of frosting. In a month, Anna had gained all the weight back that she'd had liposuctioned out. Twenty-five thousand dollars, right down the drain."

Melinda, who always worried about Anna's unhealthy habits, feels that "Anna just wants to look good. She cares about the money, I'm sure, but she really just wants to be popular. All of her life, she wanted that. Because in school, she was a nerd. She was a terrible nerd. Nobody liked her. Billy Smith was the only date she had."

Well, she'd gotten her wish. She was popular. She was a celebrity. She was someone. But at what cost?

Cocaine to keep the appetite quashed, amphetamines to do the same. Binging and purging. Using laxatives. And then the Vicodin, Xanax, Demerol, Imipramine, Temzepam, Aldactazide, Decadron, Valium, Seldane, and on and on. A prescription for big trouble if there was ever one.

Chapter 15

WHEN ANNA FIRST went to Los Angeles, she moved into a house that had once belonged to Marilyn Monroe.

Anna became convinced that she was Marilyn reincarnated or that she was Marilyn's illegitimate daughter. She had pictures, posters, memorabilia spread all over the house. Her friends and relatives knew that a Marilyn poster was always a gift that Anna would love.

Unfortunately, she didn't love the house itself. It was not in good shape, and it was very plain. The pool didn't even have a heater. The first big earthquake that came around made the house almost uninhabitable, and Anna finally gave it up.

She moved to Brentwood, a very high-priced section of Los Angeles. It became famous – or perhaps more correctly, infamous – as O.J. Simpson's neighbourhood.

Anna's new house was a two-story contemporary with four bedrooms. The master suite for Anna, one room for Marshall, one for Daniel and his nanny/companion Sam, and one that Melinda liked to call her own.

The pool in Brentwood was most definitely heated. As was the jacuzzi. And the landscaping was something of a dream-roses, roses, everywhere. Inside, outside, on the walls, and in the kitchen.

Anna had her Marilyn pictures hung in the new house, but they were far outnumbered by those of Anna.

While Anna loved the house, the atmosphere, the city, her son Daniel wanted nothing more than to go back home, to Houston.

According to Melinda, "He's got four earrings in his ears. Anna told him that she wasn't going to give him dinner unless he got his ears pierced. So he got four earrings. Two on each side. I think it's ugly And so is his hair. It's really long, and he said he looked like a girl."

His room was filled with toys, including his favourite, Nintendo. But the best thing Daniel had was "Sam."

Nassir Samirami was something of a surrogate everything to Daniel. He got the boy to school, made sure he was fed properly, dressed properly, and to the best of his ability, he tried to keep Daniel happy.

"Sam is a good man," Kay Beall told D'eva. "He takes him to school and does everything for the child. He's the only one that [Anna's] never slept with. He's the only one I really liked for Daniel to be with at all times because I know he won't hurt Daniel. Anna pulls away from everybody that gets close to Daniel. If you show him too much love and kindness, she thinks you want something for it."

Chapter 16

IT IS OUR understanding that on or about June 2, 1992, Maria Antonia Ceratto was hired by you as a housekeeper and caretaker for your son Daniel Smith. Our investigation reveals that Ms. Ceratto has a cause of action against you for each of the following particulars as a result of your actions which occurs while in your employment, including but not limited to:

a) *sexual harassment;*
b) *sexual assault;*
c) *false imprisonment;*
d) *conversion; and*
e) *intentional infliction of emotional distress.*

As previously stated, Ms. Ceratto was hired as a housekeeper and caretaker. Shortly after the commencement of her employment, she became aware in addition to the numerous relationships you had with men, you also had sexual affairs with women. Although these activities bothered Ms. Ceretto, she needed her job and decided to continue her employment as long as you did not bother her.

In the months that followed, you repeatedly asked her to accompany you in the evenings and she repeatedly refused. In addition, you showered her with gifts and told others that you were in love with her and found her attractive. Even though Ms. Ceratto informed you that she was not a lesbian and would not participate in such activities, you continued your advances and encouraged her to break her engagement so that you could have her "all to yourself."

Because of her fear of losing her job, Ms. Ceratto endured your embarrassing and humiliating treatment. These events ultimately led to your sexual assault of an intoxicated Ms. Ceratto in a hotel room in Las Vegas, Nevada. After forcing yourself upon Ms. Ceratto, you made many false promises, including the promise to marry her, so that she would continue to submit to your sexual demands.

As you are aware, Ms. Ceratto speaks very little English. Because of this language barrier, you were able to keep Ms. Ceratto a virtual prisoner in your home. You refused to allow her to go out or to have guests, and changed the phone number to prevent her communication with others.

Due to your acts and/or omissions, Ms. Ceratto had endured extreme mental anguish in the past and will continue to experience mental anguish in the future. By forcing Ms. Ceratto to leave without her possessions, you caused her great economic hardship. Ms. Ceratto was completely dependent upon you for her livelihood and support while in California, which allowed you to unjustly detain her. Furthermore, you sexually assaulted Ms. Ceratto when she was intoxicated and unable to defend herself against your advances. You then continued to force her to submit to your sexual advances out of fear of losing her job.

This letter is to serve notice that a lawsuit will be filed on behalf of Ms. Ceratto if this matter is not resolved within thirty (30) days. Prior to expiration of the thirty day period, this claim can be settled for the sum of TWO MILLION AND NO/100 DOLLARS ($2,000,000.00).

The letter went out on 3 February 1994. Maria had found an attorney who would work on a contingency basis, Martha Garza. At the time this letter was served, Anna was embroiled in another fiasco that looked like it, too, was leading to a lengthy legal hassle.

The Ceratto accusation was one more piece of bad publicity that she just didn't need. She'd lost two years of the Guess contract because of all the negative press, the opportunity to read for the Marilyn Monroe part in the remake of the movie *Niagara*, and now her agent Monique Pillar at Elite was telling her that Conair was cancelling her contract.

According to the original petition filed in Harris County, and Anna's own testimony, Anna hired Maria Antonia Ceratto on 6 May 1992, as a caretaker for her son, Daniel. Anna's friend Debbie Hopkins had in her employ a woman named Blanca-Maria's sister. Even though Maria did not speak English and Anna spoke no Spanish, they both felt the match would be a good one. No contract was signed, no agreement written. Maria was supposed to clean the house, look after Daniel, take him to school and activities, cook for him, and generally be responsible for the house and the boy on an ongoing basis. For this she received $200 per week, paid mostly in cash.

According to Ceratto's suit, Anna began sexually harassing her soon after her employment. Because she was a Honduran native and had limited use of English, Ceratto claims she didn't fully understand what was happening. It was only after Ceratto claims she witnessed a sexual encounter between Anna and another woman that the light dawned- she became aware that Anna was making sexual advances towards her. Ceratto then proceeded, as best she could, to tell Anna she was not a lesbian and would not consent to a lesbian relationship.

Even though Maria said she wasn't interested, she maintained that Anna continued to sexually harass her, culminating on 6 May 1993, with a sexual assault by Anna in a hotel room in Las Vegas. According to Ceratto, Anna insisted that she accompany her to a nightclub that evening. During the night, Anna also insisted that Maria have several drinks and take drugs, all of which, Ceratto claims, Anna provided. Then, after returning to the hotel, Anna forced herself sexually upon Maria, who was severely intoxicated at the time that she was unable to defend herself.

Because of Maria's embarrassment and humiliation that she'd been a victim of a homosexual assault, and out of fear of losing her job, she continued to endure a sexual relationship with Anna for approximately six months. Maria contended that because Anna was a famous model and actress, no one would believe her if she reported the assault. Besides, she was dependent on Anna for her livelihood and couldn't afford to lose her job. Without a recommendation from Anna, Maria knew she wouldn't be able to get work elsewhere.

According to Maria, Anna had complete control over her life keeping her financially and emotionally dependent upon her. During this time, Maria states, Anna continued to have sexual relationships with other people: men and women.

It did not end there. Maria Ceratto, in her statements to her attorney, claimed that Anna had told her numerous times that she was in love with her and wished to marry her. That Anna had given her clothes, jewelry, and other gifts, including a car. This to ensure that Maria would continue to "endure" Anna's unwanted sexual advances and to keep Maria quiet.

She states that from May 1993 until November 1993, Anna kept her as a virtual prisoner. Maria was not allowed to go out alone and could only leave when accompanied by Anna, Sam, who was then Anna's chauffeur. Maria claims that she was not allowed to use the telephone and that Anna had her phone number changed to prevent Maria from receiving phone calls.

Then according to testimony, Maria alleges that on 7 November 1993, at approximately 12:30 A.M., Anna instructed her chauffeur/bodyguard Nassir Samirami to order Maria out of the Los Angeles house. Maria was not allowed to remove any of her belongings. The police were called to make sure nothing at all was taken from the home.

That was Maria's version. Anna tells a very different story.

Chapter 17

ACCORDING TO ANNA'S deposition of 17 January 1995, Maria was very sweet, a very good person when Anna hired her. Then in September of 1992, things began to change when Maria befriended a girl named Angie. Anna maintained Angie began to influence Maria negatively, that Angie tried to get Maria to come on to Anna and to hug and kiss her and to ask Anna to marry her.

The first incident occurred in a Mexican restaurant in Houston, and Anna says she was quite shaken by the event and informed Maria that she didn't want Angie to come around anymore.

Things calmed down then and Anna bought a car for Maria for the express purpose of taking Daniel to school and doing other household chores. Anna signed the car over to Maria so that she wouldn't be liable in case of an accident. Anna also bought Maria a television set because the girl didn't have one in her room. The only other gifts Anna gave to Maria were little trinkets and knick knacks from airports and gift shops, which were given as tokens.

Anna had been very pleased with Maria's attention to the house and to Daniel until one afternoon when she, Maria, and Angie went to lunch at a Mexican restaurant in Houston. They all had a lot to drink, and Anna claims that Maria tried to kiss her right there in the booth. Maria pointed to her ring finger and in broken English asked, "You marry me." Anna quickly finished her meal and drove Maria and Angie back to her house. When Angie left, Anna told Maria that she didn't want the woman back in her home, ever again. The restaurant incident only compounded Anna's previous suspicion of Angie, whom, she said, she'd found rifling through her mail on several occasions.

Nothing untoward happened for awhile, although Anna was not pleased with the number of long-distance calls Maria was both making to and receiving from a boyfriend. That came to a head when the boyfriend called the house very late one night and woke Anna and Daniel. Anna told Maria then that the long-distance phone calls had to stop-no more calls to the boyfriend, no more calls from him.

Shortly thereafter, Anna moved to Los Angeles, to the Marilyn Monroe house, bringing Maria along with her. The move itself went smoothly, but the situation with Maria began to deteriorate quickly after that.

Anna noticed first that Maria had begun to neglect her chores. The house was no longer clean, and according to Anna's deposition, "There were spider webs all over." Second, she saw that Maria had begun to drink. White wine was the libation of choice and supposedly Maria went through quite a bit of it.

Anna later learned from her chauffeur that while she was away on business, Maria used a limousine service, charging nearly $25,000 in fees to Anna over a period of six months. Also, according to Sam, Maria would frequently rent X-rated videos, lesbian videos, and charge them to Anna.

Daniel was left with others more and more frequently. The wholesome meals Maria used to cook were replaced by fast food and microwaved meals.

Then, in the summer of 1993, Maria began drinking wine during the day, and she encouraged Anna to join her. During one two-week period, Anna testified that Maria kept her intoxicated while feigning her own drinking.

According to the deposition taken on January 17:

Attorney Todd N. Moster: So she [Maria] was giving you drinks?
Anna Nicole Smith: Yeah.

Moster: Okay, so she offered you a drink that night and you had a drink?

Smith: Right. She offered me drinks many nights, but this night I did have a drink.

Moster: Okay.

Smith: Because, you know, I can't drink when I'm working because next day my eyes are-I'm out of it. I can't work.

Moster: Okay. So you had a drink that night because she offered you some white wine.

Smith: Right. And I didn't have to work the next day.

Moster: Then what happened?

Smith: Then 8:30 in the morning [I] got up. She was drinking. She offered me some more to drink. I was drinking. We ended up drinking all day.

Moster: Why did you drink with her all day?

Smith: She just kept begging me. She said, "Come, Bicky, please, please. Bicky, please, please, please." But what I was noticing is she was not drinking.

Moster: She was not drinking.

Smith: No. She would have the same glass. She was feeding me.

Moster: So what happened after you started drinking?

Smith: I went and got in the jacuzzi. Okay. She was not drinking. She was putting hers back and kept bringing me drinks, bringing me drinks.

Moster: How do you know that Maria wasn't drinking?

Smith: Because Sam was watching her. I passed out in the jacuzzi.

Moster: You went into the jacuzzi and you passed out?

Smith: I passed out cold.

Moster: Then what happened?

Smith: She took my clothes off, my bathing suit. Sam said that I was passed out, so I don't know what happened. Okay? Sam told me, okay. Billy, he works for Playboy, he does lights. So he comes out there. Billy's worried. He goes and tells my boss, you know, I'm in trouble the next day.

Moster: Okay

Smith: Sam comes out, and he sees Maria come to me and start hugging me and kissing on me and putting her hands down there.

Moster: When you say "down there," you're talking-

Smith: Down in my personal, private area—

Moster: —genitals. Okay.

Smith: —that I don't let women touch. Sam said she was wearing a bathing suit top with nothing on down there.

Moster: So Maria was wearing a bathing suit top, but she was bottomless?

Smith: Right.

Moster: Did you see Maria or become awake during any of this time?

Smith: No. Sam put me to bed.

Two days later , also according to the deposition, Maria got Anna drunk again. Anna's friend Alexis Vogel, a makeup artist for *Playboy,* went to the bedroom to say good night, and she found Maria "just trying to attack me."

"Maria's on top of me trying to take my clothes off, and Alexis is like, 'Maria!' You know 'Leave her alone.'"

This behaviour, getting drunk and staying drunk, continued for about two weeks. Then, Anna reported she "snapped out of it."

A couple of weeks later, Anna claimed that she was taking a bath and Maria got in the tub with her, attempting again to kiss her and touch her. Anna left the bathroom shaken.

Maria asked Anna to marry her a month later. According to Anna's testimony, both she and Maria were sober at the time, and Maria pointed to her ring finger and said, "You marry me."

Finally in December of 1993, while Anna was back in Texas, she received a late night phone call from Maria. Anna was recuperating from surgery at the time and had left Maria to take care of Daniel in Los Angeles.

It was two in the morning, and Maria was intoxicated. She

wanted to go out. Anna yelled at her then, telling her she couldn't go out, that she couldn't leave Daniel.

Maria then said, "Me no wanna work here."

Anna said, "Fine. Get out." Then she called Sam and asked him to get over to the house immediately.

When Sam called Anna back, he said that Maria had some people there, in a brown car. She was loading Anna's stereo in the car. She'd already loaded clothes and jewelry, all of which were Anna's.

When Sam demanded Maria return the property, Maria tried to hit him. At that point she went to Daniel's room and packed some clothes before waking up the boy. According to Sam, Maria told Daniel, "I'm taking you to Honduras."

Sam wouldn't let her take Daniel, and at this point, he called the police. Two officers arrived in about fifteen minutes. After hearing Sam's explanation of the situation to them, they contacted Anna, who told them, "She's trying to steal my kid. She just quit. I want her out of my house. I don't want her to take not one thing."

The brown car had left before the police arrived, and it's not clear what was in the trunk. According to Anna, the stolen goods included her cellular phone, thirty-thousand dollars worth of clothes, her stereo, and hundreds of dollars worth of jewelry/

The police prevented Maria from taking anything else. They couldn't arrest her, but they could and did take the house keys. According to the police officers, Maria told them she and Anna were having a "lover's quarrel."

Maria filed suit two months later.

$\mathcal{I}$N DECEMBER 1993, Anna ran into another lawsuit. This time it was with her ex-publicist, David Granoff. He claimed she walked out on her one-year contract with him after only five months and owed him more than $17,000.

Anna's contract with David Granoff Public Relations, Inc., signed 16 April 1993, called for Granoff to represent Anna for one year for a fee of $2000 per month. It also delineated the out-of-pocket expenses that would be borne by Anna Nicole. These included photocopies, transportation, telephone, postage, press kits, messengers, etc. Anna was asked to make a $500 deposit to cover these items on the day she signed the agreement.

The final statement for services, sent to Anna through her attorney Irwin and Rowan, not only included seven months of back fees for $14,000, but also telephone, messenger services, press clipping services, and more, for a total of $17,143.13. The bill was dated 9 September 1993.

On 2 December 1993, Granoff filed suit with the Supreme Court, State of New York for breach of contract. In addition to the $17,000 outstanding invoice, the suit asked for no less than $500,000 in damages.

Oddly, the suit also included an order to pick up diamond earrings. Granoff says that on August 3, he received diamond earrings from Anna Nicole's former security agent for safekeeping. Granoff put them in a safety deposit box at the Chase Manhattan Bank in New York City. Although he repeatedly requested Anna to get the earrings, she had failed to do so.

Chapter 18

IN 1994, ANNA made her big-screen debut with a small part in *The Hudsucker Proxy*, a screwball comedy made by the talented young Coen Brothers, Joel and Ethan. A homage to the work of Hollywood masters Preston Sturges and Frank Capra in the Forties and Fifties, it starred Tim Robbins, Paul Newman and Jennifer Jason Leigh and tells a fictitious story about the rise and fall of a naive executive and the invention of the hula hoop.

Just before the film's realease, Anna's publicity machine went into high gear. *Los Angeles* magazine's Daniel Foster did a question-and-answer session with Anna in September, in which she talked about her figure. About the fact that she'd been so thin as a girl and how she shot up to two hundred pounds after the birth of her baby.

"More and more women are coming out about their weight," she told him. "I get thank-you letters all the time. Or they stop me on the street and say, 'I'm so glad you're here-that you weigh as much as you do. Finally, there's a woman and not a waif'. I used to dress up like Marilyn Monroe. I have all her songs and movies. Most men, I think, like a womanly figure."

Finally, Foster brought up the subject of breast surgery. "I haven't had silicone implants," she said. "No."

Despite the stellar cast and generally decent reviews – some hailed it as a masterpiece, others as overly derivative and too smart for its own good – the film was not much of a commercial success.

In an interview to promote the movie, she was asked about marriage. "I don't really have that many friends," she confessed. "It's been seven years since I've been trying to get married and it hasn't happened yet. I'm givin' up tryin'."

Maybe her acting wasn't so bad after all.

*T*HE APRIL 1994 issue of the *Houston Scene* magazine ran a short article about Anna Nicole. Impressed with her guest-starring roles in *The Hudsucker Proxy* and *Naked Gun 33¹/₃: the Final Insult*, Earl Ditmman asked how it felt to be called an actress.

Anna replied that she liked to act but didn't like all the waiting inherent with movie making. She was confident that after people had seen her in both movies, that she'd be taken more seriously. Once again, she told the story of her outsized breasts being a result of gaining weight during her pregnancy.

*N*AKED GUN 33¹/₃ was the final instalment in the hugely popular *Naked Gun* trilogy starring Leslie Nielsen, Priscilla Presley, George Kennedy and the soon -to-be-disgraced O.J.Simpson. Based on the character Lieutenant Frank Drebin, created by Nielsen in the comedy TV series *Police Squad!* the movies were packed with fast-paced, off-the-wall slapstick, puns and gags. Anna played one of a gang of bombers planning to blow up the Academy Awards ceremony. Several celebrities had cameo roles, including Raquel Welch, James Earl Jones, Elliot Gould and Morgan Fairchild.

Shortly after the movie was released, the cast went on the *Phil Donahue Show*. It was clear that the other cast members were nervous about Anna's involvement, afraid that she'd say something embarrassing not only about herself but about the movie. Anna was also worried about the show, and one of her friends told Eric that she handled that by getting stoned. Xanax and cocaine – the breakfast of champions.

*

Chapter 18

AT A Las Vegas video show, Anna Nicole answered questions in a round-table interview. David Salcido of *Entertainment Weekly* commented that "The bosomy blond's screen debut in *Naked Gun 33¹/₃* may mark the beginning of a whole new career. But as what isn't clear."

When asked what she liked best about making the film, Anna said, "Oh, me and Leslie [Nielsen] played around so much. Me and him were probably the funniest in the whole movie. Leslie was always using his fart cushion. He has this fart cushion, and he farts, and then he walks away. I was dying. I mean, I was just on the floor. We had fun. We played and poked. Don't tell his girlfriend, though."

In the movie, Smith plays Tanya, a fertility clinic nurse and girl-friend of bad guy Rocco (Fred Ward). For the swimsuit scene, in which money is stuffed down her suit, Smith reported, "I played right along."

When asked where she saw herself in five years, she responded, "Well, I'm either going to be a very good, famous movie star and model, or I'm going to have a bunch of kids. I would miss having a career, but I've done my acting, and I've done my modeling. I've done everything I wanted to do. If no one wants me to be an actress anymore, well, I've made my goals. And if I don't work another day, I've done what I wanted to do."

AT THE Fifteenth Annual Razzies, Anna was awarded the Golden Raspberry Award for her performance in *Naked Gun 33¹/₃*. Her title? Worst New Star of the Year.

O.J. Simpson was also awarded a Raspberry for *Naked Gun*, as Worst Supporting Actor.

ANNA'S AUNT Kay believes that her niece was a good actress. That "she can make a person believe." But she told Eric that her fondest wish was to have Anna get into a "mild movie, with [her] clothes on. I know she's getting tired of just being used for her body. That would aggravate anybody."

Although she never studied acting, as with everything she did, Anna Nicole aimed high. She said: "I want to do a little bit of everything – drama, comedy." Said by some critics to resemble a blonde Brooke Shields with the physique of Jayne Mansfield, she preferred being compared to her idol, Marilyn Monroe. "I'd love to play a psychotic woman, like Marilyn Monroe in *Don't Bother to Knock*. That's my favourite movie. She was so good in it, and I just know I could play it. I can just see her eyes. I know I could get into it."

Chapter 19

PAT WALKER, THE owner of the White Dove Wedding Chapel told a reporter for *Texas Monthly* that on June 25, an interracial couple in a black pickup truck came by and told her they wanted to book a wedding. Although they were wearing casual T-shirts, and didn't appear to be wealthy, they ordered the best of everything, which was the $1000 package. The couple assured Walker that "Money is no object."

When Walker asked to see the marriage license, she informed the couple that they wouldn't be able to wed until Monday, the twenty-seventh. In Texas, there is a seventy-two-hour waiting period, and the license had been signed at 2:05 p.m. on 24 June 1994, at Harris County courthouse.

On Monday, the bride entered the chapel wearing curlers. Someone asked Walker not to call any reporters. The bride told her "I'm not marrying him for his money. He's been begging me to marry him for over four years. But I wanted to get my own career started first."

Finally, Walker turned to the bride and asked, "Who are you?"

Stunned, the bride said, "Well, I'm Anna Nicole Smith."

Walker's next surprise was that the handsome African-American, bodyguard Pierre DeJean, who had been with Anna Nicole constantly, was not the groom. The groom was to be none other than J. Howard Marshall II, then aged eighty-nine to Anna Nicole's twenty-six.

Anna Nicole wore white. A long, hand-beaded wedding gown,

with train and plunging neckline. The dress became more famous later when she wore it to Marshall's funeral service.

Daniel was there, of course, in a white tuxedo, acting as ring bearer. While the bride dressed, her little son and a nephew, killed time by tossing their satin pillows into the air – competing to see who could throw his higher. No one in the small party seemed to mind that Anna Nicole's 22-carat diamond ring was tied to one of the pillows.

Also present were some of Anna's other relatives: mother Virgie, her aunt Elaine Tabers, and nieces and nephews. Anna was given away by a man she described at one point as her uncle and at another as her father. Marshall's nurse served as a bridesmaid.

Finally, the groom entered. A small man in a tuxedo, a white shirt, and white shoes. Old enough to be the bride's grandfather. Her great-grandfather. "I've done a lot of things," he told Walker. "I've made a lot of money. If I can make her happy, I've made her happy today."

Anna desperately wanted her groom to stand up during the ceremony, but when Pierre lifted him from his wheelchair, his legs simply buckled beneath him.

In the wedding book, under "How We Met," Anna Nicole wrote, "I was on stage. He was in the audience, and he was lonely and I started talking to him and we just started being friends." In reference to her wedding ring, she wrote, "This is the third ring I've had – the others were too small."

The chapel had been draped with white ribbons and white flowers. "She walked on white roses," Walker told *Texas Monthly*. No petals. Buds."

The music was "Tonight I Celebrate My Love For You." The groom was wheeled up the aisle. When it was over, two white doves were released from their cage.

Anna Nicole's aunt Elaine Tabers told the *Houston Press* that "It was real simple, but it was beautiful. A lot of people think it is strange, but their love is so strong it will put goose bumps on you."

Marshall reportedly told the eleven guests, all from Smith's side of the family, "I'm a millionaire. I've done everything I want to do in my life. Now, If I can take my money and see her spend it and get some of the things out of life and I can see it while I'm still living. I'll be happy."

A small reception was held in a room near the chapel. Anna Nicole, dressed in a wig, floppy hat, sandals, and a tight yellow suit, left from there to go to a photo shoot in Greece (though she actually only got as far as Los Angeles), leaving behind her brand-new husband, weeping in his wheelchair.

"Please don't *cwy*," said Anna Nicole, whose divorce from her first husband, Billy, had been finalised a year earlier. "You know it's you I love."

Then, she took Pierre DeJean's arm, waved bye-bye, and was gone.

Chapter 20

THE PRESS, OF course, went wild with the news of the eighty-nine-year-old groom and the twenty-six-year-old bride. The age difference of sixty-three years was forty years more than the one between Jackie Kennedy and Aristotle Onassis. Thirty years more than the age difference between Woody Allen and Soon-Yi Previn.

David Letterman referred to Anna Nicole and her "situation" regularly in his Top Ten lists all through 1995:

17 July 1995
"Surprises in the Mark Fuhrman Tapes"…
  4. Accuses O. J. of killing Anna Nicole Smith's husband

8 August 1995:
"Items on the Westinghouse 'To Do' List"…
  4. Have Anna Nicole Smith keep marrying rival network executives until they're all dead

15 August 1995:
"Anna Nicole Smith Dating Tips"…
 10. Forget the personal ads – try the intensive care unit
  9. Wear something that, even to his failing eyes, will look slutty
  8. Always carry some "mad money" for the paramedics
  7. Make sure the valet parkers understand, if he dies in the restaurant, you get the car

6. When he wants sex, hide his glasses and put him in bed with a car battery

5. Remind him, "Hey, when you're 160, I'll be 101."

4. Prepare candlelight dinner. If he can blow out the candle, you don't want him

3. To convincingly fake excitement during sex, just think about his stock portfolio

2. Good pick-up line: "Can I pre-chew that for you?"

1. Three words: "Bring extra plasma"

5 September 1995:
"Things Overheard at the World Conference for Women"…

8. "Anna Nicole Smith sure seems to be warming up Deng Xiao Peng"

11 September 1995:
"Excuses For Us Not Winning An Emmy"…

4. Academy disapproves of my marriage to Anna Nicole Smith

15 November 1995:
"My Retirement Plans"…

9. Bide my time till I'm 90; then marry Anna Nicole Smith

11 December 1995:
"Good Things About a Cold Snap"

4. Husbands of Anna Nicole Smith stay fresher longer

Yet those who knew Anna well felt that this was not simply a matter of dollars and cents.

David Granoff, the New York publicist who brought suit against Anna for stiffing him, told London's *Arena Autumn* magazine that Smith talked about Marshall long before they were married. "She told me how he changed her life and how much she loved him and what a great person he was. She used to get calls from lots of people when we were traveling, but his calls she always took. Or if she couldn't take them, she would get a number and call him back as soon as she could.

"It was an unusual relationship but there have been stranger things in life than that. I do believe that she had great, great personal feelings for him. The money makes someone look a little better than maybe he would if they were not a high fashion model or a movie star but believe me, they had a real relationship."

Anna's cousin Melinda said, "She loved Howard. She did love him. Many people think that she's used him for his money, but it wasn't like that. I used to spend Christmas with them. It really wasn't like that. She took care of him. Howard really needed somebody. He was very nice."

People magazine, in an article on "Odd Couples and Peculiar Pairings," titled "Wedding Shockers," quoted Anna as saying, "I'm very much in love. I could have married him four years ago if I'd just wanted to get rich."

Of course, what most people wanted to know about wasn't love – it was sex. Just what did Anna do with a nonagenarian?

Several people, including Al Bolt, some of the girls Anna worked with in bars, and eyewitness Pierre DeJean told us that Anna would bring home women, and they would have sex while Howard watched. She herself told Howard Stern that she would often take off her blouse and bra and rub her breasts on Marshall's head. Evidently, he got a big charge out of that.

In response to questions about her recent marriage, she told reporters, "Well, he's an older gentleman. He's eighty-nine. I love him. He loves me. He asked me to marry him so many times, and I just wanted to establish myself first. I didn't want somebody to say, 'Aw, she married for money,' He was very sick. His girlfriend had just died. Right before that, his wife had died. He had no will to live. I saw him, I met him, and it was just like he was my friend. So we started going to dinner and to lunch. And he's helped me a lot. And the age difference – I don't care what people think. I love him, and we're in love, and that's it."

There was even talk of children. She said, "We want to have children. But we don't know if he can. He'll be tested and if not, I'll have artificial insemination."

It was about four months after the wedding that Sandi Powledge, her former lesbian lover, saw Anna again. She had just gone in for another boob job. "I just had them lifted up a little," Anna told Sandi. Sandi nursed Anna until she began eating again and taking her pills. She took the stitches out around the nipples, but when Anna was healthy enough to begin seducing her male driver, Sandi announced through the bedroom door that she was going home.

"I can't believe you're leaving me when I need you most!" were the last words she heard.

Chapter 21

ANNA NICOLE'S BLISS at the event of her marriage might have been dampened somewhat had she known that J. Howard Marshall II had granted his son Pierce a living trust, originally dated 1 September 1982 and amended on 23 June 1992. According to the *Houston Chronicle*, two weeks after the marriage, Marshall signed control of his assets over to his son, as well as control over his life in a medical emergency.

According to the six-page power of attorney filed with the Harris County Clerk on July 15, Marshall signed over control of the living trust he established.

He also authorized Pierce to handle his business transactions. He transferred ownership of ten acres of land off Fenske Road near Rosehill-Cypress Road in Cypress, Texas, from the living trust to himself. The *Houston Chronicle* reported he kept the small ranch, valued at $960,000, for his bride.

Marshall had been estranged from his older son, J. Howard Marshall III, since the younger J. Howard had sided against his father in the dispute over control of Koch Industries. Pierce, it seemed, was now attempting to protect the family inheritance from the possible predations of Anna Nicole.

This wasn't the first time Marshall signed over power of attorney to Pierce. In January 1992, he signed a more limited document that he revoked in April of that same year, according to public records.

That document specifically authorized Pierce to handle litigation against his dead mistress, Dianne "Lady" Walker, and her children.

That lawsuit had been filed against Lady's estate in February 1992.

Marshall had give Lady more than $5 million in gifts, according to documents filed in federal court, as well as state court documents in Fort Bend and Harris counties. She had Rolls-Royces that matched her outfits and several dozen fur coats. Sources close to Lady said Marshall also paid for her last divorce.

In the 1992 lawsuit, Marshall sued Lady's estate and her children for the return of a condominium, 558,291 shares of stock in Presidio Oil, control of Colesseum Oil & Gas, and a portion of his life insurance policy he had signed over to Lady.

Just days after Lady died, Marshall wrote to Presidio, where he sat on the board of directors, and told them that the stock shares he gave Lady were "lost, stolen, or destroyed." Presidio declined to reissue the stock, according to court records.

Whether he recovered the stock from Lady's estate is a secret sealed in the confidential settlement reached in 1993. Public records indicate that the disputed condo ended up among Marshall's vast real estate holdings.

However, in October of 1995, a jury in Houston rejected claims that Marshall was a victim of conspiracy and fraud from Lady Walker. The jurors found the Marshall estate liable for over $200,000 in jewelry charges which it had refused to pay after Lady's death in 1991.

Kevin McEvily, attorney for the jeweler, said that he felt the estate, led by Pierce, was trying to get some of the money back that the old man had spent. The jury, however, felt that Marshall was competent when he bought the jewels and that he was responsible for the bills.

Chapter 22

THE 22 AUGUST 1994 issue of *New York* magazine had an article, "White Trash Nation," by Tad Friend. Anna Nicole was on the cover, sitting on the floor, legs spread, with a package of Cheese Doodles between her legs. She's grinning through a mouthful of food, and still manages, despite the crass pose, to look beautiful. The cover copy reads, "Tonya. Lisa Marie. John & Lorena. Roseanne & Tom. Paula & Gennifer & Bill. They're everywhere. Lock up your Twinkies."

In the article "A Little Ol' Chat With Anna Nicole Smith," by William Boot, Anna is described as a "strapping country girl, come to town to be photographed," and that she is "absolutely unapologetic about the size of her breasts (enormous), her diamonds (enormous), her thighs (truly enormous), and her (enormously deep) twang."

When asked about her recent marriage to J. Howard Marshall II, she states unequivocally that, "I'm happy I did it. I'm very much in love with my husband. And he's very much in love with me."

Pierre DeJean, also present for the interview, commented that "He's been askin' her for years."

Anna goes on with the story that she's told a hundred times before: that she didn't marry Marshall early on because she wanted to establish herself first. That she didn't marry him for the money. The picture inside shows Anna pointing to her 22-carat marquise engagement ring and diamond-studded wedding band.

Anna Nicole was incensed over the picture and the interview. She sued New York, claiming she'd been tricked. Although it's hard to understand how – she was smiling for the camera. Nonetheless, the suit was settled out of court, for something under $100,000.

By now, Anna had become a cultural icon. Jay Leno, David Letterman, Conan O'Brian all were taking potshots at her. The name Anna Nicole Smith had become synonymous with all the old jokes about women marrying for money. The quips don't need explanation – the country, the world – understands the significance.

She's also been made an icon, much as Oprah and Roseanne before her, as a woman of size. Of course, in this society that's a sin punishable by mass ridicule. In the August issue of *Esquire*, under the caption Things We'd Never Like to Say to a Woman We Love, is "Anna Nicole, do you really need that dessert? I can almost see the Statue of Liberty behind you."

Michael Musto interviewed Anna for *Entertainment Weekly* just before *The Hudsucker Proxy* came out. The interview didn't cover much new ground but was used for fodder for countless magazine articles to come.

"Are you a feminist?" Musto asked.

"I don't understand that question."

"Do you fight for women's rights?"

"Whoever started that," Anna replied, "I could kick them in the head. I believe in women staying home and watching the children while the husband's at work – the traditional way. I would have been home with my family right now, except for my husband."

And her opinions about Sharon Stone and Madonna?

"She doesn't have a womanly figure," Anna said of Ms. Stone. On Madonna, Anna said, "She plays good music – that's all I can say. She should definitely stick to that."

In another spate of interviews, Anna decided to let her feelings about models be known. "I think thin models look so unhealthy," she told one reporter. "Who wants to hug a skeleton?"

"I wouldn't change my body for anything, Besides, I hate exercise," she told the *Star*. "I just love sweets."

Chapter 23

ON 29 AUGUST 1994, Pierre DeJean signed an employment agreement with Anna Nicole Smith. The contract, from the law firm of Myman, Abell, Fineman, Greenspand & Rowan of Los Angeles, was not just an employment agreement, but a confidentiality agreement.

The contract begins with, "You hereby expressly acknowledge and agree that Ms. Smith's privacy is highly valued and that you will make all efforts to maintain confidentiality with respect to all information and other material of any kind concerning Ms. Smith."

It goes on to specify that, "you shall not, at any time during the term of your employment or thereafter, use or disclose, directly or indirectly, to anyone any of the following described information: pictures, recordings, audio and/or visual tapes acquired by you in the course of or in connection with your employment by Ms. Smith...and all such information shall be deemed to be...private, secret and sensitive; and such information...shall not be removed or copied by you without Ms. Smith's prior written consent.

"Further, you shall not...give any interviews (whether oral or written), write or prepare or assist in the preparation of any books or articles.

"This letter agreement and the representations, warranties, covenants and acknowledgments shall be deemed to be a binding agreement between you and Ms. Smith and shall continue in full force and effect to the fullest extent provided under the law notwithstanding the termination of your employment."

The agreement was signed I. E. DeJean aka Pierre DeJean.

On October 4, *Star* magazine came out with a story that claimed Anna Nicole was "living in fear of her bodyguard." The article states that Pierre, whose real name is Patrick Irwin, trashed her apartment in a rage. Police were called to Anna's Manhattan apartment at 8:30 a.m. on September 14 after neighbors complained about excessive noise, including screaming and smashing objects.

Witnesses reported that Anna Nicole was "covered in bruises as she fled."

When asked by a police officer if she needed help, she told them that Pierre, thirty, had "wrecked her apartment, throwing and breaking furniture while screaming at her at the top of his lungs."

"My ex-bodyguard, that is," she is quoted as saying.

No charges were leveled against DeJean, and Anna went immediately to Donald Trump's Plaza Hotel. Not just to his hotel, but into his arms.

Anna and Donald had dated before he wed Marla Maples. It was clear that the relationship was still cordial, as Trump "assured her he would keep her safe."

DeJean claimed, in several tabloid stories, that he and Anna Nicole had been lovers for more than two years, and that the incident at her apartment was nothing more than a lovers' spat.

He told the *Star*, "I never hit her, not once. She was bawling all night long and that's why the police were called. We are two people who love each other. The fact is, our relationship has happened. Nobody can take that away from us."

The *Star* tried to get a comment from Anna's representative at the William Morris Agency in Los Angeles but was refused comment.

In the Newsmakers column in the *Houston Chronicle*, DeJean is quoted as saying, "She asked me to leave and I left. Every time we have a fight, she fires me. It's an emotional thing. Women are like that."

DeJean was fired after the episode in New York and decided that, regardless of the confidentiality agreement he'd signed, he was going to go public. On *Current Affair*, DeJean told viewers that he tried to leave, but Anna slapped him. He warned her to let it go, but she hit him again. He also claimed that he saved her life when she'd tried to commit suicide by slashing her wrists. He said that she was high on cocaine and that she begged him not to leave because she was in love with him.

The reporter called his claims outrageous and that it was hard to believe that Anna Nicole, this beautiful supermodel, had to force DeJean into having sex with her. DeJean's response? "Anna Nicole is a monster."

Of course, the reporter then told how Pierre DeJean is not his real name and that he'd served six years in San Quentin for manslaughter. It's painfully clear that no one believed one word the ex-bodyguard said.

Even so, DeJean didn't let it go. He made financial deals with several news groups, appearing full of outrage on camera. The charges grew with each show. He swore Anna forced him into a sexual relationship during her "honeymoon." He said he was constantly threatened. And, of course, the *piece de resistance* – he told reporters that she was carrying his child as she walked down the aisle.

"The deal was," he said, "the baby would be raised under J. Howard Marshall's name until he passed, God forbid, then I would be able to claim my own baby. Like a big dummy, I went along with the deal."

His assertions were called preposterous by Anna's attorneys. The reporter shook her head and turned to the next story.

We met with DeJean in February 1995, in Los Angeles. DeJean repeated the story about how Anna had planned to have his baby, but that the child would be adopted by J. Howard Marshall II. Anna, he claimed, wanted to make sure that she got more than her share of the money. DeJean was adamant that Anna had married Marshall strictly for the money, that love played no part in the transaction. He said that Anna had Marshall wrapped around her little finger and that Anna had told her aged husband that she was going to get pregnant somehow, but that he shouldn't ask her any questions. According to DeJean, all this was agreed to complacently by Marshall.

DeJean said that he and Anna planned on raising the child together after Marshall passed away, which they both knew would be soon. What hadn't been planned was the miscarriage, and that changed everything.

"I guess looking back," DeJean said, "it was stupid of me to even think that Anna would honestly have ever stuck by me in the relationship, or do what she said she was going to do...which was marry me after Howard was gone. We were supposed to raise our child and live happily ever after."

Another afternoon in Los Angeles, DeJean arrived at the restaurant in a black Rolls Royce he claimed was a gift from Anna Nicole. He was dressed in black pants with a silver belt, black and gold Versace glasses, a white shirt, and a white headband. It came up early in the conversation that he speaks several languages: French, the patois of Jamaica and Haiti.

DeJean was quite upset at that lunch. It was December 1994, and he'd just been charged with stalking Anna Nicole. The Los Angeles Police Department had been called by Anna Nicole, who claimed that DeJean had phoned her numerous times, and threatened her.

*S*USPECT (DeJean, Pierre) phoned Victim on above date and time and stated, "If I can't have you, no one will. I will kill you."

Suspect phoned victim's residence numerous times and demanded money and jewelry from Victim. Suspect also phoned Victim on above date and stated that he would be over [to] her residence to pick up his clothing. Victim terminated Suspect's services 9/1994 due to suspect's physical abuse towards her.

Witness 1 (Hazel Snyder) observed Suspect knocking on Victim's door on 12-11-94 at approximately 1300 hrs. Witness 2 (Sam Nassir), Victim's current housekeeper, was advised of above incident and notified Bel-Air Patrol.

Witness 2 ordered Suspect to leave location. Suspect refused and stated, "I want to speak with Anna." Witness 1 is a neighbor of

Victim and observed incident from her front lawn.

An emergency protective order was requested at Victim's location on 12/12/94.

The order was denied by Judge McBeh.

Also listed, as Witness 3, was Gerald (Clay) Spires. He gave Anna's address as his own but with a separate phone number.

Then on December 19, a complaint was filed with the Superior Court for the State of California by Anna Nicole Smith against Patrick Doe, a/k/a Pierre DeJean.

Case Number SC034122 was a complaint for a temporary restraining order; preliminary and permanent injunctions, and damages for: 1) Harassment; 2) Extortion; 3) Intentional infliction of emotional distress; and 4) Breach of Contract.

Paragraph four of the complaint states: "In about February, 1994, SMITH hired DEFENDANT to act as a bodyguard for herself and her son. Thereafter, on or about August 29, 1994, in partial consideration for his engagement as a [sic] employee of SMITH, DEFENDANT executed a Confidentiality Agreement, a copy of which is attatched hereto, made a part hereof and marked Exhibit 'A.' Pursuant to said agreement, DEFENDANT was contractually precluded from divulging or otherwise disseminating any information regarding any fact of SMITH's entertainment activities or personal life.

At about the time of SMITH's marriage to her present husband, in June of this year, DEFENDANT began to grow extremely possessive of SMITH and to make demands upon SMITH that were not appropriate for an employee. SMITH discovered that Pierre DeJean was not the DEFENDANT's real name and that the DEFENDANT had spent many years in prison for the commission of various violent criminal acts.

On or about September, 1994, while in New York on a modeling assignment, the DEFENDANT's behaviour towards SMITH became increasingly threatening and abusive and ultimately resulted in his physical attack upon SMITH. SMITH immediately terminated his employment.

Subsequent thereto, beginning on or about October, 1994, and continuing to the present time, DEFENDANT has wrongfully and unlawfully engaged in a pattern of threatening, abusive and harassing behavior towards plaintiff, her husband and other members of plaintiff's family and household. DEFENDANT has made numerous phone calls to plaintiff's residences in Los Angeles, Houston and New York harassing her, threatening her personal safety and well-being, threatening the safety and well-being of plaintiff's husband and family, and demanding the payment of money. In addition, DEFENDANT has been caught trespassing on SMITH's gated property in Los Angeles, lying in wait for plaintiff's arrival.

DEFENDANT's acts of harassment include, but are not limited to, telephone calls of varying lengths commencing on or about September of 1994, up to and through the present; jumping the security fence around plaintiff's Los Angeles residence and lying in wait for her on December 11, 1994 in the early afternoon; and calling plaintiff on December 12, 1994 and stating "If I can't have you, no one will; I will kill you."

SMITH has repeatedly demanded that DEFENDANT cease and desist his threatening behavior and refrain from contacting SMITH or any member of her family or household. DEFENDANT refused and still refuses to refrain from his threatening conduct.

SMITH has suffered substantial emotional distress as a direct and proximate result of DEFENDANT's conduct; the same course of conduct would likely cause any reasonable person to suffer like emotional distress.

In furtherance of DEFENDANT's scheme and systematic strategy of harassment and blackmail, he has on numerous occasions made unlawful demands of money on SMITH under threats and duress specifically threatening to publish and disseminate defamatory and disparaging information regarding SMITH and her family all with a view towards overwhelming SMITH's will and judgment.

DEFENDANT's course of conduct has been outrageous and was

performed with the intent to cause or with reckless disregard of the probability of causing SMITH's emotional distress.

A temporary restraining order was then issued.

Chapter 24

PIERRE DEJEAN HAD a completely different story about the fight in New York that made the papers. Although Anna told reporters that he'd hit her, DeJean claimed that was completely untrue.

He said that Anna had come home very late that night, completely drunk. She told him that she'd misplaced her purse, which contained her credit cards and $7,000 cash. She asked DeJean to go back to two hotel rooms and ask if the occupants, whom she'd been with earlier, had found her purse. It was four in the morning, but DeJean did just that.

No one had seen the purse, and they didn't appreciate being awakened. By the time DeJean got back to Anna's room, she'd found the purse. It had been with her coat all along.

DeJean was angry and wanted to apologize to the people he'd disturbed. Anna told him not to, to let it go. In fact, if he did apologize, he would be fired.

Anna then started to fight with DeJean, and he claimed that he never struck her. He did try to restrain her, especially when she grabbed a knife and threatened to slit her wrists. She managed to hurt herself but not badly.

After he'd patched her up with Band-Aids, he left. According to the story he told Eric, he walked to the Hyatt Regency Hotel and got a room. Once he was settled, he called Anna to make sure she was all right. Anna told him she was fine and that she was going to sleep.

According to DeJean, the next morning, he got a call from Carolyn, Anna's representative at Elite Modeling, who said he was in the papers, that he'd beaten Anna.

DeJean said, that after he'd phone Anna, she'd called Donald Trump. DeJean insisted that Anna and Trump had once been an item, that three years earlier they had been intimate friends.

When Eric asked him if it was true that Anna's room had been torn apart, DeJean told him yes, but that it was Anna who had done the tearing.

One last thing – Anna had been so angry at DeJean that she cut up his credit cards, canceled his flight home to Los Angeles, and made sure none of her people would help him. He had to ask a friend to lend him the money to leave New York.

Though DeJean told a nice tale, we had learned by that time to take everything he said with a grain of salt. Melinda had told us many times that DeJean was a bully, that she knew for a fact that DeJean hit Anna. On the other hand, we saw a Western Union telegram from Anna Nicole to Pierre DeJean, after the hotel incident, with $2,000 and a brief message: "I love you."

Then there was DeJean's claim about Anna carrying his child on her wedding day. He had Marshall saying, "Yes, dear. Anything you say," after Anna told him she was going to get pregnant and he was not to ask questions.

Melinda and Aunt Kay reject this all as nonsense. Not only was Anna never pregnant with DeJean's child, Melinda has said Anna was afraid of DeJean. She was terrified of his temper and finally she ended up getting the restraining order to keep him away.

Kay Beall, who had known DeJean from the beginning, told us that she wanted to "wring his neck." Shaking her head, she said, "I've met him and I don't know what to think about him. He tells me one story and a week later he tells me a different story."

"Was he telling the truth about Anna being pregnant with his child?"

"No. I was up there with Anna at that time. That child was not pregnant. She married Howard because Howard was a good man. I knew him. He was a wonderful man. Anna didn't even go to the hospital. She had her period. It wasn't a miscarriage. Just a normal period. You can tell him you asked Kay, and Kay said she was in the house with Anna. She knows the truth."

"Do you think Pierre actually beat her up in New York?"

"I wouldn't put it past him."

"Why do you think he's saying those things about Anna?"

"He's trying to scare her into giving him money. She got him a car to drive. The Rolls Royce. Also a white Mercedes. He just don't like it that his money's been cut off."

When D'eva asked why Anna had bought him the Rolls, it was Melinda who responded. "He wanted a Rolls Royce because he wrecked his. I got mad about that because she's never bought anybody in the family a Rolls Royce or anything that expensive. My Aunt Virgie has to work three jobs. Two extra jobs just to make it. That's her own mother. If she would have given her the money for the Rolls Royce, my Aunt Virgie could have retired."

$\mathcal{D}$EJEAN, ANGRY about the stalking charge, angrier about the $15,000 in attorney's fees, fought as hard as he could to get Anna to back off. He had made tapes of Anna's phone messages and kept them. One call in particular was damaging to Anna's claim that she wanted DeJean kept away.

She'd had her phone number changed, and shortly after that, DeJean recorded the following message:

"Oh, honey, I miss you," Anna said, in that patented baby talk of hers. "Honey, I miss you and I really want to meet you, and here's my new phone number, but don't tell anybody I gave it to you."

This message was left in December, during the same period Anna claimed in her lawsuit that she wanted nothing to do with DeJean.

DeJean was able to get the criminal charges against him dropped. He still had the threat of a civil case over his head, but he'd run out of funds.

Todd Moster, the attorney for Maria Cerrato, had asked Eric to set up a meeting where he could meet DeJean. He wanted DeJean to testify on Cerrato's behalf, but DeJean refused. He was worried about the civil suit.

Another interesting slant came up about the tapes DeJean had made of Anna. She claimed that Pierce Marshall, Howard's son, was having affairs with two strippers. Anna was convinced DeJean could get their names, get some evidence she could use as leverage, given that Pierce held Howard's power of attorney. We listened to DeJean's tapes, and it was definitely Anna Nicole's voice on each one.

DeJean and Pierce had a meeting, also. Pierce showed up with three armed bodyguards. He asked DeJean to sign an affidavit stating that he'd had sexual relations with Anna Nicole before and after her marriage to J. Howard Marshall II. Money was offered, but DeJean would never say how much. He didn't sign the affidavit, and he didn't take the money, although he told Eric that perhaps he should have.

Oddly, during all of this, DeJean told D'eva that he still had strong hopes that he and Anna would reconcile.

They met back when Anna was still going out with Daniel Ross, at a nightclub in Los Angeles called Tatou. DeJean and Ross knew each other, and after a long night of dancing and drinking, DeJean went up to Anna and whispered, "You were born and bred to be with a black man." Evidently, the line was quite effective, as later that night Anna got DeJean's phone number from Ross. She called DeJean several nights later and asked him to come to her home for an interview.

Their conversation must have been a good one, because later that same day DeJean was given keys to Anna Nicole's home and the job of bodyguard.

DeJean told us that he'd been a bodyguard since he left prison and that he'd worked for Zsa Zsa Gabor, Arsenio Hall, and Eddie Murphy. Eric discovered later that he, in fact, hadn't worked for Hall or Murphy.

DeJean also confided that his salary while working for Anna Nicole was $8,000 per month (although Clay Spires says that's nonsense – it was $2,000 per month) and that his employment ran from June of 1993 to January of 1994. Not only did he travel with her, he acted as her road manager. He was the man that went to Greece with Anna the night of her marriage to J. Howard Marshall II.

DeJean told us something fascinating not long ago. He respected J. Howard Marshall II very much, he said. They had had many philosophical discussions, during which J. Howard would recall conversations he'd had with Freud, Jung, and Machiavelli (who died in 1587)!

Chapter 25

ACCORDING TO MANY reports, including a piece in the 24 January 1995 issue of the *National Enquirer*, Anna spent that New Year's Eve at Hugh Hefner's big bash. After much drinking, champagne mostly, Anna jumped into Hef's swimming pool – fully clothed – at the stroke of midnight.

Guests were startled, to say the least. One unnamed attendee told the *Enquirer* that they were "surprised she didn't sink like a stone with that gigantic rock around her finger." Of course, that was a reference to the 22-carat diamond engagement ring Anna had gotten from hubby J. Howard Marshall II.

The *National Enquirer* titled their piece about the incident: Thar She Blows!

Clay Spires, her bodyguard and lover, also mentioned that after midnight, when Anna had dried off, that she and Judd Nelson went to the grotto and brought the New Year in with a bang.

Shortly thereafter, the media went on a feeding frenzy when Anna Nicole made her infamous stage debut with Bruce Willis at the opening of yet another Planet Hollywood, this one in San Diego, California. Anna's pictures, in the skintight red dress that had earned her a prominent place on most "Worst Dressed" lists, sang, cavorted, and of course, showed off the body that had made her millions. Several tabloids ran photos revealing Anna's naked breasts as they slipped out from underneath the tight garment.

It was reported that the Planet Hollywood publicist was quite unhappy with Anna's shenanigans, and that Demi Moore was furious at Anna's unabashed fondling of husband, Bruce, and that she insisted that Anna Nicole be barred from all future openings.

Next up was the debacle at the Academy Awards. Anna went to the ceremonies with Branscom Richmond, an actor who appears regularly on the syndicated television show *Renegade* and who also starred in Anna Nicole's last movie *To the Limit*.

The pictures of Anna, larger than she'd ever been before, waving and smiling, wearing a skintight red gown, appeared in tabloids, newspapers, and magazines. She was ridiculed and pitied. It was a far cry from her debutante pose on the cover of *Playboy*.

Chapter 26

ONLY TWO WEEKS after the wedding, Howard Marshall not only gave his son Pierce power of attorney over his affairs, but amended the J. Howard Marshall II Living Trust, making it irrevocable and severing Anna from "the use and enjoyment of (its) assets."

After that, according to a lawsuit Anna Nicole filed, no one paid her American Express, MasterCard, and Visa bills. Also unpaid were her light and water bills, causing a termination of those services at her residences.

In September, challenges arose over the legality of presents Marshall had given Anna: a 1992 Mercedes, 1,000 shares of Compaigne Victoire – a company he intended to fund to further his young wife's career with deals for perfume, a clothing line and other businesses – and the fifteen-acre spread outside Cypress, valued at $960,000.

At this point, Texas Commerce Bank refused to honour a $965,388.75 cheque Marshall had written to jeweler Harry Winston. Winston sued Anna Nicole to either return the baubles or pay up.

By 26 May 1995, Marshall had apparently grown unhappy with his son's efforts to restrict Anna's visits. In her suit against Pierce, Anna included a statement by Marshall.

"Your honour, this is Howard Marshall. I am not a member of the Bar of Texas, but I am of two other states and the Supreme Court of the United States. I want you to know that I am perfectly competent. I think that my son Pierce has overreached a little bit in trying to make himself my guardian.

"I want my wife to be aided and supported by me. She's the light of my life. I don't think Pierce quite understands that. And maybe he's a little jealous."

Pierce had also previously hired private detectives to follow his father while he visited Anna at her California home. He claimed it was because of his concerns about violent bodyguard Pierre DeJean, but undoubtedly he used the gumshoes to keep tabs on Anna.

On June 1, Anna pressed Judge Scanlan for the right to see her husband. She said she was not "permitted to stay in the home with Mr Marshall longer than thirty minutes, after which time an armed officer indicates that it is time for her to leave."

That rule appeared to have eased, court documents suggested, and the suit became mostly devoted to "discovery" matters as both sides continued to prepare for the courtroom.

According to Kay Beall, Marshall adored Anna. She remembers him saying that Anna was supposed to get money when he died. He wasn't crazy. He was very smart. But, Kay added, she didn't think Anna would ever see any of that money.

"Howard loved Anna and he wanted her to have that. It was his choice – not his son's, but Howard's. If she was trying to take it without Howard loving her, that would have been different. She went with Howard a long time. She could have married him years ago. He asked her over and over to marry him, but she wanted to get her career and her own money before she wed him.

"He was a sweet old man. There wasn't nothing that he would not do for you. He would ask you if you needed something."

Melinda also remembered that about Howard and that "he could eat three of those chocolates with alcohol in them and get drunker than a skunk. We used to laugh at him all the time."

"But Howard was always real supportive," Kay continued. "He always told [Anna] that she didn't have to work a lick if she didn't want to. He would tell her that he would take care of her, but she wanted her career.

"One thing, she was scared of him being old. Scared that he would get sick and she wouldn't know what to do. She always had Uncle Melvin or me or somebody there with her in case something happened. Melvin was real good with Howard. When they went out on trips, Melvin would go. He'd help him get up and get dressed. Up and down steps. They got along real good.

"I know for a fact that that old man just loved Anna with all his heart. I know that."

NNA NICOLE went to probate court for the hearing on the guardianship of her husband on Thursday, February 16. Dressed in a simple flannel shirt and pants, her hair pulled back in a ponytail, wearing no makeup, it was clear to see that she was terribly upset by the proceedings.

Judge Jim Scanlan awarded E. Pierce Marshall temporary guardianship, despite Anna's entreaties. Pierce had petitioned the court for guardianship, claiming that his father was mentally incapacitated. Basing his petitions on the reports from Dr Stephen Rosenblatt, Pierce claimed that Marshall was cogent to answer direct questions by nodding his head.

Anna Nicole did come away with visitation rights, although someone from Pierce's camp was required to be present.

Piece also made sure that his father's millions were put in trust, which, of course, guaranteed a lengthy, ugly lawsuit.

Anna was clearly devastated by the proceedings and went on television to talk about it. In an interview with *News 2 Houston*, she said, "I'm not asking for millions and millions. I just want my bills paid and to have my salary back." Tear stained, wearing no makeup, her hair now in pigtails, Anna said of Pierce Marshall, "It hurts me, because I've kept his father alive for four years. He should be praising me. He should be happy. Howard told people that I saved his life. He has told me numerous times that I save d his life, and that he is here for one purpose – to take care of me and my son."

On the same day, in the same outfit, she told *Current Affair* that, "I could have been a rich snob. I did not marry him for his money. That's not me, that's not my character."

The reporter asked how Marshall's family viewed her. She replied that she couldn't say that on television.

"The most I worry about," she said, "is having to leave his side just to make money to live on, you know, I don't want to ever, ever leave him. I'm a total basket case, going to see my psychiatrist. I'm almost having nervous breakdowns all the time."

Anna also told the reporter that she took care of her husband in a "sexual way." She said that she did her "wife duties" even before they were married.

J. Howard Marshall's secretary was present during some of Anna's visits to the hospital. Several times, Anna brought Ray Martino with her. He'd directed two of Anna's films, *To the Limit* and *Skyscraper*. He wasn't above asking Marshall to put up some money for the films. He also made a point of putting rosary beads and crucifixes all over the room, telling Anna that he was trying to cast the devil from Marshall.

Kay also witnessed Martino's odd behavior. She was concerned when Ray started trying to get the "devil" out of Anna, as well as Marshall.

"He's not helping her by feeding her full of this devil stuff," she said. "That's not what she needs. She's not full of the devil. She's full of mischievousness, and she's mean sometimes. But she shows a lot of love. She's a lovable person. She don't need that Martino."

Chapter 27

IN JULY 1995, Anna and her entourage went to the Bahamas for a photo shoot – a topless one. Things went haywire when island security guards put a strong-armed stop to the proceedings.

The *Globe* reported, in its July 4 issue, that the two gendarmes, responding to complaints by other beachgoers, asked Anna to leave the beach. When she resisted, they "slammed her to the ground, then dragged her from the beach."

Anna Nicole was outraged. She told *Globe* reporters, "My whole life revolves around my breasts. Everything I have is because of them."

Interestingly, there is no law against topless sunbathing in the Paradise Islands. But something certainly stirred up the usually sanguine police.

Anna vigorously protested the police intrusion but was pushed to the ground for her efforts. Then, one of the native guards got her in an arm lock and dragged her off the beach.

Anna's publicist Tony Angellotti told *Globe* that Anna wasn't arrested, and no charges resulted from the incident.

As an aside, he also mentioned that Anna makes $18,000 a day for modelling, but the fee doesn't include bail.

What Anna didn't know, was that while she was being man-handled on the beach, Pierce Marshall was busy selling off some of Marshall's estate at auction in Houston.

Chapter 28

TALK SHOW HOST Jay Leno latched on to the Anna Nicole Smith story with a vengeance. For weeks, his monologues included at least one mention of the newlyweds:

"Did you hear about the twenty-six-year-old *Playboy* centrefold who married an eighty-nine-year-old guy? J. Howard Marshall II – I don't know how old the first is. The only thing they have in common is that they both grew up listening to the Rolling Stones."

"Now that Dole is seventy-one – that's an awkward age – too old to be on *Beverly Hills* 90210, but too young to marry Anna Nicole Smith. You remember her – she married an eighty-nine-year-old man worth five hundred million – and today, Tom Arnold proposed to both of them."

"She's twenty-six, he's eighty-nine – they had their first fight today over a sensitive issue. He wants to be cremated after he dies, she wants him cremated now."

"Let's strap Anna Nicole Smith in a lie detector and find out if she's really in love with that eighty-nine-year-old guy. That's what I want to know."

"I don't want to say he's old, but yesterday she told him to act his age – and he died."

"Anna Nicole Smith –you know her – in *People* magazine they show her with her eighty-nine-year-old husband. Hey want to have children. Hey Anna, to an eighty-nine-year-old guy, you are children."

"She did say they are more and more in love every day. She lives to hear him say those three little words…'I can't breathe.'"

"Last night in the monologue I did a joke about Henry Gonzales, the congressman from San Antonio. A rather elderly gentleman. Seventy-seven to be exact. I said he looked like the 2,000-year-old man, and today Anna Nicole Smith proposed to the guy."

"Anna Nicole Smith – you know who she is, right? She's the *Playboy* centrefold married to the eighty-nine-year-old millionaire. In the paper today, she described their relationship. She said they're like two peas in a pod. You've seen the picture in *People* magazine? It's more like two cantaloupes and a prune. Please. Enough."

"Here's the oddball story of the week – I'm not making this up – twenty-six-year-old *Playboy* centrefold and Guess Jeans model Anna Nicole Smith, you know her? I'm not making this up. She's married to an eighty-nine-year-old Houston man who's worth something like five hundred million dollars. I'm not making this up. She married an eighty-nine-year-old guy. Here's my question. Where does a twenty-six-year-old woman go to meet eighty-nine-year-old guys? You think she's bar-hopping with a bunch of girlfriends at some after-hours club, and she looks over and says 'Whoa, who is the guy with the aluminum walker? He is hot, yeah. Hey, whose teeth are on the bar, are they yours?' He's eighty-nine-years-old. Forget about sex – just carrying her across the threshold would kill him. Anyway, I guess they got married, spent their honeymoon alone, just the two of them alone up there in Niagara Falls, in the honeymoon suite, rewriting his will."

"Scientists in Europe have recovered the fossilized remains of a man reported to be 500,000 years old…the man is half a millions years old, and today Anna Nicole Smith proposed to him. I heard about this, and just for fun I looked up the *Playboy* data sheets – under turn-ons, she said 'old geezers with bad hearts.' Now she's twenty-six, he's eighty-nine, she says she's happy taking her clothes off for a living, and he says he's happy if he's living after she takes her clothes off. It works out great. Actually, they were married last month, but just today he got her bra off. But she did say that he is an incredible lover, just incredible, all night long – of course, that could be the rigor mortis setting in, I don't know."

Chapter 28

"The story we've been talking about all week – Anna Nicole Smith, anyone here from Texas? Ever hear of that guy? Is he famous? In the paper today, Smith called it a May/December romance – I guess she figures he may last till December. During the marriage ceremony, you think she laughed at the part 'Till death do us part?' Actually, there have been a few problems with the honeymoon couple. You know at first I understand that she was very encouraging. She said. 'Don't worry, honey, about having sex. Where there's a will, there's a way.'"

"She says that he's a great lover, you know something? Every guy with five hundred million bucks is a great lover."

On *Geraldo*, during his Friday afternoon gossip show, the wags went berserk. One tattler said, "God bless her. She found her sugar daddy."

Another complained that Anna wasn't giving any in-depth interviews.

Still another recalled a meeting with Anna at Las Vegas Video Show. The reporter, a regular contributor to the *Star*, said Anna seemed very out of it mentally. Was it drugs?

Not one reporter regarded her seriously. In every way, they sneered, lifted their brows, snickered.

Jon Stewart did a parody on his late-night television program. He called it a one-woman show, "Anna Nicole Smith, Up Front and Beautiful."

"It is Texas, it is hot, and I am born," he said, wearing a skintight dress and a long blonde wig. "I'm fifteen, and I will not fry chicken for the rest of my life, I want love. I want a baby. I want nice earrings. I want to be rich."

"Why, Mr Hefner. Me? Pose nude? Why you could charm the honey out of the…things that makes honey."

"Wait, it's too much. Chicago, Austin, Beverly Hills, Jed, Ellie Mae, Xanax, are you gonna finish those fries?"

"I realized then that life is a box of chocolates – and I'd eaten the whole damn box."

Chapter 29

J. HOWARD MARSHALL II died of pneumonia on 4 August 1995, at the age of ninety, in Houston's Park Plaza Hospital. His obituary appeared in newspapers all over the world.

He was survived by his third wife, Anna Nicole Smith; son J. Howard Marshall, III and daughter-in-law Ilene Marshall of Pasadena, California; son E. Pierce Marshall, daughter-in-law Elaine T. Marshall and grandsons E. Pierce Marshall, Jr. and Preston L. Marshall of Dallas.

Anna hadn't spoken to him for a month.

Donations to the George School, his old Quaker prep, were requested in lieu of flowers. Friends said it would be a shame if Marshall was remembered only for his bizarre wedding to Smith and the circus show it provoked. "'I learned a great many things from him," said Jay Grubb, who knew Marshall for forty years and worked for him at Union Texas Petroleum. "He's done a number of wonderful things for a lot of people, a lot of companies, his government and the universities."

Elliot Powers, an associate who assisted in editing a chapter of Marshall's 1994 autobiography *Done in Oil*, said, "I think he should be remembered by all his accomplishments in the field of geology and the oil and gas business. He was a great man to work with and for."

And Oscar S. Wyatt Jr., chairman of Coastal Corp, where Marshall had been a board member, said, "J. Howard Marshall made legendary contributions to the energy industry in America. He significantly shaped American public policy on energy issues throughout his life, and he helped build some of America's most respected oil companies, including the Coastal Corp., where he served as a director for many years."

Not everyone was so complimentary. The *Houston Press* described Marshall as "one grasping old man with an enormous appetite for pretty young women," and remarked, "He is chiefly remembered today as a most astounding old lecher."

His death triggered yet another legal battle between Anna Nicole and Pierce. Anna's attorney, Suzanne Kornbilt, said her client was adamant that Marshall's body be buried, preferably in a mausoleum. Pierce wanted his father's body cremated.

In addition to the dispute over the remains, Anna's attorney filed suit to gain spousal support from the J. Howard Marshall II Living Trust. She wanted half his earnings since the marriage on 27 June 1994.

An employee at the office of attorney Diana Marshall, who also represented Anna, said Anna wanted to use funds from Marshall's estate for her living expenses, which Pierce had managed to keep from her.

According to the *Houston Chronicle*, "Kornbilt acknowledged that Pierce Marshall's lawyers have done a masterful job at hamstringing Smith's every effort at utilizing her husband's funds. They likely will keep up their efforts at denying her a share in Howard Marshall's estate."

"It's really up in the air what we'll be able to achieve in court,' Kornbilt said. 'They've been pretty mean about everything, but I think when this is over, the public will feel sorry for Anna Nicole."

Joseph S. Horrigan, attorney for Pierce Marshall, declined comment.

*T*WO FUNERAL services were held for J. Howard Marshall II. Anna's private affair was held Monday, August 7, at Geo. H. Lewis & Sons chapel, complete with a white baby grand piano and candelabra. Pointedly, the eminent businessmen who paid fulsome tributes to Marshall when he died chose to stay away.

Anna wore her wedding gown and veil. Her son Daniel wore a white tuxedo. A little black dog ran up and down the aisles when Anna sang "Wind Beneath My Wings."

Anna was inconsolable. She sobbed as she viewed the white flowers adorning the casket and the white stuffed bear draped with a rosary sitting beneath the casket. Although she tried to read a Bible passage to the congregation, she only managed to say, "The swords of the just are in the hands of God..." She fell apart after that.

J. Howard Marshall II lay in a burnished wooden casket draped in white roses and lilies, and adorned with a gold-glitter banner reading "From Your Lady Love." Nearby decorations included two white teddy bears and a framed picture with a label identifying it as Mr and Mrs J. Howard Marshall II. As harp music played, some thirty mourners gathered. Conspicuously absent was anyone who appeared to have known Marshall during his first eighty-nine years of life

Surprisingly, Diana Marshall, Anna's attorney, was the one to stand and eulogize. According to *People* magazine, Marshall said, "I am here today to talk about love. I have never known a relationship that embodied love as much as this one. Anna, if Howard were here today, he would say to you, 'Don't cry, Precious Package, my Lady Love.' And in years to come, when you see yourself succeeding, as you will, because you are strong, you will say to yourself, 'Hello Howard. I'm succeeding. I've got my chin up.'"

Ray Martino, who was so new to Anna's life that he'd only met Howard a few times, said that those brief moments with Anna and Howard "taught him the meaning of love."

Although most of the media were held outside the sanctuary, Smith did allow the Houston bureau chief for *People* magazine to sit among the mourners, as well as cameras from *Extra*, a daily entertainment television program. She said after the service, "He called me his Precious Package. Even when he couldn't talk, when he was on his deathbed, I was there ... I gave up much of my career to sit by his bedside, day after day, and nurse him."

J. Howard Marshall's death was treated like sideshow entertainment. The news stories all included pictures of Anna Nicole looking her most lascivious.

David Letterman quipped that his ovation lasted longer than an Anna Nicole Smith mourning period.

Not to be outdone, Jay Leno included her in his monologue. "She said she's getting tired of defending her feelings toward her late husband – she says she worshiped the ground he struck oil on."

But why shouldn't they have their fun? It's not as if the wedding and the funeral weren't all played out in every tabloid and magazine.

Extra filmed the candelabra, her white gown, the piano player. When Anna broke down, whispering, "I'm sorry, I can't right now," it was said to a reporter and caught on film.

Oddly, caterers from Magnolia Grill stood by outside with the rest of the journalists. They served hors d'oeuvres of goose liver and salmon pâté and Perrier. A harpist strummed as mourners filed out at the end of the service.

Anna didn't stop to eat. A black limousine waited for her at the entrance. She left with Daniel and new best friend Ray Martino.

MAXINE MESINGER, the gossip columnist for the *Houston Chronicle* wrote, in her August 11 column, "If anyone has any idea of trying to 'crash' the memorial service Sunday, August 13, for oilman J. Howard Marshall II, forget it. His son is in charge of Sunday's services and said, 'All I want is to honour my dad here in Houston, where he lived most of his life.' The family expects friends and business associates to fly in from both coasts for the memorial; Marshall had many friends in high places. There will be heavy security at Geo. H. Lewis & Sons on Sunday, both before and after the service. The funeral home's head honcho, Bob Jones, will be given the list of invited guests, and only persons on that list will be admitted. Pierce Marshall pointed out that his father came from a small Quaker family in a suburb of Philadelphia. Litany is limited in a Quaker funeral, and Pierce will stick with its customs for the memorial."

Mesinger quoted Jones saying, "I handled the Howard Hughes funeral, and this one's worse."

Of course, at the time of both funerals, the decision had not been reached as to what to actually do with Marshall's body.

Under Texas law, the widow is supposed to have first say on such matters as disposition of the body, but Pierce Marshall contended that his power of attorney entitled him to arrange for the funeral, and dispose of the body.

In a bizarre aside, *People* magazine quoted a Geo. H. Lewis & Sons staffer as saying "[Anna Nicole] wanted to take the coffin out to her ranch and set him up on the patio deck. I had to talk her out of it – I could just see him sliding into the swimming pool."

Chapter 30

ON MONDAY, 14 August 1995, Anna had her day in court. Although she'd already had a funeral for her husband, the body had yet to be interred.

Pierce insisted that he had signed a funeral contract in January designating him to make arrangements, including the cremation of his father's remains.

Anna's lawyer Suzie Kornbilt was quoted in *USA Today*. "Our position is that it's extremely inappropriate for the son...to make this contract without consultation with the wife. If it were Howard's wish to be cremated, Anna would have honoured his wish."

Kornbilt's contention was that Pierce made the contract when "his dad was sick in the hospital and Anna was at his bedside."

In preparation for the upcoming, bigger legal battle over Marshall's estate, Kornbilt made it clear that "Howard slept the night at their ranch many times. He's also slept the night at her L.A. house ... She has slept the night with him in his Texas house."

The disagreement about Marshall's body ended with an out-of-court settlement.

Probate Judge Jim Scanlon decreed that Pierce and Anna would equally divide Marshall's ashes after he was cremated.

Anna had opposed the cremation on religious grounds. It seems she had recently converted to Catholicism. It was alleged that Pierce Marshall secretly arranged a cremation contract with a funeral home before his father's death. A court protest by Anna

Smith called Pierce Marshall's tactic a "gesture of spiteful contempt for his father's marriage."

ACCORDING TO her cousin, Melinda, it was the influence of movie director Ray Martino that had Anna questioning her beliefs. After working on one of her movies, Ray supposedly persuaded Anna that her immortal soul was in danger and that converting to Catholicism was the answer. Melinda also reported that Ray was still trying to "cast the demons" out from Anna, using candles, prayers, and other rituals. A priest was not present during these ceremonies.

However, Anna did speak with Father Bruce Noble after Marshall's death. He assured her that cremation was accepted by the Catholic Church. That conversation took place prior to the hearing, so Anna was willing to concede the issue to Pierce.

She didn't fare so well at the actual hearing, however. According to the *Houston Chronicle*, Anna had to be led from the courtroom due to an attack of nausea.

The attorneys from both sides went behind locked doors to negotiate the finally reached agreement late in the afternoon.

Pierce and his attorneys did not comment, but Anna told the *Chronicle*, "I think it's fair. I'm glad it's over. Thank you for coming."

After that, Diana Marshall read the following statement to the press: "E. Pierce Marshall and Anna Nicole Smith reached an agreement today whereby J. Howard Marshall's remains will be cremated, and the remains will be divided and disposed of by agreement of the parties. Each of the parties believes that this agreement best serves the interests of J. Howard Marshall II with respect."

According to those in attendance, Anna's main argument with regard to the entire proceeding was that she wanted acknowledgment from Pierce that as Howard's widow, she was entitled to some respect.

This court session dealt only with one issue – the disposition of Marshall's body. Nothing was settled about his estate.

Interestingly, Maxine Mesinger, in her August 16 column, stated that insiders told her that although Howard Marshall "lived very comfortably...his wealth was enormously exaggerated – including *Forbes'* multi-million estimate in the early 1980s."

O̶N AUGUST 18, a Los Angeles court found that Anna Nicole Smith Marshall had failed to follow through on her lawsuit against Maria Antonia Cerrato and therefore had to pay out damages. Anna's attorney declared that no guilt was admitted and that she would immediately file an appeal.

According to Kelly Moore, another of Smith's attorneys, Anna's countersuit was effectively dismissed because she failed to comply with an evidence procedure. Moore told the Associated Press that "There is no admission of guilt in this."

At the same time, ex-bodyguard Pierre DeJean was busy talking to the press. He told the *National Examiner* that "I can put the brakes on that inheritance so fast, it will make your head spin."

DeJean reiterated his claims that he had an affair with Anna after her marriage to Marshall. He also said he had an explicit videotape to prove it, but as of this writing, this tape has never surfaced.

He also told the *Examiner* that, "Pierce and Anna Nicole cannot stand each other. Even before Marshall's death, Pierce's people came to me. I substantiated my relationship with Anna."

Of course, this comes from a man who has lied, on several occasions, to us. He had once embellished on his bodyguard-to-the-stars story, saying when he worked for Arsenio Hall, he, Hall, and Eddie Murphy had been together in the Polo Lounge on a certain night. Eric found out that DeJean hadn't been there at all, and neither had Mr Hall or Mr Murphy.

Anna Nicole responded to the *National Examiner* reporters that "pictures taken of them kissing and cuddling prove absolutely nothing. If I like someone, I'm very touchy-feely. He's just out to cash in."

On August 19, the *Globe* printed yet another damaging report about Anna Nicole. Daniel Ross, the guy she'd been seeing a year before her marriage to Marshall, claimed that Anna "had a whole wardrobe full of sexy lingerie, see-through stuff. She also had leather ties and gags. And canes, you know, for sadomasochistic sessions."

Ross said that she asked him to try on some costumes, including a pair of leather trunks.

In the terribly unflattering piece, Ross is quoted about how much Anna likes to eat. The whole article was ugly – and completely irrelevant to anything going on at the time. The *Globe* clearly had nothing relevant to say, so it dug for dirt in order to run something.

Another item that made the paper was the emergency surgery that took place on 28 November 1994. One of Anna's breast implants had ruptured and was leaking inside her body. Anna had opted for saline implants and one was defective.

Anna herself told *Globe* reporters that "My left breast was shrunken and withered. It was half the size of my right one. I called my doc and screamed, 'This is my life, my whole world. I can't look like this!'"

The surgery took three hours, and according to Anna, "They had to fight to wake me from the anaesthetic. I nearly lost my breasts – and my life."

One of the hospital staff commented that "Anna was a total pain in the ass. A big crybaby." She ordered people around, demanded drugs, and when she couldn't get them, she went off on the nurses.

Two interesting things came out of that hospital stay. One was that Anna ended up with larger breasts, and the other was her bodyguard Pierce DeJean was out, and Clay Spires was back in.

ON NOVEMBER 6, 1995, paramedics were called once again to rescue Anna Nicole. It was reported in the *Star* that she was at boyfriend Ray Martino's home, and he called 911. The *Houston Chronicle* placed Anna in her Brentwood home with her housekeeper calling for help.

In either case, paramedics found Anna limp on the floor. They were told she'd had several seizures. They took her to St. Joseph's Medical Center in Burbank where she was listed in critical condition.

Diana Marshall insisted her client had another reaction to pain medication prescribed for migraine headaches. That was the same story offered the last time Anna had been rushed to the hospital after she'd mixed alcohol, painkillers, and tranquilizers.

"Anna was packing at home to go to London for a modelling assignment," Diana Marshall told reporters. "She even had her plane ticket in her bag. People see her as invincible and healthy, but she gets these very bad problems with headaches. It is not a drug overdose."

An Anna spokesman, Tony Angellotti, continued the headache theme. "Anna gets migraines a couple of times a month and takes medication for them. She's been through a lot of trauma, and it takes some time for her to come back."

The news was all over the media. News shows, including those on CNN, reported that Anna had been rushed to the hospital. Although the reporters dutifully gave the migraine explanation, every one of them implied she had overdosed.

Anna was released on Sunday, November 12, but didn't go home. First reports had her recuperating at an "undisclosed location." It wasn't long before the location was disclosed. Anna had checked into the Betty Ford Clinic, the drug rehab centre popular with movie stars and rock idols.

Friends were interviewed, and the enterprising *Globe* managed to get a quote from reclusive Billy Wayne Smith, Anna's first husband. Smith said, "She seems to have a serious drug problem, and I'm worried about Daniel. I want to find out if I might be awarded sole custody of our boy." (Eric wonders about the veracity of that quote. The *Globe* had Billy speaking in full, grammatically correct sentences. When Eric tried to interview Billy Wayne at his parents' house in Mexia, Eric got the impression that Anna's ex was mentally challenged. He used to infuriate Anna by sending notes written with crayons.) An unnamed source said in the same article, "Everyone knows Anna's fond of certain pills."

Hard Copy, which broke the news of Anna's visit to Betty Ford, ran pictures of her in a wheelchair. Not to be outdone, the *Globe* headlined the same pictures with "Texas tycoon's pinup playmate fights for her life in Betty Ford. Drug nightmare puts Anna Nicole in a wheelchair."

Worst than the headline was the possibility raised in the article that Anna had suffered brain damage. Someone characterized as an "insider" told the supermarket tabloid, "Doctors are worried her heart may have stopped, causing permanent brain damage. There seems to be some sort of impairment – doctors hope it's temporary." Clearly, something had gone seriously wrong. One of the rules of the clinic is that no matter what, no matter how rich, famous or powerful, patients must walk to and from the cafeteria for meals. Patients, as part of their therapy, were also required to fraternize with other patients. And yet, Anna Nicole was in a wheelchair and not talking with anyone.

Another source stated, "Anna acts very depressed and seems ashamed of the way she looks. She hides her face in the cafeteria. Right after she arrived, she wouldn't or couldn't get out of bed until they brought in a woman to do her hair."

Still, Diana Marshall gamely stuck to the bad-reaction story.

"That's baloney," a friend of Anna's said. "She was admitted as an OD. Doctors are afraid there's permanent brain damage. They haven't established that yet. She's scheduled to have a lot of tests done."

Anna checked herself out after a few days, not a great fan of the clinic. "They were so mean to me there," she reported.

There was no further talk of brain damage, at least not from that particular drug overdose.

Chapter 31

IT MIGHT HAVE been easier for everyone if Pierce Marshall hadn't despised Anna Nicole as much as he did.

We came to know Pierce after Anna Nicole's marriage to Marshall Senior (his son, J. Howard Marshall III, was known as Marshall Junior) and grew to like and respect him. Pierce told us, "I wouldn't fight Anna one moment in court if I thought she loved my dad."

But we all knew she didn't love J. Howard, despite all her protests to the contrary. Did anyone really believe her when she appeared on *Larry King Live* and declared, "I mean, I just loved him so – I've never had love like that before. No one has ever loved me and done things for me and respected me and didn't care about what people said about me. I mean, he truly loved me and I loved him for it"?

The most important part of that declaration was "and done things for me." Those things included what was estimated in court documents as more than $6.5 million-worth of gifts and baubles Marshall gave her to show his respect. (Some reports had the amount of the gifts a couple of million higher.)

At one point, Pierce defiantly said to us that he would go to jail before paying Anna a dime. To which D'eva immediately replied that she'd join him in the Big House and keep him company. Observing Anna Nicole over the years, D'eva had come to dislike her. The nicest thing D'eva had to say about Miss Cleavage was that she was a "gold digger." This assessment came after hearing Anna complain frequently that she "dreaded" her lunches and dinners with J. Howard, that it was nauseating watching him eat, and she hated having to spoon-feed him.

We observed her trying to get J. Howard to drink two or three glasses of wine so he would go home and immediately fall to sleep. Plying him with wine did nothing to improve another problem she complained about. I'll give this to Anna, it was difficult dining out with J. Howard because of his incontinence. Even wearing adult diapers, he would wet his chair. Despite the mess, his money and clout made sure he was welcomed back – and some smart restaurant owners kept chairs he'd soiled on hand for his next visit.

That didn't bother D'eva, who found him a delight to dine with. She was impressed by his intelligence and engaging conversation. More than once, she wondered what Anna and he discussed when they were alone. Here was this savvy businessman who graduated from Yale Law School magna cum laude and the near-illiterate high-school dropout. What did they talk about?

One thing is for sure, neither would have guessed that thirteen years later Anna Nicole would be watching Judge Ginsburg as still another battle in the Pierce-versus-Anna Nicole, Anna Nicole-versus-Pierce war was fought. If Pierce had been willing to throw Anna a few tens of millions, she might have been happy to settle. But not a dime.

$\mathcal{T}$HE NEXT battle after the cremation conflict came in Texas over J. Howard's estate. According to Texas law, even though Anna was not mentioned in Marshall's will, half of what her husband earned during their fourteen-month marriage went to her, as his legal wife. Pierce's side argued that she already gotten that and more in the form of the gifts J. Howard gave her.

Then the accusations and animosity really began to fly.

Anna's lawyer, Diana Marshall, questioned the "blizzard of documents that were put in front of Howard Marshall to sign two weeks after his marriage. He signed all of them in an almost illegible fashion, which makes sense because he couldn't read at the time, according to his doctors." Among those documents was the power of attorney giving Pierce control of the J. Howard Marshall II Living Trust, the full beneficiary of the will. Diana Marshall claimed that the power of attorney was "basically an attempt to remove Howard Marshall from control of his estate." It would be her strategy to produce repeated declarations of love between husband and very young wife. Later, Anna's side would try to prove that J. Howard had wanted to set up a separate trust for Anna, but had died before doing so.

"The important thing people miss is that this was a long-term relationship," commented Diana Marshall. "J. Howard Marshall discovered Anna before Guess jeans did; he knew her before any notoriety, any word of publicity, before a single modeling contract. He fell in love with her when she was unknown to the world and they loved each other deeply, and anybody who was around him will tell you Howard really lit up when she was in the room."

But matters got nastier and nastier as Pierce went on the offensive. According to *People* magazine, he cut off her $50,000-a-month allowance and accused her of defrauding his father "by way of excessive gifts or transfers of community property to strangers of the marriage, with some of whom she has had adulterous affairs." It was alleged that Pierce was so upset with what he felt was his father's excessive generosity, he sent a private investigator to California to make sure J. Howard didn't sign away anything to Anna Nicole. Pierce claimed he sent the detective to check out reports Anna had hired a bodyguard with a felony record.

Apparently, J. Howard never did sign anything to Anna, which left her with only the "he promised me half his estate if I married him" claim. She was, however, able to produce a letter from J. Howard that read, "I don't object to his [Pierce] being guardian of my affairs, matter of fact he runs a lot of businesses and does very good. But he has no business coming between my wife and myself."

If Diana Marshall's contention was true, that J. Howard could no longer read, we have to assume this note was dictated to someone. Be that as it may, Diana Marshall was definitely not on Pierce's favourite people list. He didn't like her implications that somehow he had been underhanded in getting control of the trust and called her comments to the media a "smear campaign." He took his objections to court where he sued her, the firm of Schechter & Marshall and attorney Suzy Kornbit, for defamation of character. The case was reported to have been settled in Pierce's favor, to the tune of $800,000.

Estate cases go to state probate courts. That of J. Howard's became even more interesting when his other son, J. Howard Marshall III, jumped into the fray in January 1996, siding with Anna Nicole in that he was contesting the will as well. The petition filed on his behalf maintained that Pierce "embarked on a concerted course of conduct to gain control of assets" when J. Howard II "could not see what he was signing." Howard III's lawyer called for the estate to be divided three ways. What could be fairer?

Pierce didn't see it that way. He contended that his brother was not in the will because his father didn't want him to be. The bad blood dated to 1980 and the battle for control of Koch Industries, the mega energy and agricultural company, when the younger Howard had made a tactical – or should we say, really stupid? – miscalculation in voting against his father's wishes in a bid to appoint a new board. The outraged father demanded Howard III return his shares in exchange for $8 million. Pierce claimed that the $8 million was in lieu of any inheritance and that, as a result of the oldest son's perceived treachery, his father had disinherited Howard III in multiple wills dating from 1982.

Howard Junior remembered things differently. "J. Howard Marshall III says he agreed to sell and his father then withdrew the threat of disinheritance, promising he'd share equally in the estate," reported the *Dallas Morning News*. "That promise amounted to a contract that should be enforced, he says."

This was the mess that faced Judge Mike Wood of the Harris County, Texas, probate court. One side (Howard III) saying they had received verbal contracts, the other (Pierce) with a will that may have been signed under suspect circumstances – or may not have been. Added to the mix in a three-way dispute was the claim of Vickie Lynn Marshall (Anna Nicole's legal name in the proceedings) to a substantial share of her late husband's wealth.

The opening statements finally began in October 2000, with Pierce's attorney, Rusty Hardin, saying the case was not about the love of J. Howard II for Anna, but her love for him and how she treated him. He said he would paint a darker side to their relationship, in contrast to the love story portrayed by her attorneys. Hardin said she was left out of the will because of her lavish spending. "I can't train her. She doesn't understand. She just spends," J. Howard was supposed to have said.

A breakdown of his gifts to Anna was presented during trial:

L.A. House – $597,000
Jewelry – $2,804,000
Living Expenses – $318,000
Modeling/Acting Clothes – $699,000
Ranch – $693,000
Ranch Furnishings – $230,000
Toyota – $20,000
Mercedes – $82,000
Misc. Disbursements – $439,000
Total – $6,607,000

After opening statements came weeks and weeks of accusations, rebuttals, denials. Did Pierce use armed guards to keep the loving wife from her sick husband's bedside? Was he trying to have Anna killed? Was Howard Senior of sound mind, or did the 1994 video of him reciting limericks indicate diminished capacity? Did Anna Nicole bar J. Howard from her bed? And what about the choking incident when Anna fed her ailing husband chicken soup?

Hardin set out the case that Howard's interest in marriage stemmed from wanting to avoid taxes on the millions of dollars in gifts he had given Anna. He said she agreed to the marriage because her career was on a downturn and she was gaining weight and had other problems. "This is not a woman who loved him," he said, "but a woman who took tremendous advantage of him."

Hardin noted that Howard Senior purposely left her out of his will when he discovered that she had an insatiable appetite for money. One person quoted him as saying, "I can't train her, she doesn't understand, she just spends."

"No one resented the fact that he loved her," said Hardin. "What they didn't appreciate is the way she treated him."

Attorney Don Jackson told jurors that Vickie's claim that she was promised half of everything Howard Senior owned did not surface until three years after his death. In a 1995 interview on the Howard Stern show played for jurors, Vickie told the radio host, "I've got to fend for myself."

"You're not getting a million?" asked Stern.

"Nothing," she replied.

Her first claim concerning the promise didn't come until 1998. "She has no witnesses, nothing in writing, no evidence," said Rusty Hardin. "She has only her contention that she was offered half. She has nothing, nada."

Yet there seemed little doubt that Howard had intended to support Anna. The key question was whether or not he had ever intended to leave her a share of his company stock or personal wealth. A document referred to in court as the "New Community Memo" gave some indication of his intentions. Written in December 1992 by attorney Harvey Sorensen, it stated:

> JHM (Marshall II) has asked me to assist him in achieving a personal goal of his. He would like to provide his future wife, Vickie, with a gift of a half interest in his 'new community' without triggering any gift tax and in a legally enforceable way.

However, he had also signed a new will and living trust that did not name his wife as a beneficiary, indicating clearly that he did not intend to provide her with a share of his estate.

Witnesses testified that Anna did not visit her husband during the last thirty days of his life, and would upset him by bringing other men with her when she came to visit. A nurse also said Marshall almost choked to death while Anna was feeding him soup, against the nurse's recommendations. Another witness testified how the eighty-nine-year-old oilman would keep everyone up waiting for a call from his young wife, which often never came. "The only thing he wanted in life was to hear her voice before he went to bed," he said.

Things got really interesting when Anna/Vickie took the stand, despite the best efforts of her legal team to keep her from testifying, at the end of January 2001. Clutching a picture of her late husband, she reprised her past career as an exotic dancer, telling jurors it took "thirty minutes and a few drinks" to convince her to strip at a Houston topless bar. It took her a further two weeks before she did her first table dance.

Her clashes with Pierce's tough attorney, former Huston prosecutor Rusty Hardin, were characterized by *Time* as "a pouting, flirty, girly Anna Nicole against a pit bull of a Texas lawyer." Hardin said that Howard's lavish spending on Anna was "unusual behaviour." Anna responded that she thought the millions of dollars in cash, cars, homes and jewelry "was great behaviour." Nor did she dispute that she received at least $5,000 a week in cash from her late husband.

"Did you put the money in the bank?" asked Hardin.

"No," Anna replied, "I put it in my purse."

Asked how should could go through so much cash so quickly she told jurors, "It's very expensive to be me."

Anna also made some bizarre new claims concerning Pierce Marshall. She said that he had wanted his father to die in 1991, and was angry when she "brought him back to life." She offered no evidence to back her allegations. She also claimed that Pierce had armed guards limit access to her husband when he was ill in 1995. "Pierce cut me off," she said. "He only let me see him thirty minutes a day." Her attorneys said she was intimidated by the off duty Houston police officers that provided protection at the Marshall home. Ironically, she hired two off duty Houston police officers as part of her entourage for her appearance in court.

Anna concluded her first day on the stand by telling the jury, "Pierce bought all my friends, took everyone away from me. Every single person turned on me when he (Howard Snr) got sick."

When the question of why she couldn't pay her bills came up, Anna explained her jewelry had been stolen. "Although it is commonly known that my husband gave me a large amount of jewelry that cost him several million dollars," she said, "all of this jewelry has been stolen from me over the past eighteen months, I suspect by relatives, former bodyguards, former friends, and my son's former nanny. The only jewelry I have left are the two pieces I wear constantly – my wedding ring and my inexpensive watch."

How could anyone lose this much jewelry? she was asked. "I used to be a real ditz," came the answer.

Her bodyguard, a convicted felon, told police he had the jewelry, but it was never recovered. Hardin pointed out that she carried the jewelry in a shoulder bag and never declared it to customs officials when she left or returned to the United States. She described as "rude" the Los Angeles Police Department officers who investigated her claim that the jewelry was stolen, saying they asked "if I was on something." The police ultimately concluded the jewelry, which has never been found, was "neither lost nor stolen." Hardin strongly suggested that Anna finally agreed to marry Howard because she had lost the jewelry, she faced numerous lawsuits, and her career was in a downward spiral.

Hardin pressed her so hard in cross-examination that on one occasion she blurted out, "Screw you, Rusty!"

Anna continued to insist that off-duty Houston police officers that worked at the Marshall home "dragged me out of my husband's room." She claimed the officers were armed and in uniform, though other witnesses contradicted this.

She did make one statement that brought no argument from anyone. "My whole life seems outrageous. It's like a crazy soap opera."

Hardin challenged Anna to produce a document or even a witness who would say that her late husband promised her half of his estate.

"I'm sorry. I'll have to get back to you," Smith said. "I can't tell you now."

Anna Nicole also told the Houston jury today that she wanted to be buried in the same crypt as the late Marilyn Monroe, and that her late husband wanted to be buried with her. "I told him that I wanted to be buried in the same concrete thing as Marilyn Monroe," she said. "He wanted to be buried there also." Her fixation with Monroe was already well known. She rented a home Monroe once lived in and sometimes flew under the name Norma Jean.

She denied causing Pierce Marshall emotional distress, which must have had the jurors wondering if she thought falsely accusing someone of trying to have her murdered might not be a tad upsetting. When Anna brought up the murder claim, Judge Wood said he would hit her with a perjury charge with a dash of contempt of court if she couldn't prove it.

Anna had another murder theory she told us about privately. She was convinced that Pierce had tampered with the morphine drip of his father's longtime mistress, Lady Walker. She went in for a routine nose job and came out dead. Anna also told us she was determined to get into J. Howard's will. She knew what he had given Lady Walker and wanted the same. Luckily for Anna, Judge Wood never heard any of this. (It is believed that after the trial, some of Anna's testimony led the FBI to open an investigation into whether *she* had put a hit out on *Pierce*.)

On her final day of cross-examination, Anna showed up in court in a dress emblazoned with the word "Spoiled" across her ample chest. Subtle it wasn't.

She recalled a tearful interview she had given on the TV program *A Current Affair* during which she claimed that Howard only stayed alive because she saved his life.

"He only responded to me," she told jurors.

"Do you feel responsible for his being alive?" she was asked.

"Yes, I do. Me and Jesus," she replied.

In another bizarre twist, Rusty Hardin asked if she took off her blouse to entice her husband when she coached him to record a tape saying she would inherit half of his money.

"Oh, Rusty," said Smith. "You're a pervert."

Then, accompanied by her bodyguards and her "personal attorney," she finally flounced out of Houston.

There were other witnesses whose testimony was equally intriguing. Nurse Betty Morgan took the stand and told jurors about the dark side of Anna's relationship with Howard Senior. Morgan, who began working for the Marshall family in 1991, said Anna would call as often as five times a week demanding still more money. "She would begin to scream and holler, she needed the money," Morgan testified. "She said he had to send her the money, he was her husband."

Morgan described an attempt by Anna to claim her late husband's body so that she could put it on display at a pool party, and says she once stopped Anna removing all the books from her husband's home so she could replace them with pictures of Marilyn Monroe and Elvis. "In the beginning he was happy to give her things," testified Morgan. "But as time went by she was demanding, really demanding. He told her at the time, 'Vickie, I can't afford to pay the gift taxes.'"

Marshall's driver and traveling companion, an ex-marine called Arnold Wyche, told jurors his version of the choking incident story. He said Marshall choked when Anna was feeding him soup, and Anna, who he described as "hysterical and freaking out," summoned Wyche to the room. Wyche called 911 and began relaying instructions to Anna on how to clear his airway and give him mouth to mouth resuscitation. But she gave up after breathing into her husband's mouth only once and remained hysterical throughout the incident. Wyche said he had to take over and finally got Marshall breathing before an ambulance crew showed up at the house.

Wyche also described how she humiliated her husband when he

asked to be placed in her bed at her home in California so he could take a nap. "'Arnold, just throw me in bed next to her,'" Wyche said Marshall suggested. Anna allegedly told her husband, "Oh no, Howard, you know you don't get in the bed with me. You pee the bed." Anna denied this.

Eyvonne Scurlock, who ran Marshall's office, kept a log of Anna's comings and goings during her marriage. According to the log, Anna spent only seventeen days with her husband between 27 June and 31 December 1994.

Mercifully, the trial finally went to the jury in March 2001, after twenty-two weeks. The verdict: the entire estate went to Pierce. And the loser? Howard Junior. It was decided that not only did he get nada, he must pay the Pierce side $35 million in damages for what the jury deemed a "frivolous lawsuit" that tied up the estate in court for more than five years.

And what of Anna Nicole? Well, a funny thing happened on the way to probate court. Remember Maria Antonia Cerrato, the nanny who claimed Anna had sexually assaulted her? Well, she won an $850,000 judgment that Anna couldn't pay. In 1996, Anna filed for bankruptcy in California. And that's where things really got interesting, because should the grieving widow receive anything from the estate, that money becomes part of the bankruptcy proceeding.

In a strange turn of events, before the probate case got going, the U.S. bankruptcy judge, Samuel Bufford, hearing much the same testimony that came in Judge Wood's courtroom, found Anna Nicole's version more credible than Pierce's. He even sanctioned Pierce for withholding evidence and making changes to the will, the *Dallas Morning News* reported. Oh happy payday for the widow when Bufford ruled she should receive damages in the neighborhood of $475 million, which came out to about half the estate.

Naturally, Pierce appealed. This time the case landed in the courtroom of U.S. District Court Judge David O. Carter. Judge Carter found the earlier testimony so at odds, he needed more than court transcripts to make a decision. He would have to hear from Anna, Pierce, *et al.* After wading through the swamp of who did whats, whys, and how bad they were, in March 2002, Judge Carter came to the conclusion that while Anna's marriage to Marshall was "driven by greed and lust," the happy husband loved her, and she was deserving of more like $88 million.

His seventy-nine-page judgment, described by *Time* as reading in part "like a paperback novel," said:

Vickie dreamed of becoming the personification of her idol, Marilyn Monroe. Both became international superstars, traveling far from home under assumed names. Norma Jean's fame thrust her into the arms of an American baseball icon and a dashing young politician, while Vickie Lynn found herself in the company of a Texas oil baron. But her notoriety never reached the same heights or longevity. Her life is best described as that of a person who was rescued by her wealthy pursuer and taught to spend money at a breathtaking pace that most Americans cannot fathom. While she detested being thought of as a gold-digger, her actions leave little doubt that money was the central facet of her relationship with J. Howard. Her appetite for money, once developed, was incessant and outlandish by everyday standards.

Vickie appeared before the Court to testify for three days. Her communication skills were poor as she frequently had trouble engaging counsel. Her illiteracy is striking. Examples are too numerous to chronicle but include writing "25.00" meaning $2,500 and "4500,00" meaning $4,500–she testified that she has trouble with zeros. In fact, she has only recently started learning to pay her own bills after years of managers and relatives managing her money. Vickie also finds herself in difficult times and is being treated for depression.

But education is no guarantor of integrity and a discredited profession does not mean a person lacks truthfulness. While Vickie certainly drew a more noble image of herself than the facts bear out, her testimony on the statements made by J. Howard are credible.

Perhaps the person who came out of his judgment worst, though, was the late J. Howard Marshall II:

J. Howard was a well-trained lawyer. Oddly, however, he did not appear to have much regard for the profession. He was reputed to dislike lawyers and the details of lawyering. To his mind, a legal document should never be more than one page long. (It is ironic then that his death has created the largest volume of legal filings in the history of the Southern Division of Central District of California.) J. Howard is also described as being irascible and demanding. Perhaps to those who knew him, those personality traits were endearing. To outsiders, he was viewed simply as impatient and hostile. His tendency to bang the table to make his point was viewed as being in command of a situation. However, the Court's view is that, at least late in his life, J. Howard's theatrics were transparent.

In addition, J. Howard's disregard for the tax codes was a pattern he followed his entire life. For ninety years, he showed nothing but contempt for the IRS and the tax codes of this country. Throughout his life he surrounded himself with excellent legal counsel who were creative in attempting to circumvent the tax codes. He ignored gift taxes until he could no longer evade the issue. He railed against the inheritance tax provisions, claiming that being forced to pay estate and income taxes was "double taxation," while at the same time he avoided paying substantial income taxes by: writing off as business expenses the gifts to his paramours Lady Walker and Vickie, whom he claimed were consultants; financing his lifestyle by taking a line of credit against his valuable stock holdings, the proceeds of which are not taxable income; and hiding and manipulating his assets in aggressive accounting gimmicks.

In summary, this court is not impressed with the character of a man who had the finest private school and legal education and who consciously avoided the very taxes that millions of American families comply with every year. It is in the collection of these taxes that the government must rely on the good faith and honesty of our citizens to fund our nation's needs in time of peace and war. The fact that J. Howard could not see fit to comply with these laws, despite the great advantages that he was afforded by American society, speaks poorly of his character.

Judge Carter's federal interference with what was traditionally a state matter – probating of wills – did not sit well with Judge Wood, however. He, after all, was the probate judge, and probate judges are in charge of settling estate squabbles. Pierce's lawyers had contended all along that Anna Nicole had been, in essence, venue shopping when she filed for bankruptcy in California, or as Charles Lane of the *Washington Post* put it, she went "shopping for a favorable new forum in the federal courts as if she were shopping at Neiman Marcus."

Three members of the 9th U.S. Circuit Court of Appeals agreed, and threw out Carter's judgment. Just before their decision was announced, Eric exchanged e-mails with Rusty Hardin. Hardin predicted, "I bet my partying tonight will be much more grand than hers." And so it probably was. Though who knows with Anna Nicole.

Speaking to the press, Hardin said, "Basically, this means Anna Nicole Smith gets zilch. I think it's safe to say we are all totally comfortable that it's all over but the shouting, and we're about to start shouting."

That was somewhat optimistic on his part.

Anna Nicole's lawyers were left with three choices. One, they could drop the whole thing (and probably be out their legal fees). Two, they could ask to go before the full 9th Circuit. Or Door Number Three, hey, why not see if the Supreme Court will hear the case?

Which brings us to Anna Nicole Smith meet Ruth Bader Ginsburg, Associate Justice on the Supreme Court.

Chapter 31

When they chose Door Number Three, a lot of people were wondering what they were smoking. Anna Nicole Smith, tenth-grade dropout, Wal-Mart cashier, stripper, Playmate of the Year, *that* Anna Nicole Smith before the Supreme Court? Sure?

As it turned out, the case was of interest to the court, but not for the tug-of-war over the millions or the tawdry details of the courtship and marriage. It was that little jurisdictional matter. Did what is known as probate exception, which cedes probate proceedings solely to the states, have no exceptions? Could the federal courts never intervene?

The case came before the US Supreme Court in August 2006. Anna arrived dressed in black and shielded by enormous sunglasses. Rusty Hardin was there and told me he almost didn't recognize her, she had had so much plastic surgery on her face. She sat two rows in front of Rusty and his gang. One of his staff members later told Rusty that Anna said to her attorney, Howard K. Stern, "Rusty keeps looking at me." Rusty figured that the very insecure Anna was intimidated by the turnout of her adversaries.

The Vickie Lynn of *Marshall v. Marshall* had an unexpected ally – the Bush administration. The federal government had a vested interest in reducing the sweep of the probate exception, since it must often file claims on estates to collect taxes. And from the start, Pierce Marshall's attorney, Eric Brunstad Jr., was in trouble. Justice Stephen Breyer went along with the California District Court that decided Pierce "had forged three pages of J. Howard Marshall's will." Later Breyer almost seemed to chide poor Brunstad because, "They hired private detectives to keep her from [her husband's bedside] … this is quite a story."

Justice David Souter wanted to know why Vickie Lynn shouldn't be allowed to claim in court that "I just want some money from this guy."

In the end, Ruth Bader Ginsburg, in a unanimous decision, swept aside "misty understandings of English legal history" and held that "the Ninth Circuit had no warrant from Congress, or from decisions of this Court, for its sweeping extension of the probate exception ... The probate exception does not bar federal courts from adjudicating matters outside those confines and otherwise within federal jurisdiction." Further, she wrote, that Anna's accusations of misconduct on the part of Pierce made it more than a probate case.

Anna Nicole wins.

Well, sort of. All this meant was the Supreme Court found the 9th Circuit in error and the case would return to federal district court. Two issues would be decided there: whether or not E. Pierce Marshall interfered with Anna Nicole's claim against her husband's estate, and whether or not she was entitled to inherit $88 million. "Actress and model Anna Nicole Smith can add another line to her colorful resume: a winner in the US Supreme Court," reported CNN.

Rusty Hardin wasn't surprised by the outcome. After the day of listening to arguments and the questions lobbed at the lawyers, he said he had a gut feeling the justices were sympathetic to her cause. For his part, Pierce Marshall told the Associated Press that he would "continue to fight to uphold my father's estate plan and clear my name," promising that Anna Nicole and her lawyers "can take that to the bank."

*B*UT YOU never know.

On 23 June 2006, sixty-seven-year-old Pierce died of what was described as a "brief and extremely aggressive infection." The family later told Eric that it was septic shock brought on by a combination of drug-resistant staphylococcus and streptococcus.

We were shocked. Eric had spoken with Pierce only two days earlier about getting new pictures for this book.

Pierce might have been dead, but he continued to call shots from the grave. His will, Rusty Hardin told us, had a provision calling for his wife, Elaine, to carry on the fight against Anna Nicole – and not give his father's widow a dime.

After Anna's death the *New York Times* reported that the case over the Marshall fortune "is likely to continue in the name of Ms. Smith's infant daughter.

You never know how things will play out.

Chapter 32

FOUR HUNDRED AND seventy-five million dollars. Eighty-eight million dollars. In a sense, this was all make-believe money. Pierce and his lawyers were making sure not a cent was ending up in Anna Nicole's bank account, and, of course, a girl has to eat. Granted in Anna's case, it might have been better if she had eaten a lot less.

Anna picked up TV and movie work. She guested as herself on the TV show *Naked Truth*, with Tea Leoni, in 1995. It was a singularly strange episode involving a gynaecologist's office and a urine sample. In the same year, she starred in a Ray Martino film called *To The Limit*, and two years later teamed up with him again for a little something called *Skyscraper*. There were plots, but it seemed that the main function of the scripts was to get Anna Nicole out of her clothes as often as possible. A friend of Anna's said about *Limit* that she "really hoped this movie would catapult her career. But it nose-dived." Both movies went straight to video.

Then with her enormous weight gain, it wasn't likely there'd be another Guess jeans contract in the works. Enter Lane Bryant.

Lane Bryant, in business since the beginning of the twentieth century, caters to what were once called "stout women," today referred to as "plus-size." Through most of its successful corporate history (it now has more than 800 stores), the clothes were considered somewhat fuddy-duddy and matronly. In 1995, the company decided to change its image, sell fashionable clothes, and use models that weighed more in the range of its customers.

Chapter 32

Signed up as celebrity spokeswomen were Kathy Najimy, who appeared in *Sister Act* with Whoopi Goldberg and many other films; the glorious singer and actress Queen Latifah; one-time *Sports Illustrated* swimsuit girl Carré Otis; and Mia Tyler, Steve's daughter who isn't Liv. And who better to change the company's staid image than Anna Nicole Smith? Nobody would associate her with dowdy and conservative.

Anna Nicole hit the runways for the company's shows, with the splashiest one being its lingerie extravaganza in 2002 at which Chris Noth, who played Mr Big in *Sex and the City*, also appeared. (It's unclear what kind of message Lane Bryant wished to send since Mr Big's love interest was the Sarah Jessica Parker character who was too small for a size two.)

Held in the legendary Roseland Ballroom, the rock group Kiss performed, and celebrities such as Roseanne Barr showed up. (Roseanne and Anna Nicole were old pals, known to take private planes to get to where the action was.)

Anna Nicole and an entourage that included lawyer Howard K. Stern checked into the Essex House hotel on Central Park South. According to *New York* magazine, the widow Marshall was greatly put out that her room was not filled with chocolates and flowers. To make up for her disappointment, she sent out a minion in search of pickles. Since the name of her favorite deli was buried deep somewhere in her temporal lobe and wouldn't come out, the pickle person had to hit several delis and pick up different types in the hope of hitting the pickle jackpot.

New York also reported that Anna Nicole went into a weeping fit in her dressing room after the show. Someone present told the magazine that "she said she was upset because she was upstaged by Kiss. She thought the event was going to be just about her."

Howard explained away the sobbing jag as a "happy cry."

But showing off undies for Lane Bryant was nothing compared to where Anna Nicole would get her next pay cheque.

She owes a major debt to Ozzy Osbourne *et familia* for it was their hit show, *The Osbournes*, on MTV that started the stampede to find other eccentric or dysfunctional types to star in their own cameras-follow-you-everywhere programs.

Osbourne, another Betty Ford Clinic alum, first gained fame as a member of the hard-rock band Black Sabbath, and for biting off the head of a live bat during a concert performance. (He's always maintained he thought it was a rubber toy someone threw onto the stage.) MTV aired the first show on 2 April 2002, and ratings were phenomenal, making it the highest-rated show in MTV history. After too many years of drinking and drugging, Ozzy's slurred speech was almost unintelligible except for the frequent f-word. Wife Sharon was unpredictable, once threatening to pee into a Jack Daniel's bottle. The many dogs couldn't be trained not to poo on the floor. And the kids, Kelly and Jack, were not your typical children next door. But many viewers – at times as many as six million – found the family engaging and funny, if somewhat bizarre.

Other cable networks casted around for likely reality-show candidates. E! executives remembered a 1997 segment of *True Hollywood Story* that looked at the improbable life of Anna Nicole Smith. It was a ratings hit. Hey, Anna Nicole, she's wacky, unpredictable, over the top, and despite abusing her bathroom scale by tipping in at 200 pounds (if she ever weighed herself), she was still glamorous – sort of.

You have to wonder about Mindy Herman, president and CEO of E! Networks, who said, "From Marlo Thomas in *That Girl* in the sixties to Mary Tyler Moore in the seventies, Anna Nicole is the real-life version of these classic female TV characters struggling to find their way in the big city. Unlike Mary Tyler Moore, however, Anna Nicole will throw caution and not her hat to the wind, and have a lot more fun along the way."

Huh?

Judging by what Tim Goodman wrote in the *San Francisco Chronicle*, even before the first show aired, disaster was in the air.

It is customary for actors to plug their new shows at the Television Critics Association meeting before the start of the season. Goodman wrote that the critics were treated to a "thankfully brief clip of some scenes, then sat slack-jawed as Anna demonstrated that if she is indeed a cult of personality, it's not because she has scientifically engineered some new rocket.

"As presentations go, this one was a disaster. The Smith from the clips, all hammy vacancy on camera as she desperately tried to emulate Marilyn Monroe, seemed disconnected and strangely subdued in person. Also – and there's really no nice way to put this – she comes off as dumb as a post." (She referred to her breast implants as transplants.)

Perhaps the saddest part of the Q and A came when Anna Nicole was asked if she was worried her son, Daniel, would be teased at school. Goodman wrote, "He hasn't said anything about being teased, she said. Um, maybe that's because the show hasn't been on yet?"

The show did go out, on 4 August 2002, and made the E! people very happy with 4.1-million people tuning in. E! never had a premiere with such a number. Who cared if those elitist critics at the *Hollywood Reporter, Tampa Tribune, Christian Science Monitor,* and *Hartford Courant* likened the show to a "train wreck" (the *New York Times* and *San Francisco Chronicle* called it a "car wreck"). You know you should drive on with eyes averted, but you are drawn to the mayhem. And let's not forget the critic who said watching the show was comparable to going to a vomitorium. Talk about elitist. Who has a vomitorium these days?

The people spoke by tuning in. And that's what E! cared about.

What were they thinking?

August 4 was, coincidentally one can only hope, seven years to the day after J. Howard's death. How better to commemorate that than have the animated opening credits depict Mr Marshall and buxom Anna being married and the aged bridegroom leaving the scene in a shroud of smoke? Want it more tasteless? Try Marshall being replaced with piles of currency landing next to Anna.

You want worse? Anna Nicole went looking for a new rental in Episode One and finally found one to her liking after temper tantrums and pouting. She announced no house would be a home without her beloved J. Howard. Okay, Episode Two finds our heroine taking the box containing the urn with her share of Marshall's ashes on a tour of the new place.

She finally finds the best place for the remains of her husband. Where else than beside the VCR in her bedroom? Pierce and other Marshall family members were reportedly appalled by this episode. The *New York Post* pointed out that it took the grieving widow five years before one of her lawyers retrieved the ashes from a Houston funeral home because she "feared it would become an issue in her bid for her husband's estate."

The urn became a blur in later shows.

Subsequent episodes contained an eating contest between Anna and her faithful retainer, Howard K. Stern; fights with decorator Bobby Trendy (who seemed only capable of showing up with pillows and more pillows, but not the box spring for Anna's bed); the star yelling and screaming at assistant Kim Walther (who showed her devotion by being tattooed with Anna's likeness); poor little Sugar Pie, the small black dog on Prozac that Anna took everywhere; Anna on hands and knees carrying on a conversation with her breasts; and Daniel, the reluctant A-student participant.

Dale Sherman, who had the thankless job of reporting episode after episode for Reality News Online (which he did hysterically), wrote of Episode Four that "Daniel, by the way, does a marvellous job of hiding his face for most of the shots in the first part of this segment. This kid may be brighter than anyone else on the show." Sherman made many similar comments in praise of Daniel as the season progressed.

One of the low points of *The Anna Nicole Show*, and there were many, was when she went to see the *Puppetry of the Penis*. If you haven't heard about it, two guys manipulate their genitalia into – it doesn't matter. The show has gotten great reviews around the world. On the *Anna Nicole Show*, it seemed liked the Chippendales without jockstraps.

Wait, there was a lower point. Anna and entourage were limoing to a party when she became interested in what was happening in the

Middle East. "Who's killing the Jews?" she wanted to know. Howard told her about suicide bombers. "Why would they do that? Don't you think it was kinda painful?"

Then a funny thing happened. Viewers began to notice that watching *The Anna Nicole Show* was kinda painful. It was a half-hour of Anna bitching and whining and verbally abusing everyone around her (except for Daniel, though some people found her baby-talk do-you-love-me unsettling), eating pickles covered with Cheez Whiz, and complaining she hadn't been laid in two years. Somehow this wasn't that entertaining. Ratings plummeted.

But never underestimate the spin of a network. Mark Sonnenberg, E!'s executive vice president of entertainment, went on the offensive. "If you want to hold it against us that we had a phenomenal premiere, go ahead. The show is averaging close to a 2 rating. Yeah, compared to a 4 rating, it's down ... but it's still the highest-rated show on the network and has improved its timeslot average by almost 25 percent in households."

Writer Dan Snierson of *Entertainment Weekly* came up with an *Anna Nicole Show* Drinking Game to make the guilty pleasure of watching it even guiltier. He described the show as "just like *The Osbournes*, but with less metal and more slurring."

Some of the rules were:

Every time Anna Nicole noshes, take a drink.

Every time she's seen without her attorney, Howard, take a drink.

Every time she addresses the camera, take a drink. (If she comes on to the camera, do a double.)

Every time she talks about masturbation, take a sip of blush wine.

Every time she mentions the fact that she hasn't had sex in two years, take a drink while fastening a chastity belt around your waist.

Every time she flaunts her breasts, adjusts them, or refers to them by name, take two drinks. (Caution: Please have an EMT standing by in case of alcohol poisoning.)

Every time she converses with her pooch, Sugar Pie, share a Milk-Bone with your dog.

Every time Anna Nicole herself mounts an object or person, close your eyes, plug your ears, and chant, "La-la-la-la-la-I'm-not-listening!"

Every time she mispronounces a word, throw a dictionary at the TV.

Every time she engages in a sweet-'n'-awkward conversation with her son, Daniel, call your mom and tell her that you love her.

Any time she seems embarrassed by her own behavior, game over.

AMAZINGLY, E! renewed the show for a second season. It would be different, however. No more no-script, come what may. The next episodes would be themed and plotted. Let's see, Anna has been manless. Okay, there would be a *Bachelorette* ripoff. Men yearning to date Anna Nicole would be culled by Howard asking if they liked pickles (obviously very important), if they wanted to date Anna because she's famous, if they masturbated to photos of Anna, and most important, "Do you like cunnilingus?" She would then choose from the chosen five.

Not exciting enough? How about Anna Nicole taking driving lessons, acting lessons, camping?

The series was cancelled in February 2004, and Lane Bryant executives, not happy by how their spokeswoman comported herself, cancelled Anna as well.

Anna was quoted as saying she hated the show's second season. "The first season I thought was okay. You know, it was good, because it wasn't prepared or anything. But the second season, they were telling me like, oh, like do this and do that, and it just didn't work."

But the girl had to work. So let's think. You've been described as morbidly obese, you have name recognition, let's think, let's think. Bingo. Endorse a diet pill.

TRIMSPA was one of those over-the-counters diet pills. Originally, it contained ephedra, an herb the federal Food and Drug Administration had issues with. TRIMSPA took that out of its formula and added Anna Nicole when she proclaimed she was losing weight using the product.

She said, "I just came across TRIMSPA. And I started taking that. And then, amazingly enough, TRIMSPA called Howard, my manager and my best friend. And they called him and wanted me to be a spokesmodel for TRIMSPA. And I was like, this is great. It's absolutely working."

"That really shrinks your stomach," Smith announced on *The Early Show*. "It really shrinks until you can't eat much, and you're not hungry. So, I've had to taper off the pills. I take like two a day now. I don't take six a day anymore."

She added, "It's really hard to eat, because, for me, it's like I've lost my appetite. So I have to really, really push myself to eat."

She did look better and better, but there were those who questioned the magic pill despite the ads where she proclaimed weight loss was because of "TRIMSPA, baby."

How many people actually thought that she, completely absent of discipline, lost seventy pounds on TRIMSPA? Think again. Think tummy-tuck. Think maybe a rumoured more than twenty plastic surgeries done in Palm Springs, California, on not only her tummy, but also repairing her breasts, which looked awful after the earlier implant surgeries, and to mold her face. Also, she reportedly modified her eating habits and used a colon cleanser that had her "on the pot all the time."

Every time the Anna Saga might appear to be winding down, the judicial system adds to it – and then, true tragedy strikes, making you almost sympathetic to Anna Nicole until her worst gets the best of her.

ANOTHER COURT action involved a former lover. Mark Hatten, all 6ft 5in and 255lbs of him, met Anna shortly before the 2000 Academy Awards. They had a brief sexual relationship that ended that June when he approached her with a knife at her home. He continued to call, leaving messages on her home and cell phones, and in 2002 he said he was coming over with a gun. "I was holding my son and we were just freaking out," said Anna.

Hatten, who went by the nickname "Hollywood" and who had two tattoos of Anna on his back, arrived at her home, where he punched and kicked neighbour Rene Navarro, who had gone to ask him to leave. Navarro needed surgery to damage ligaments in his hand.

Jurors found Hatten guilty of assault and making threats, despite his denials and his claim that he and Anna had dated on and off for two years. He was jailed for nearly seven years. He would later claim, ludicrously, that a sample of his sperm had been frozen and had been used by Anna to conceive her daughter Dannielynn.

Chapter 33

IN 2006, ANNA Nicole was gaining weight again and was struggling to find work. There were rumours that she'd done a deal to join Channel 4's *Big Brother* house but organisers instead opted for her compatriot, the basketball star Denis Rodman. Some Anna-watchers thought she was back to her old, horrendous eating habits. There were many others who believed the thirty-eight-year-old was pregnant.

Ever-faithful Howard K. Stern issued a statement saying, "If Anna Nicole is pregnant, she obviously doesn't want anyone to know yet. If she is not pregnant, she's not denying the rumour because she thinks it's funny how much of a stir it's causing."

Then on June 1, the lady, via a video on her website, broke the news herself. Sprawled on a raft drifting in a swimming pool, and with a poodle yapping in the background, Anna said, "Well, let me stop all the rumours. Yes. I am pregnant. I'm happy. I'm very, very happy. Things are going really, really good, and I'll be checking in and out periodically on the Web, and I'll let you see me as I'm growing."

There was no mention of the father but the announcement sparked the usual media feeding frenzy, with one report claiming the dad was a sperm donor who was now seeking cash. Photojournalist Larry Birkhead, with whom Anna Nicole had had a brief fling, emerged as the most likely candidate, claiming he had been pressurised by Stern to deny responsibility. "I have been told that I am expecting a child, I have seen the ultrasound and have spoken to doctors," he said. "I am very excited about the possibility of becoming a father. Howard needs to get past his own jealousy about the relationship between myself and his only client."

On his website, he said he still hoped to play a part in the baby's life – and wished his ex well. "My thoughts and prayers are with you. I wish you a healthy and safe delivery."

Birkhead had come on the scene the previous year, when Smith was spotted behaving outrageously in Myrtle Beach, South Carolina. After entering a wet T-shirt contest, she become involved in a loud dispute with Birkhead, slapping him in the face. He later revealed that he'd had a picture of Anna Nicole tattooed on his back while they were still an item.

Anna Nicole repaired to the Bahamas to get away from the media during her pregnancy, according to her Bahamian lawyer, Michael Scott. She moved into an oceanside mansion on the island of New Providence.

All was quiet on the Anna Nicole front until the birth of her daughter, weighing six pounds nine ounces, by C-section on September 7 in Doctors Hospital, a private facility in New Providence. We remember as far back as 1991 when we first met her that Anna had a small, cedar hope chest filled with clothes and dolls for a baby girl. When once asked by a reporter what was her fondest wish, she answered that she wanted a little girl. "I pray with my rosary every evening. Honestly, I beg God to protect me and my son, and that he will give me another great love with whom I could fly away – like Peter Pan in the storybook."

Anna wanted Daniel to see his new half-sister and asked that he fly in from California. No matter what else can be said about her, Anna seemed to have genuine love for her son.

Daniel, now twenty years old and a student at Los Angeles Valley College, was one of the producers of his mother's latest movie, a dark, psychological drama reminiscent of Ingmar Bergman. Actually, it was something called *Illegal Aliens* and co-starred Joanie Laurer (better known in the professional wrestling world as Chyna). The International Movie Database describes it as "*Charlie's Angels* goes sci-fi, with a touch of *Men In Black* thrown in for good

A brochure featuring Anna Nicole from the Executive Suite, the Houston "gentleman's club" where she worked as a topless dancer.

Christmas for Anna Nicole and son Daniel.

Anna with Warren Moon, former Houston Oilers quarterback. She wasn't happy posing with Moon because, she told Redding, she couldn't stand black men. Not long afterwards, she began an affair with her black bodyguard.

Anna Nicole poses with Eric and D'Eva Redding in front of her outrageous white Christmas tree.

Anna Nicole and author/former manager Eric Redding "seeing eye to eye".

D'Eva and Eric Redding with Anna Nicole at the Reddings' home.

Anna Nicole on the set of her movie *To the Limit*, with co-star and ex-lover Clay Spires.

Anna Nicole and her former maid, Maria Cerrato, who won an $830,000 judgement against Anna for assault and sexual harassment.

Anna Nicole during her Houston trial.

Anna Nicole leaves court with the attorney Howard K. Stern, in February 2006.
(Getty Images/Evan Agostini)

A plus-sized Anna modelling lingerie for Lane Bryant in 2002, before her TRIMSPA days. *(AFP)*

measure, when three aliens morph into super-hot babes and arrive to protect the earth from the intergalactic forces of evil."

The movie's director, David Giancola, told *People* magazine that Daniel wasn't feeling well the day of his departure and "they weren't sure if they should put him on the plane." (*In Touch* magazine reported that Daniel was in the hospital a couple of months earlier with chest pains and high blood pressure.) *People* assigned eight people to track Daniel's movements on September 9 from Los Angeles to Nassau, where Howard Stern picked him up at the airport.

They went directly to the hospital, where happy family photos were taken and Daniel spent a few hours bonding with his half-sister. The *People* story even had what Stern bought when he made a convenience-store run – chips, sodas and chicken fingers.

Daniel was seen helping his mother to the bathroom at about half past six in the morning. The story has Alex Goen, the head of TRIMSPA, saying Daniel "complained to no one in particular that he was tired." Stern was to say, "In hindsight, I wish I had seen that as some of sort of signal and seen that wasn't right." But regrettably, he didn't.

When Anna woke up at about 9:30, she tapped her son, only to realize he wasn't breathing. She yelled for Howard, who ran for help. Doctors tried to resuscitate Daniel for more than twenty minutes before pronouncing him dead. Stern said Anna refused to accept that and continued trying to revive him. "We stayed there," Stern said, "and we were at the foot of the bed and she was hugging Daniel's legs. And she was praying to Jesus to take her and not take Daniel."

Anna Nicole had to be sedated before she could check out of the hospital with her newborn. She was reportedly so overcome, she didn't remember what had happened and later told Stern she wanted to watch a movie with Daniel.

Reginald Ferguson, assistant commissioner of the Royal Bahamas Police Force, told reporters Daniel Smith was found sitting upright in a chair after going to see his mother and his new half-sister. "It would appear from our report that the mother had gotten up, saw him in the chair and he appeared to be sound asleep. She tried to wake him up, he was unresponsive and she sounded the alarm."

During a press conference on September 12, Barry Rassin, President and CEO of the hospital, said, "We can confirm that Daniel Smith arrived at the hospital late evening, 11 p.m., Saturday, September 9. He spent the entire evening in the room and remained as a visitor with his mother and newly born sister. On Sunday, September 10, at 6:20 a.m., it was noted by one of the associates that Daniel was attending to his mother's comfort." According to Rassin, later in the morning Daniel was "observed to be asleep," but at 9:38 a.m. a nurse was called and doctors were summoned after Daniel was found to be "unresponsive." After CPR "resuscitation efforts using advanced life support protocol continued for twenty-two minutes without response," Daniel Smith was pronounced dead at 10:05 a.m.

Also on September 12, Her Majesty's Coroner Linda P. Virgill announced that the cause of death was "suspicious." She quickly clarified that didn't necessarily mean foul play was suspected, adding, "The cause of death is not natural. However, we wish to reserve the cause of death at this time pending the toxicologist examination and report for confirmation of cause of death. Friday is the likely release date for the autopsy and toxicology report"

Virgill announced that an inquest would take place in late October or early November to determine how, when and by what manner Daniel came to his death. "All persons who are relevant witnesses, like his mother and hospital staff and airline personnel who had contact with him, will have to testify."

There was talk of blood and vomit in the hospital room (there wasn't any), that maybe Daniel committed suicide, that the resuscitating team couldn't find needed oxygen tanks, that the death was caused by a drug overdose. Maybe he was murdered.

Murder claims were fuelled by his grandmother, Virgie, who hadn't seen her daughter or grandson in years yet was suddenly an authority on his condition. "It was murder," she told the now-ubiquitous TV cameras. "The levels of drugs in his body are way too high. Someone has to pay. He didn't take an overdose." There were reports of a mystery third adult in the room at the time of Daniel's death. That conspiracy theory was soon put to bed when Stern confirmed he was present, but Virgie had more to say, including how she rang her daughter to commiserate, only to discover her almost incoherent.

"She was so drugged up, I imagine [because of having to deal with] Danny's death," claimed Virgie. "You know, she was so medicated, I think, I could not understand a word, other than, 'Danny's dead.' And she was crying, and trying to talk and mumbling – you couldn't understand hardly anything she said. And as soon as she said that, the phone went click, so I don't know if she hung it up, or if somebody else hung it up for her. I don't know."

On September 14 Anna Nicole's attorney, Michael Scott, read a prepared statement, giving the fullest version, so far, of Daniel's death. This is his account:

Anna Nicole recently moved to the Bahamas to avoid the intent media scrutiny in the United States that she has received throughout her career. She wanted to give birth to her new baby girl in a peaceful environment. Shortly after Anna Nicole gave birth, her son Daniel flew to the Bahamas to share in the joy of his sister's arrival.

Howard K. Stern picked up Daniel from the airport at 10:30 p.m. on Saturday, 9 September 2006. They drove straight from the airport to Doctors Hospital. With one exception, Anna Nicole, Daniel and Howard spent the entire evening together in Anna Nicole's hospital room. The one exception was when Howard left to get food because everybody was hungry.

When Daniel arrived in the hospital room he went straight to his baby sister. He embraced his mother and sister and told them both that he loved them. Daniel was very helpful to his mother and baby sister. On several occasions throughout the night, Daniel assisted his mother to the bathroom, as she was still in a lot of pain from her C-section.

Anna Nicole, Daniel and Howard spent the entire night together and had a wonderful time together with Ann Nicole's newborn baby. At all times, the hospital staff knew that Howard was in the room with Anna Nicole and Daniel. The chronology prepared by Doctors Hospital states that Daniel was observed by hospital personnel helping his mother at approximately 6:20 a.m.

Later in the morning, Anna Nicole awoke and noticed that her son appeared not to be breathing. Anna Nicole frantically awakened Howard with the alarm that Daniel was not breathing. Howard immediately checked Daniel's neck for a pulse and the nurses were immediately summoned. According to the Doctors Hospital chronology, this occurred at approximately 9:38 a.m.

Hospital personnel came immediately to administer emergency aid and assistance. Unfortunately, despite their best efforts, the medical staff was not able to revive Daniel. Even after Daniel had been pronounced dead, Anna Nicole and Howard frantically continued resuscitation efforts.

Anna Nicole was so distraught at the loss of Daniel that she refused to leave his side and it was necessary to sedate her in order to check her out of the hospital. This step was taken upon the recommendation of Anna Nicole's attending physicians and because of the realization that as soon as Daniel's death became public, worldwide media would descend upon the hospital.

The devastation and grief over Daniel's sudden death, coupled with the sedation, has been so extreme that Anna Nicole experienced memory loss of the event. It was necessary for Howard to tell Anna again that Daniel had passed away.

Anna Nicole, Howard and their close friends are obviously shocked and appalled after experiencing such devastation that they have not been allowed to privately grieve, as they ought to have been able to under these circumstances. They have been relentlessly besieged by cameras at Anna Nicole's home and unfair and intrusive media scrutiny.

Anna Nicole has been informed that a coroner's inquest will be convened to inquire into the circumstances surrounding Daniel's *death and she now asks the media and the public to await the outcome of this proceeding before leaping to sensational speculative and unfounded conclusions as to how Daniel died. It is Anna Nicole's wish that this sensational and irresponsible journalism cease immediately out of respect for her privacy.*

On her official website, a statement was posted: "Anna Nicole is absolutely devastated by the loss of her son. He was her pride and joy and an amazing human being." It said that drugs or alcohol were not believed to be a factor. Her son had travelled to the Caribbean country "to share in the joy of his baby sister," the statement said. "Please do not make any press inquiries at this time so that Anna Nicole can grieve in peace."

Friends and family struggling to make sense of Daniel's loss recalled a polite, quiet young man, far from a party animal, who loved video games like *Mortal Kombat*, Japanese cartoons and Ben Stiller movies, particularly *Zoolander*. "He never missed saying, 'Please' and 'Thank you,'" said friend Chelsey Leon, aged seventeen, who attended the same private school as Daniel until tenth grade. "He was really intelligent and well-spoken."

Anna Nicole's half-sister, Donna Hogan, who was finishing a book about the relative she barely knew, told reporters the death was "horrible," and a "real shock."

When it became known Anna Nicole was hiring an outside pathologist to probe her son's death, coroner Virgill said, "It is nothing unusual for families to want their own pathologist to confirm or look for something that may have been overlooked." A first had already been performed by forensic pathologist Dr Govinda Raju.

Predictably, Anna chose a famous pathologist, seventy-five-year-old Cyril Wecht, who appeared often on TV to give his opinions on everything from a plane crash in Greece to the confessed killer of six-year-old JonBenet Ramsay. The murder of Ramsay, a child beauty queen, was a case which had gripped America.

Wecht had been around or had opinions on many of the famous deaths of the previous forty years, from Marilyn Monroe to Elvis

Presley to Scarsdale diet doctor Herman Tarnower. He disagreed strongly with the "single bullet" theory in the assassination of John F. Kennedy and argued that Sirhan Sirhan did not kill Bobby Kennedy. Robert Dvorchak of the *Pittsburgh Post-Gazette* called Wecht "a man who never met a TV camera he didn't like, a man who never had an opinion he didn't share."

When Anna Nicole hired him, Wecht was facing a time problem. He had to get back to Pittsburgh, where he had been Allegheny County coroner, in a few days to face charges of misusing his public office for his private gain. Among other things in an eighty-four-count indictment, Wecht was accused of giving unclaimed cadavers (worth between $1,800 and $4,000) to a local university in exchange for lab space used in his private practice.

Wecht performed his autopsy Sunday, September 17. He could find no evidence of heart disease or stroke. Nor was there evidence of "anything that would cause me to believe there is something in terms of some traumatic injury that was inflicted, or somebody having done something to him in some cryptic manner that could not be observed."

While he had to wait for the toxicology report to say anything definite, Wecht did inform the press the next day that the psychiatrist who had recently treated Daniel for depression had put him on a low dosage of the antidepressant Lexapro and that his psychological state was brought on by girlfriend problems. Wecht added that neither he nor Linda Virgill believed Daniel killed himself.

The lab results found that in addition to Lexapro, Zoloft and methadone were present in Daniel's system. It was not known if Daniel had been prescribed Zoloft, also given to combat depression, and where he had gotten the methadone. Methadone is used to help addicts withdraw from heroin and by some people for pain relief. What is known is that taking Zoloft and Lexapro at the same time can kill you. Ann Blake Tracy, director of the International Coalition of Drug Awareness, explained that "the [pills'] residue can stay there for some time, and if they're prescribed one after they've taken another, they end up in trouble."

A few weeks later, Wecht reported that the autopsy revealed Daniel had taken more drugs – another antidepressant, Amitriptyline, and two non-prescription cold medicines. However, he told *People* that "the levels are insignificant and they don't mean a thing. They're of no consequence." Wecht said that because Daniel was taking three drugs and not a large dose of a single drug, paired with the fact that he was celebrating a happy occasion with his mother, those factors pointed to a "tragic accidental drug death."

Asked why Daniel may have been taking methadone, which is sometimes used to help heroin addicts end their addiction, Wecht said the drug is "a legitimate prescription drug for pain relief" and that Daniel had "no known history of morphine addiction."

Wecht explained that methadone can alter the cardiac rhythm, in what is referred to as a "prolongation of the S/T segment." He said, "When that is prolonged, the individual could even lose consciousness, and suffer cardiac disrhythmia. And that is something that can happen from methadone alone, and in the presence of Zoloft and Lexapro, it is more likely to happen. I don't mean frequently, and certainly not predictably, so tragically, with this young man this is what happened. So I have no question at all as to the cause of death."

Anna Nicole accepted Wecht's findings. Wayne Munroe, another of her Bahamian lawyers, said, "At least she knows the attacks on her son's reputation can be put to rest because it's clear he didn't intentionally take his life."

Howard K Stern said Anna Nicole's baby daughter was now "the one thing that is really keeping her going. Through it all, even with all the pain, she has been a great mom, a very attentive mom," he said.

Finally, on September 20, authorities in the Bahamas issued a death certificate for Daniel, although the cause was listed as "pending chemical analysis," Chief Magistrate Roger Gomez said. If it didn't clear up all the doubts, it at least meant Anna Nicole could bury her baby.

Chapter 34

THE CONTROVERSY OVER Daniel's death may have been temporarily put to rest, but another remained. Who was the father of Anna's baby?

Ever-dependable Howard K. Stern answered that question on *Larry King Live*. With the host obviously pleased he was getting a scoop, Howard announced that he and Anna Nicole had been an item for years and that he was the daddy. "Right now," Howard said, "we have to somehow get through what we're going through. And I'll tell you, our baby is the one ray of hope. Anna and I have been in a relationship and we love each other, and it's been going on for a very long time, and because of my relationship as her lawyer, we felt that it was best to keep everything hidden." Stern said he and Smith were confident he was the father, and "based on when the timing of when the baby was born, there really is no doubt in either of our minds."

Stern was also asked if they were going to get married. "We'll have that happiness one day," he replied, "but first we have to get through the grieving process."

So who is Howard K Stern and how did he come to play such an important role in the final months of Anna Nicole Smith's life?

Not to be confused with the shock-jock radio presenter with the same name, he is a graduate of UC-Berkeley and the UCLA School of Law. Stern, a tall, dark-haired man now in his late thirties, co-founded a firm that handled Smith's modelling and show business contracts in the mid-1990s.

When her husband J. Howard Marshall died in 1995 and she entered into litigation with his family over his $1.6 billion estate, Stern helped out. "Howard assisted capably as a resource," her lead counsel, Philip Wendel Boesch, Jr. told *People*. "He presented Anna's direct examination in the court trial. I did the closing argument and the cross-examination of witnesses."

A search of legal databases did not show any cases in which he had been the attorney of record. He started his career pursuing a mix of entertainment, corporate and personal-injury law, according to his sister, Bonnie Stern. Several lawyers who have worked with him describe him as sharp and painstakingly methodical. Former law partner Dave Shebby said Stern led a "frugal" life, driving a twenty-year-old Jaguar.

Public records also showed that the Californian, the youngest of three children raised in the community of Sherman Oaks, maintains an apartment in Santa Monica, California, from which he operated a business with the intriguing name HotSmoochie Lips Inc. More about the nature of the business is not known but plenty were willing to speculate.

By the time Stern's law firm dissolved around 2002, he had become more involved in Smith's affairs, negotiating her E! show and even appearing with her in the 2003 B-movie *Wasabi Tuna*. Stern concedes that Anna Nicole, who first met in 1996, was dating other people during their relationship, but says he was relaxed about that. He also served as a kind of valet. In the *Anna Nicole Smith* reality show, Stern is continually fetching things. Anna sits while he brings her food from the buffet, and then she complains he didn't bring everything she wanted. He carries her bags and smiles when, at one point, she shoves him. His shirt is always untucked, his eyes too eager.

But there are many readings of the man. Some who know Stern paint him as a canny planner who insinuated himself into Smith's life for venal reasons. Others call him far worse.

Stern's sister begged to differ. She said her brother brought Anna to holidays at their parents' house, for Thanksgiving, in 1998. Anna was dressed formally and seemed "pretty shy." Later, they took pictures. "I was asking her to show me how she poses sexy," Bonnie said. "So she was posing, and I was snapping pictures." For years, Anna and Stern publicly denied any romantic relationship. Bonnie Stern said she had a feeling they were in love, but they wouldn't admit it.

Larry Birkhead, who was to testify later that he dated Anna from 2004 till 2006 and claims he is Dannielynn's father, has said Stern had a "fantasy" about being Anna's lover, but Anna never felt the same way. Birkhead said that while he was in bed with Anna, Stern used to sleep on a couch on the floor below.

It was clear to many of those who knew Smith that Stern was indispensable to her. "She relies on his opinion for everything and he takes care of every aspect of her life," one source told *People*. "He was always there for her, even when she was dating other guys. He fell in love with her the moment he met her. He has always been madly in love with her." Anna was equally indispensable to him – she was his only client. As it would emerge later, he relied almost totally on Anna Nicole for financial support.

Anna told the world that it was she who initiated the romance. In interviews on *The Insider* and *Entertainment Tonight*, she said, "I just kind of attacked him, and that was it. I kissed him first. He was the shy one."

At first, Stern was reluctant because "he always had to go by the books." That didn't discourage Anna. "I knew I was in love the first time I kissed him."

Ahh, but true love proved rocky as almost immediately after the Larry King announcement, Anna's former boyfriend, photographer Larry Birkhead, came forward to say that *he* was the father, sparking a vicious war of words between the two rivals. He told *Us Weekly* magazine that he wasn't surprised by Stern's claim, but was "laughing at it. Larry King didn't even believe Howard."

Birkhead, who met Anna while photographing her at the Kentucky Derby, wanted a DNA paternity test. In a statement, he said Smith told him he was the child's father, and that he had proof. He said he accompanied Smith to doctors' appointments until a "minor disagreement" took place while she was pregnant. He suggested a DNA test be conducted to determine the child's paternity.

In response to Birkhead, Stern said, "I think, first, you have to look at what his motives are. If he honestly believed he was the father, based on when the baby was born, he should have handled it appropriately … handle it through the proper channels, not through television and through the media. Anna has had problems with people going to the media in the past about her, and for that reason, most people around her, including myself, have signed confidentiality clauses that we won't go to the media about her. I'm just very shocked at how he's handled this, under the circumstances."

Asked whether Smith and Birkhead had a relationship, Stern said, "she never considered him her boyfriend."

When it looked as if Anna wouldn't comply with his demands for DNA tests, Birkhead went to court. His lawyer, Debra Opri, questioned Anna's decency. "Where's her fairness? Can Anna Nicole Smith not allow Larry Birkhead the peace of mind in resolving the question of whether he is the father?" She claimed that Anna told Birkhead he would never see the baby.

Debra Opri is something of a mini media personality in her own right, as she often appears on TV shows as a legal expert. She has also represented singer James Brown and members of Michael Jackson's family. She boasts her own website, with a section where the media can click instantly for photographs.

Birkhead's motives were brought into question. In California, child support is determined by comparing incomes of the parents. With the possibility of Anna Nicole getting a massive chunk of J. Howard's estate, well, you see how some people might think Birkhead was in it for the money. (Of course, that could also be seen as Howard Stern's motive for wanting to be the daddy.)

Naturally, Opri disagreed with this theory. Her client "truly wants to be involved in that child's life. This is his first child, and he does not want to lose that child."

Opri said her client wanted Smith and her child to return to California for DNA testing. "He wants to establish legally that which he already knows personally – that he is the father and he has rights," Opri said. She also told *USA Today* that Birkhead was seeking "a presence in this child's life." She added, "He is concerned for the health and safety of the child based upon drug issues and manipulation by a third party for purposes contrary to the interests of the child."

According to Ron Rale, the attorney representing Anna in this case, she did not want to appear in person because she was in mourning. "She is grieving. She lost her son, she's had a baby. She's obviously in bad condition, and here we are appearing in court. So it's not a good time for Anna Nicole."

As legal wranglings often do, this got complicated. Anna's lawyer claimed that California was the wrong venue for the paternity case. Opri took it to Anna by flying to Nassau in pursuit of a deposition. Anna was a no-show.

*I*T TOOK the death of her son, but finally it seemed as if Vickie Lynn might have had public opinion on her side.

That lasted as long as it took for word to get out that she had sold hospital-room pictures of Daniel taken a few hours before he died to TV shows and a gossip magazine for hundreds of thousand of dollars.

Linda Massarella, news editor of *In Touch* magazine, said, "When we heard that the photos were available, my immediate reaction was we have to get them." And get them they did for a reported $600,000, give or take.

Apparently, *Entertainment Tonight* and *The Insider* had similar reactions and bought rights to show the photos on TV.

The grieving mother profiting from the death of her son? Some people felt this was exploitative to the *nth* degree.

Anna's former PR guy, David Granoff, disagreed. "These photos should be seen. It's one of their happiest moments together, and, I mean, she's not going to give them away. That's not the way the world works. What is she going to do, donate them?"

How about put them in the family photo album and keep them private?

Then it hit the news that on September 28, Anna and Howard were married aboard a forty-one-foot catamaran named *Margaritaville*. Well, not exactly "married." It was not a legal ceremony, merely a spiritual one. That was good enough for *People* magazine, which coughed up money for photos of the ceremony.

The magazine described how, in the early morning hours, Anna Nicole, Stern and a nanny clutching her three-week-old daughter Dannielynn Hope, slipped aboard the vessel and pushed out to sea off the coast of the Bahamas' Paradise Island. Later that day a Baptist minister and some of the couple's close friends were ferried to a nearby island called Sandy Cay, where they met up with Smith, thirty-eight, and Stern, thirty-seven, before setting sail again on the catamaran. At around 3 p.m., Stern, in a black dress suit and white shirt, and Smith, holding a bouquet of red roses, exchanged vows and Bible verses – as well as temporary rings, because the real ones weren't yet ready.

John James, an actor who played Jeff Colby in the nighttime soaps, *Dynasty* and *The Colbys*, was one of the guests in attendance. He told *People*, "We all cheered, and Anna wanted to jump into the ocean. But there were sharks out there, so we sped back to [Sandy Cay], and then Anna and Howard jumped in."

The guests were treated to Champagne, apple juice, and Kentucky Fried Chicken, which arrived by boat.

"It was fun and Anna was smiling," says James. "Howard and Anna were both crying and kissing and holding hands. It was kind of sad and happy at the same time."

All of this became too much for attorney Michael Scott. After announcing that Smith and Stern "needed a little adrenaline boost because things have been so hectic and devastating in their life recently," he quit.

He told the AP that he was disturbed by Anna doing the vow

thing with Howard before arranging for Daniel's funeral. His embalmed body was still in a Bahamian funeral home a month after his death. Another factor Scott gave for resigning was that he and Howard didn't see eye to eye "on a commercial transaction [that] made it difficult for us to remain as counsel." Scott characterized the parting as not really "amicable."

In a statement Scott, who had represented Anna for just six turbulent weeks, added: "We have in fact terminated representation of Anna Nicole Smith because of differences that have arisen in relation to strategy and matters arising out of the death of Daniel Smith."

But, in an interview with *Entertainment Tonight*, Stern defended the timing of the ceremony. "For anybody to try and judge us and to try and say we're doing what's right or what's wrong, there's no way for anybody to understand what Anna was going through when Daniel passed," he said. "For Anna and for myself, we felt like we needed it and Anna needed it," he continued. "She didn't want to be alone in life."

The fallout from Daniel's death rumbled on. Although a private pathologist has said the death of Anna Nicole's son was caused by a lethal – but probably accidental – drug interaction, Bahamian police were still investigating.

Reginald Ferguson, assistant commissioner of the Royal Bahamas Police, revealed that four officers from the island nation had travelled to California. "They interviewed a few different people – doctors – and tried to determine drugs and prescriptions and who may or may not have issued them," said Ferguson. "All of those things have to be looked into because at the end of the day, when we send this file to the coroner, it will be expected that all these questions have got to be answered by the investigation."

Police had to extend their investigation to the US to investigate Daniel's background, Ferguson said, because he died roughly eight hours after he arrived in Nassau after travelling cross-country from California through Texas to Florida, where he boarded a flight in Miami for Nassau. Ferguson concluded, "Nothing that our investigators have found indicates any sort of criminality."

The waters became even murkier when it emerged that a witness had come forward claiming that shortly after Daniel died while visiting his mother in hospital, Howard K. Stern appeared to have "flushed [a couple] of prescription drugs down the toilet" in the house he shared with Smith.

He told police Stern returned to the house and checked Daniel's clothing. Shelley said two white tablets fell out of Daniel's jeans pocket and that Stern then "went immediately to the bathroom" and "seconds after, I heard the toilet flush." Stern, he said, told him "that he had taken care of a problem." The claim was denied by Stern's legal team, along with allegations that Anna Nicole's lover administered medication, including methadone which was kept in a fridge, to the former model.

ANNA NOW prepared to bury her son. As was the case with her second husband, Marshall, there would be two services for him.

While Anna continued to mourn in the Bahamas, family and friends gathered on October 7 at a church back in Mexia, where the saga had its roots. About fifty people attended an hour-long memorial service at First Baptist Church of Mexia, including Anna's first husband and Daniel's father, Billy Smith. He looked grief-stricken during and after the service, the *Waco Tribune-Herald* reported.

Most relatives, including his father, hadn't seen Daniel in years, but they recalled that when he was a child he liked to wear cowboy apparel and ride horses. Cousins recalled playing Teenage Mutant Ninja Turtles with him, and full-size cutouts of the cartoon characters lined the front of the church.

Shortly after Daniel's death, Billy Smith, interviewed outside his Mexia home, had said he hadn't seen his son since Daniel was two years old and only learned about his death "when my brother read it on the computer." Still, he said he had "no hard feelings" toward his ex-wife and added that his memories of Daniel were fond ones: "He was a good baby, well-loved."

Twelve days later, thirty-nine days after his death, Daniel's body was carried in a gold-coloured hearse to a cemetery in Nassau. A ceremony was held inside a green tent from which could be heard screams and cries.

People quoted a passage from the funeral's program from Anna Nicole. "My dearest son Daniel, you were my rock, you were the only one that could keep me solid. Why God took you away from me I do not understand. Perhaps some day I will. It is so hard to think of you, but I do every second."

The service also likened Daniel to "a comet, blazing across the evening sky" who "died too soon like a rainbow fading, the twinkle of an eye gone too soon."

Stern, who read a eulogy, said, "Anna Nicole Smith laid her son to rest today. It was the most difficult day of her entire life."

He would later give a moving account of the final moments before Daniel was laid to rest. "She had the people open the casket and she was just inconsolable and hugging Daniel and grabbing onto him, and she wanted to go down with Daniel right there," Stern said. "She said, 'If Daniel has to be buried, I want to be buried with him.' Anna and Daniel were inseparable. Daniel was without question the most important person in Anna's life." He said after the young man died, Anna sometimes cuddled with a poster-size picture of him.

Daniel was buried at the island's Lakeview Memorial Gardens wearing a trucker cap, T-shirt and blue jeans – items said to be his favourite type of clothing. He was laid to rest in a pure mahogany casket with brass trim. His grieving mother wore a black dress and veil specially made for the occasion by close friend Pol Atteu, the Beverly Hills couture designer who also fulfilled her last-minute request to make the lavish gown for her commitment ceremony to Stern.

Smith went to her grave without official confirmation of the reason for her son's death. An inquest, to be held in the Bahamas, will make a ruling. Chief Magistrate Roger Gomez explained, "There are a lot of unanswered questions surrounding Daniel's death that we want to clear up."

Chapter 35

AT LEAST ONE matter had been resolved: the baby girl's name. It was on the birth certificate as Dannielynn Hope Marshall Stern. In a typical gesture by Anna, she ensured that the memory of Daniel lived on in his half-sister's name. Oh, the Stern part? Howard was listed as the father.

Self-described "Proud Father" Stern had said the couple would reside in the Bahamas to escape the media spotlight and start a new, more normal life.

That wasn't going to happen right away as Larry Birkhead upped the ante and filed another lawsuit. He accused Anna Nicole of fraud and conspiracy. Fraud? That would be for listing Howard Stern as Dannielynn's father.

The suit requested that the Bahamas' registrar general change the baby's last name on legal documents from Stern to Birkhead. "It will be up to this government entity to pursue any criminal investigations against Anna Nicole Smith and/or Howard K. Stern," Birkhead's attorney Debra Opri said.

Speaking from LA, Opri added that she was afraid Smith would flee the Bahamas to avoid the charge. "My main concern is this child," she said. "While I do not anticipate that Anna Nicole Smith will be going to Disneyland here in California anytime soon, I do have every concern that she might go to another jurisdiction with my client's child, and we will then be forced to pursue her."

Birkhead issued his own statement: " I just want to say that I am the father of Dannielynn and I think this is a crime, what these people are doing to me, and I expect to be reunited with my daughter with the help of my attorney."

In yet another bizarre twist, Anna Nicole was accused of dyeing her baby's hair. Birkhead claimed he saw the child with dark hair in leaked snippets from a television interview with Smith. The reason, according to Birkhead's attorney, may have been be to make her baby look like Stern. "It's horrendous," Opri said. "We are calling our experts right now to see if dyeing an infant's hair is any way toxic or harmful to a child."

At least Anna Nicole had her safe haven in the Bahamas. Or maybe not.

To be granted permanent residency in the Bahamas, you have to own a home that's worth more than $500,000, have enough money to live there without needing a job, and have two "testimonials of good character."

Anna's qualifications for permanent residency were called into question – and it wasn't the good character part.

A Myrtle Beach, South Carolina, businessman, G. Ben Thompson, claimed he owned the house, not Anna. Different versions came out. At first, it was reported that as a kindly gesture, he bought the property in August 2006 and that Anna agreed to get a mortgage and buy the place from him. Thompson said he and Anna had a brief affair and that at one point, she told him *he* was the father of the baby. Later, the Associated Press reported that he had loaned her the money and that she wasn't making mortgage payments.

In either case, by the end of October, Thompson claimed Anna had not lived up to her obligations and sought to have her evicted. The letter telling her to move on was hand delivered the day after Daniel's funeral.

Thompson said he purchased the house for a bit less than $1 million as a favour to Smith, whom he befriended after he met her through neighbours in mid-2005. Smith was then supposed to sign a mortgage to buy the house from him, but refused to do so. "She said it was a gift," Thompson said. "I never said that. I don't have that kind of money."

If Smith did not leave, Thompson threatened to pursue a formal eviction. "I don't want to embarrass her or humiliate Anna," he said. "I just need my money, or collateral, back."

All of which got Vernon Burrows, Bahamian immigration director, to thinking. No house? No permanent residency.

Anna certainly didn't want to return to California where she faced a paternity suit from Birkhead. "We're going to get that paternity test," Birkhead's lawyer, Debra Opri, said. "It may not be today, it may not be tomorrow, but I'm not going away."

Burrows started an investigation and went looking for an explanation from the law firm of Callenders & Co., Michael Scott's law firm. It was not immediately forthcoming.

Anna's other lawyer, Wayne Munroe, said he personally saw a document that conveyed the mansion to Anna Nicole. Anna, he said, had bought the house from two men, not Thompson. Anna was saying Thompson had given her the mansion as a gift. She brought a case to the Bahamian Supreme Court asking that Thompson's claims be declared false.

Meanwhile, Thompson's lawyer, Michael Scott, said no deed with Anna's name on it had been filed. Michael Scott? Gee, that name sounds familiar.

And so it went in the twisty, turning life of Anna Nicole Smith.

We only hoped that for the sake of Dannielynn, Anna would secure a more stable life. But we realized that probably would take a while, what with the court cases and the bills to be paid. (Did Howard K. have any clients other than Anna?)

Regretfully, we tended to doubt that Anna's life would ever settle down. Not with her deep-seated need to be someone, to be famous, to be a Great Big Beautiful Doll.

Chapter 36

YEARS AGO, WE paid a visit to Anna's cousin, Melinda Beall. She was seventeen and living in a small trailer with her mother, Kay, and Kay's new husband. It was obvious that life hadn't been easy for them. The furniture was old, the carpet worn, and there was very little of any beauty. Except, that is, for a large portrait of Anna Nicole when she was still Vickie Lynn Smith.

She was holding baby Daniel and looked young, innocent, and full of promise.

Melinda remembered how close she and Vickie had been, how Kay used to say that she loved Vickie more than Kay.

"The only thing that I know that would make Anna happy was me and Daniel. The only thing that ever made her happy."

Then the fame came, and Vickie Lynn became Anna Nicole. Things changed, although the cousins stayed close for a while. Melinda began to worry about Anna's behaviour, especially when it involved Daniel. She remembered being told of an incident when Anna put a gun to her head and threatened "to blow her brains out" in front of her son.

In what can only be characterized as a gross understatement, Melinda said, "I don't think that's good for Daniel."

With all the craziness that swirled around him, it is amazing Daniel turned out to be as grounded as he did. Those who knew him often remarked about his intelligence and sanity – and his devotion to his mother. He was the one positive anchor in Anna's life. Lovers came and went. Family and friends were cast aside. Her drug preferences changed. Daniel was always there. She never had to question his motives. He wasn't out to exploit her. He seemingly loved her with no strings attached.

Then Anna got the daughter she always wanted. We didn't think anyone could replace Daniel, but maybe the child would soften the blow of his loss.

The girl's father? Only DNA would tell.

And how long would Howard K. Stern last? He had longevity, but would he run out of usefulness?

And all of J. Howard's coveted millions? It may be the Supreme Court decision did nothing more than prolong Anna's greedy hopes.

We were once friends and admirers of Anna Nicole Smith. But over the last ten years, we'd watched with despair and then disgust as she transformed into a travesty of that sweet young woman we once knew. We watched as she ill-treated a wonderful man for the sake of a big payoff. We despised the way she put Pierce through years of court-induced hell. We recoiled at her hedonistic behavior and tasteless cavortings.

But we had observed all this with great sadness as our once long-ago friend warped into a garish, valueless, tantrum-throwing me-me-me.

We ended this book ten years ago with Anna's Aunt Kay hoping for a reconciliation. "She's a good girl. If people would just love her for who she is and not for what they think she should be. I love her. I will always love her ... She's still one of my kids."

Aunt Kay, she was not the girl you loved, and that was more the pity. We could only hope that with time our Vickie Lynn would return to us.

But tragically, that was not to be.

Chapter 37

ANNA AND HOWARD K. Stern checked into the Seminole Hard Rock Hotel, an eighty-six-acre resort with a 130,000-square-foot casino in Hollywood, Florida, on 5 February 2007. The hotel, with its cascading fountains, was way over-the-top. Yes, it was Hollywood – but on the wrong coast – and Anna Nicole and Stern's suite on the fifth floor, costing $600 a night, was by no means the best in the house. In the days before she died, she'd shared the elevator with all the other guests. It was not A-list.

There are no stars on this Hollywood Boulevard: it has pawn shops and car lots and a buffet of all-you-can-eat fried chicken, and eventually gives way to cheap motels and apartment buildings yearning for a fresh coat of paint. The street cuts through State Road 7, which is lined with a vacant mall and an adult video store, and leads through an urban Indian reservation to the Seminole Hard Rock Hotel & Casino, situated in Miami's northern suburbs.

It was familiar terrain. She had been here as recently as the previous month. A concierge said her stays were often compliments of the hotel. Mounted to bedroom wall of the suites are two fixtures resembling bunches of silver-stemmed tulips with illuminated white blossoms; hanging from the ceiling is an orb of glass that looks like a transparent, motionless disco ball.

The living room has an orange corduroy couch and behind pale orange curtains, windows with a view of a pool even more curvaceous than Smith, and just past, a parking garage and freeways. The sitting area connects to two bedrooms, including the master, separated by two massive floor-to-ceiling sliding doors with frosted glass.

Inside is a four-post canopy bed with a simple duvet of subtle white stripes. The sheets are soft Egyptian cotton. A display on the nightstand phone reminds the guest that the casino is always open.

The master bathroom has a deep whirlpool tub with a jar of green bath salts, an orchid and a loofah near its rim. The glassed-in shower has a stainless-steel head that makes the water fall like rain. A copy of *Rolling Stone* is within reach of the commode; the rolls of toilet paper are sealed by either a red sticker resembling an admission ticket or a band of bright yellow paper sporting the singer Steve Winwood's line, "Roll with it, baby."

Gold-wrapped chocolates arrive with turndown service, the minibars contain lubricant and glow-in-the-dark condoms, a leopard-print ironing board is stowed in a wardrobe closet.

Smith planned to leave this haven four days later aboard a new yacht her companion Stern was arranging to buy. Since the death of her son, in September, in the Bahamas, Anna had clearly been struggling to cope. In early November she was treated for pneumonia at the Doctors Hospital in Nassau, where her daughter was born, and spent a week there recuperating.

"She has a slight case of pneumonia," her new Bahamian attorney, Wayne Munroe, told the Associated Press. "We've had a sudden change of weather here due to a cold snap."

Munroe explained that Smith was hospitalised as precautionary measure, because she recently gave birth. "The impression I got is they took her in because her ribs were hurting, and then they discovered she had pneumonia," he added. "I didn't gather it was anything serious."

However, Stern revealed that she underwent a procedure to drain fluid from a lung that had partially collapsed.

In what proved to be her final interview, at her Bahamas home before flying to Florida, Smith was clearly upset over the battle to prove her baby daughter's parentage, but told *Entertainment Tonight* that she would continue fighting.

"Everyone in my life has stabbed me in my back," she said.

"My whole life, it's just been rough for me…it's always a battle. I feel strong. I'm tired. But…I'm not going to stop fighting." She was scathing about Birkhead, claiming that he was merely interested in her former husband's millions. "I think he is after money and fame. He will never see that money if that is ever to come about."

Speaking about Daniel, she added: "I don't understand why God took him and didn't take me." She also said of daughter Dannielynn, "She looks like Daniel. If I didn't have Howard, or my baby, I wouldn't be here."

Sern, who was at her side during the interview, added, "We're following the law…What people don't understand is that we've got a lot of things that are going on right now, the most important of which is that we're trying to deal with Daniel's loss. All these things, they're like distractions, but just look; Larry Birkhead saying, 'I want a paternity test' doesn't mean that Anna Nicole automatically has to give a DNA test. It just doesn't."

Mark Steines, the *Entertainment Tonight* reporter who conducted that final interview, said Anna's failing health was all too obvious. "Yeah, I could tell that she was starting to fail in that interview," he said. "You could see, even though she said there was fight left in her, it was a false front, if you will. I think she knew that was – it was piling on."

He painted a picture of Anna as a prisoner inside her luxurious home, behind drawn blinds to keep out prying eyes. "There is a pool no one uses, gardens no one visits and terraces no one stands on to take in the very warm night air," he said. "Anna and her baby live pretty much like prisoners inside this home, and we were actually some pretty welcome guests. From the moment I saw her enter the room, I knew this was not the Anna Nicole I had interviewed before. She seemed calmer, sadder, a bit of a broken bird, yet she looked quite beautiful."

Ominously, Steines reported that as the day wore on Anna Nicole became less lucid. "She seemed to be very under the influence of something," he said.

It also emerged that, as she tried to come to terms with Daniel's death, Anna almost died after being found face down in a swimming pool at her home. Howard found her there and screamed for help, and her bodyguard Moe Brighthaupt, who is also a paramedic, came to her rescue. He pulled her from the pool, administered CPR and saved her life.

Anna Nicole's former nanny, Quethlie Alexis, was later to give a statement claiming that Smith tried to take her own life twice after her son's death – first by drinking a sleep draught and then throwing herself into a pool. In legal documents relating to the custody battle for Anna's child, she stated, "On the first occasion, she drank in my presence an entire bottle of what I believed to be a sleeping aid. When she awoke from the resulting forty-eight-hour coma, she said, 'I wanted to die. I meant to kill myself.' She also tried to drown herself in her swimming pool. Howard K. Stern rescued her. I heard him say to her, 'If anything happens to you, I would go to jail.'"

The sworn affidavit, written in the Bahamas in December 2006, also reveals Anna Nicole was obsessed with keeping her baby slim because she wanted her to be "sexy." Alexis claimed, "Ms. Marshall [Anna] was obsessed with making sure that her baby was 'sexy'. Ms. Marshall knew that the correct amount of baby food was three ounces every three hours. Ms. Marshall insisted that the maximum I was to give was 2.5 ounces. She monitored my feeding of Dannielynn by making sure the baby monitor was kept on all the time. The child is badly underweight and not thriving as a baby should."

Danielynn subsequently came into the care of a Mrs Gibson, the mother of a high-ranking Bahamanian official who was a friend of Anna and Howard. Mrs Gibson had met Anna in hospital after the death of Daniel. They became close and Anna even called her "Mommy."

Mrs Gibson later told a TV interviewer, "We spoke for a while and I asked her did she believe in God and she said yes. I also said, 'Would you like me to pray with you?' and she said yes. So everyone who was in the room at the time, we all held hands together and I prayed. After the prayer, we continued to talk, and during the course of our conversation, after she took a pause, she said, 'You know, I wish you were my nanny.'"

She said Anna would spend most of her time in bed, watching movies on TV, and rarely ate a decent meal. Sometimes she would say, "I want to go where Daniel is" and she would often question, "Why did God take Daniel? I wish it was me instead."

Anna stayed at the same Florida hotel she had visited at least three times before, this time arriving with a small entourage on the evening of Monday, February 5. With her were Howard K. Stern, her nurse, her bodyguard and two unidentified others, leaving Dannielynn in the Bahamas with Mrs Gibson.

It was clear from her arrival that all was not well. According to one witness she appeared "woozy" as she walked through the lobby. There were also reports that Anna had flu-like systems, running a fever as high as 105 degrees. Her private nurse reportedly immersed her in an ice bath to bring down the temperature.

Her final days unfolded along these lines:

Tuesday
Anna stays in her room most of the day, suffering from stomach flu. She had come to South Florida to close on the purchase of a yacht, *The Cracker*, which would enable her to commute to her new home in the Bahamas.

Wednesday
Anna slipped in the hotel bathtub and hit her head and her back. Shortly before midnight, she went down to the video bar at the center of the casino floor and had several nonalcoholic drinks.

Thursday
1:40 p.m. Smith's nurse finds Smith unconscious in bed. Smith's bodyguard comes in. The nurse calls the front desk of the Hard Rock, which sends up security personnel. Her bodyguard and security try to revive Smith to no avail. She was

dead. The Hard Rock calls the Seminole Police Department, which oversees the Indian reservation.

1:42 p.m. Hollywood Fire-Rescue gets a call from Seminole police about a white female "who is not breathing and not responsive … It's Anna Nicole Smith."

1:48 p.m. Seminole police and Hollywood Fire-Rescue arrive at the Seminole Hard Rock. Paramedics try to revive Smith, to no avail.

2:15 p.m. Emergency crews leave Seminole Hard Rock with Smith, heading to Memorial Regional Hospital in Hollywood.

2:21 p.m. Emergency crews arrive at Memorial Regional Hospital.

2:49 p.m. Hospital staff pronounce Smith dead.

According to Bonnie Stern, Howard's sister, he was not in their hotel room when Anna was discovered on the bathroom floor

And then the insanity began.

Anna Nicole had always wanted to be larger than life, the new Marilyn Monroe. She became even larger than Marilyn in death. When Monroe died, there had been only conventional media – newspapers, magazines, TV, radio – to report and then speculate on suicide or murder. In the Information Age of 2007, there were those outlets and so many more. When the news broke, the *New York Times*, the eminent gray lady of journalism, posted on its web site links to blogs.

Stories ran in every outlet imaginable. Her death made it into the *Herald Sun of Australia* under a subhead that declared "Anna Nicole Smith's journey of celebrity ended at a venue as colourful as her life when she collapsed at the Seminole Hard Rock Hotel and Casino near Miami." The story went on to report "nearby residents and casino patrons said she frequented the Indian-run [hence the casino] hotel and was known for partying loud and late."

*

$\mathcal{E}$VEN IN death Anna was afforded no dignity, as her final moments were hawked for sale and entertainment.

A shadowy video of the emergency team wheeling Anna to the ambulance, stopping to perform more CPR, was aired on the German TV station, RTL, following a media bidding war which went to a reported $500,000.

After viewing the video, Christopher Spinder, a producer with Fox News, said, "You cannot see her face, you cannot see hair flowing out from underneath the mask. Again if someone didn't tell me this was Anna Nicole Smith, I totally would not have known it. You can't even tell it's a woman."

ABC presented a forensic analyst, Dr Michael Welner, who speculated on the possible cause of death. Maybe accident, maybe suicide, maybe homicide. But even the autopsy wouldn't be definitive, he maintained. "Even if Anna Nicole Smith is found to have a toxic combination of substances in her system, the possibilities of such an event happening still include accident, homicide and suicide." Thanks a lot, doc.

A Boston DJ offered the theory that Daniel committed suicide because he was Dannielynn's father, and Anna committed suicide because of the upcoming paternity test. As ludicrous as that might have sounded, it was already being repeated in Denver by the next day.

Seemingly, everyone wanted a piece of Anna now. Larry Birkhead turned his website into a tribute to mother and child. He posted two photos of Smith embracing him and an audio file playing Willie Nelson's song "Angel Flying Too Close to the Ground." And in a written memorial, he said she called him "her angel" and he called her "my sweet potato."

"Chance brought us together, our love couldn't keep us apart," he wrote. "We loved, we laughed, we shared a connection that couldn't be broken, regardless of the challenges. I loved her in life and I will love her long after. Every night before we went to sleep, she made me say to her … GOODNIGHT MY SWEET ANNA BABY."

"No matter what our differences have been over the years, Anna was still our blood and she will be missed terribly," said her half-sister, Donna Hogan. "She was a woman who was determined to get out of her small town in Texas and make a name for herself. We feel that the death of her son left her deeply saddened, a sadness she hid from everyone. As a mother of three children, I am anguished by this tragic event and the fact that her new baby daughter, Dannielynn Hope, is now without a mother." In the coming weeks she'd have plenty more to say.

Anna's father, Donald Hogan, also felt moved to comment. "It's hard you know, to lose … a daughter, no matter if you haven't been around them in a while," he told *Inside Edition*." Hogan, a retired carpenter living in the Houston area, said he wanted answers about Smith's death, especially so soon after the loss of her son.

"I stayed out of everything with Daniel … I thought it was just an accident," he added. "I'm not going to sit around this time. I'm going to get some answers."

Even the Marshall family, through lawyer Eric Brunstad, offered condolences. "Pierce Marshall himself passed away last year, and then to have her die this year, it's obviously sort of a tragedy compounded by a tragedy," Brunstad said. "We're all, obviously, very shocked by what's happened. And the Marshall family extends its deepest condolences."

Ron Rale, the attorney who represented Smith in the ongoing paternity case over her infant daughter, expressed some bitterness at a news conference about the legal assault Smith faced. "Part of me is angry because I don't believe Anna Nicole should have had to endure this," he said. "I can't imagine any mother who has had to endure this – her loss of a child and litigation on multiple fronts."

Associated Press ran a reaction piece to Anna's death, including statements from many of the high-profile people who had known her:

Hugh Hefner: "I am very saddened to learn about Anna Nicole's passing. She was a dear friend who meant a great deal to the Playboy family and to me personally."

Alex Goen, CEO and founder of TRIMSPA: "Anna knew both the joy of giving life, and the heartache of losing a child. We pray that she is granted the peace that eluded her more recent days on earth, and that she find comfort in the presence of her son, Daniel." Part of the peace that eluded her was a class-action suit naming her with TRIMSPA for deceptive business practices – read that false advertising – shortly before her death.

Paul Marciano, chairman of Guess, the jeans company which helped make Anna a household name: "This is a very tragic and sad day. Personally I feel she did not survive the loss of her son, Daniel, who was the love of her life. Her personality was very complex, but yet she had a charming, sexy and seductive side that reminded me so much of Anita Ekberg from Frederico Fellini's film *La Dolce Vita*. In the fall of 1992, we went on tour with Anna Nicole to the Guess store openings in Hong Kong, Jakarta, Tokyo and Singapore. Thousands of people showed up at every single opening. It was simply overwhelming to see such a large crowd for a model who had just launched her career in the Guess campaign six months prior. I did two more campaigns with Anna Nicole before her personal life took precedence over her career."

Jeff Shore, head of E! Studios: "For those of us who worked closely with Anna Nicole and got to know the woman behind the public persona, this is devastating news. She was a sweet person who adored her son, made us laugh and cry with her, and who was never afraid of what others may have thought of her. There will never be another like her, and I already miss her."

Anna Nicole's former assistant, Kim Walther, told *Entertainment Tonight* that her greatest role still was ahead of her. "She wanted five more kids, and she had whole chests full of girl clothes that she had been saving over the years," said Walther, who was known as "Kimmie" on the 2004 E! reality program *The Anna Nicole Show*. "I hope I'm given the opportunity to tell baby Dannielynn about her mother one day. I just want her to know that her mom really was an amazing person, and loved her, and I would like to tell her the good things."

Of Stern she said: "I would never think that he would do anything to harm either Daniel or Anna. Anna was his entire world. I can't even imagine what he's going through. I know what I'm going through is hard, but Howard, he's been with her for these last couple of years that I haven't been there, and I really wish people would leave him alone."

$\mathscr{A}$CCORDING TO *Broadcasting & Cable* magazine, "Coverage of the death of former *Playboy* Playmate Anna Nicole Smith in the week ending Feb. 11 sent ratings for syndicated magazine shows through the roof." *Entertainment Tonight* viewership was up 13 percent from the previous week; *Inside Edition* up 11 percent; *The Insider*, 7 percent; *Extra!*, 4 percent.

The Pew Research Center found that in the two days following Anna's death, 24 percent of all news was devoted to this story, and incredibly half of all cable news time was about the death. In a survey, 61 percent of those polls said there was too much coverage. But someone had to be watching.

$\mathscr{O}$UR PHONE started ringing almost immediately. It had been ten years since publication of the US edition of this book, *Great Big Beautiful Doll*, but people wanted to hear what we had to say. Hannity and Colmes, *The Big Story* with John Gibson, *Big Story Weekend* with Julie Banderas, the *Nancy Grace* show. At one point, Eric had seven back-to-back interviews. Appearing on *Good Morning America*, he said something that needed to be said to put Anna's death in perspective. "After thirty-nine years of partying hardy and taking all these medications, to have her die at thirty-nine years old is not surprising, in the least." Eric also pointed out that Anna's fame had "offered a lot of hope to the woman out there that wanted to make it, that was a little larger size."

By the Friday afternoon, results of the preliminary autopsy report were made public. The Broward County, Florida, chief medical examiner, Dr Joshua Perper, said that he found no pills in Smith's stomach, and that the final determination of the cause of death would require another three to five weeks.

Speaking at a packed press conference, Perper said her death could have been caused by one of three things. The first, he said, was "solely to natural causes." The second, "due to some medical and chemicals." And the third, "a combination of natural causes and medication. At this time we don't have the results that would allow us to make a final determination."

Citing police sources, CNN reported that a "large amount" of medicine was retrieved from the hotel room and that the prescriptions, among them antibiotics and Valium, were in the name of Howard K. Stern.

Foul play was, however, not on the agenda. "At this point no evidence has been revealed to suggest that a crime occurred. We have found no illegal drugs, only prescription medicines," said Charlie Tiger, Seminole Police Chief. "We are not releasing the names on those prescriptions. We have taken sworn statements from all the parties involved; everyone has cooperated fully."

Anna Nicole's mother, Virgie, now using the name Arthur, weighed in with her opinion. "I think she had too many drugs, just like Danny," Virgie told ABC's *Good Morning America*, referring to her grandson Daniel. "I tried to warn her about drugs and the people she hung around with," Virgie said. "She didn't listen. She was too drugged up. She was so wasted."

Virgie also claimed that Anna Nicole's inner circle thwarted her attempts to help her daughter: "The people she was around wouldn't let, you know, let us get close to her or talk to her." Still, Virgie said she was proud of her daughter. "She had come so far, made a big name for herself" – though she said Smith's claim that she came from a dirt-poor background was exaggerated.

"Well, she didn't come from a small town, as she said she did," Virgie said. "I asked her, 'You were born in Houston, middle-class family. Why do you tell that story?'" According to Virgie, Smith said a "rags to riches" story would get more press. "'If my name is out there in the news, good or bad, it doesn't matter … good or bad, I make money so I'm going to do whatever it takes,'" Virgie said her daughter told her. "And she did. She was savvy."

Next to express an opinion was Anna Nicole's bodyguard, Moe Brighthaupt, who had rescued her from the swimming pool a few weeks after Daniel's death. It now emerged that he was the last person to see Anna alive in her hotel room. According to Brighthaupt, Smith was sinking into a very dark depression shortly before she died, but the only person that lit up her eyes was baby Dannielynn, he told ETOnline. "The depression was unreal, The only thing that gave her any ray of hope and light was Dannielynn. When she got in the depression mode in the house in the Bahamas, it was easy to just bring Dannielynn to her, Dannielynn would open up her big beautiful eyes and look at her mama.

"She always had a laptop and she Googled her name, and she would read these articles that spoke badly about her," said the bodyguard, who goes by the name of Big Moe. "She was just, was sad about that."

He said he was especially worried about Smith during her final four days in Florida, because Dannielynn was in the Bahamas and not around to cheer her up.

Brighthaupt, who stands six feet six inches tall and guarded Anna Nicole for four years, revealed a few details of those last minutes before she was declared dead. He was called by his wife, a nurse, who was part of Anna's entourage. He found her on the bathroom floor of her Florida hotel room and saw that her lips were discoloured.

"I looked at her lips. If you know Anna, she has the most beautiful pink, full lips. … [But] they were blue. I knew I had to go to action," he said. "I saw that she was just there lying still, and so I slapped her in the face and said, 'Anna, wake up, wake up!' I decided to pick her up and put her on the floor, and then I gave her two breaths. I saw they went in, and then I checked for a pulse; I could've sworn I felt a little light pulse, so I just started getting on top of her and giving her CPR and then giving her rescue breaths, and waiting on rescue to come there.

"I was talking to her, saying, 'If you got anything in you, baby girl, please come back. We all need you. Dannielynn needs you.'"

Ten minutes later, ambulances arrived and took Smith to hospital. "My personal opinion. I thought she was gone ... even though I was denying it to myself. I knew she had gone because of what I do for a living. I'd seen dead bodies, and I know the signs," said Moe.

He travelled with Smith to the hospital emergency room. When they got to the hospital, he requested a chaplain and prayed for her. "I leaned down next to her and asked her to keep going and I said a long prayer for her," he said. He was convinced that her life ended because of one thing – the loss of Daniel. "It doesn't matter what they say, I know what she died of – a broken heart.

"It's hard to think about it; I haven't stopped thinking about it," he continued. "I think that's what bothers me more than anything, is knowing that I was the last person to put their lips around her lips, to try to breathe life into her, and there was nothing there."

The bodyguard said Stern was distraught as Anna died. "He was out of control," he said. "He was on the floor, inconsolable; the people in the room were trying to calm him down."

As for Anna Nicole's memory, Moe said: "I want her to be remembered as a wonderful, beautiful woman who loved life – and anyone that has met her, actually met her, knew she was full of life."

*M*ORE DETAILS emerged about the reason for Anna's trip to Florida. She and Stern were looking forward to enjoying their newly purchased Carver motor yacht, which they had christened *The Cracker*. There were two bedrooms, a forward deck to sunbathe and a salon living area. Their plans were to redecorate it to their tastes and they'd hired an interior designer to work with Smith to choose bedspreads. New flat-screen TVs and electronics had already been installed while *The Cracker* was in a Fort Lauderdale marina, being readied for the eight- to ten-hour sail to Nassau at the end of that week, with a Bahamian captain at the helm, but without the couple. Stern was at the boat when he got the call about Anna's collapse.

Meanwhile, out in Los Angeles, Larry Birkhead's lawyers filed a request for Anna Nicole's DNA. Debra Opri explained they wanted the sample to make sure another baby wasn't substituted for Dannielynn when the paternity test was finally taken. While the Circuit Judge Lawrence Korda turned down the emergency DNA request, he did order that Anna's body be stored and not embalmed or buried until a hearing could be held in ten days. (When Korda was given the case, his response was "Why me?")

The DNA wrangling went on until finally, Broward County Circuit Judge Larry Seidlin had enough. Even though experts had said no additional samples from Anna Nicole's body were necessary, Seidlin ordered an additional cheek swab to eliminate a potential exhumation. "When we bury her," he said, "I want it to be forever."

As if the "who's the father" row was not muddied enough, from out of the wings on the day after Anna's death stepped another potential daddy. Prince Frederick von Anhalt, better known as ninety-year-old Zsa Zsa Gabor's younger-by-thirty-years husband, announced he had had a ten-year affair with Anna prior to her death. In an interview with the AP, the prince said, "If you go back from September, she wasn't with one of those guys, she was with me." He added that Anna had always wanted to be a princess.

Von Anhalt's title and credibility were quickly questioned. The AP reported that "Von Anhalt's royal credentials have been the cause of speculation over the years.

"According to stories in the British press, he was born Robert Lichtenberg, the son of a German policeman, and bought his title after being adopted as an adult by a bankrupt daughter-in-law of the last kaiser."

A former Gabor publicist, Edward Lozzi, called von Anhalt a "chronic fabricator."

The *Los Angeles Times* spoke with Zsa Zsa and von Anhalt's attorney of fifteen years, Ronald Jason Palmieri. Did he think Prince Freddy was Dannielynn's daddy?

"I have to believe my client, but it's still surreal," he said. "I would find it completely implausible that he is the father of that child, to put it lightly." So much for a ringing endorsement.

But wait, the prince was not the last of the pretenders to the Dannielynn daddy throne. Appearing February 13 on the TV show *Extra*, Alexander Denk, Anna's bodyguard for two years, claimed to have had an affair with her after he got the role of the chef on the *Anna Nicole Show*. It wouldn't be Anna's first bodyguard fling. Remember Pierre DeJean?

Denk, who is listed by IMDB as having had three movies minor roles – does playing a mercenary in *George of the Jungle* rank as minor? – described Anna as "a very sensitive and emotional woman. A very good kisser, I must say."

At the end of the interview, Denk revealed something that *Extra* described as "a bombshell," although in retrospect, they should have been expecting it. When asked if Anna had ever revealed the identity of Dannielynn's daddy, he said, "She always told me she wanted to have her kids with me."

Uh, so did Denk think he was the father? "There's always the possibility," he said. And to cover that base, Denk hired a high-powered Beverly Hills lawyer, Cyrus Nownejad. If the child is his, he wants to raise her, he said. Some cynical others have suggested the baby claim is attempt to jump-start an acting career.

Body-builder Denk was taken to the mat by Nancy Grace on her show. She didn't appreciate his attempt to sell pictures of him and Anna before appearing.

Wayne Munroe, the Bahamian lawyer who was now handling Anna's estate, didn't sound happy with all the "I'm the daddy" claims when interviewed by the AP. He predicted a lot of "bad behaviour" as the fight continued. "Some German chap came into my office … and claimed he is the father."

The terms of Anna's 2001 will might serve to discourage the emergence of other daddies from out of the woodwork. She stipulated that Howard should hold her estate in trust for Daniel.

"I have intentionally omitted to provide for my spouse and other heirs, including future spouses and children and other descendants now living and those born or adopted."

That will was written when Daniel was fifteen. Now he was dead, she was dead, and that left Dannielynn. The baby could be worth millions if Anna's quest for some of J. Howard's fortune ever proved successful. Or the designated father might be raising the girl out of love for her and not money.

The most outlandish claim was made by half-sister Donna Hogan who, according to papers seen by the *New York Daily News*, alleged that Anna Nicole froze the sperm of J. Howard Marshall years ago. She believed Anna Nicole may have used it to become pregnant.

But what of Dannielynn? Where was she when her mother died? It was believed she was in the Bahamas under the care of the mother of Shane Gibson, the Bahamian Immigration Minister who had granted Anna residency there. If the apparent cosiness of that relationship raised eyebrows then, it was nothing to what was to come.

Chapter 38

ON THE SUNDAY after Anna's death, the baby and Howard were reunited in the Bahamas. Predictably, Stern's arrival home was captured by the television cameras. He was said to have picked up Dannielynn and hugged her, saying tearfully, "This is the only piece of Anna I have left. I had to get back to Dannielynn. I know Anna loved her more than anything in the world."

He also had a warning for Anna's mother, Virgie, who had also flown into the Bahamas, seeking protective custody of the child. "Anna despised that woman. As long as I have breath in my body, that woman will not see Dannielynn," said Stern. It was claimed that Virgie was siding with Birkhead, believing him to be the father. Stern, however, was defiant: "She has no right. She can't take my baby. She can't take Anna's baby."

He revealed that he and Anna had been planning to marry for real, on February 27, a claim which was supported by his sister, Bonnie, who said the rings had been bought. But, it was also to emerge later, Anna had also been preoccupied with death and had been working with a seamstress on a dress for her own funeral.

Howard was equally furious to discover the locks had been changed at Horizons. It seems that G. Ben Thompson's son-in-law, Ford Shelley, the witness who claimed to have seen pills being flushed by Stern, had gone into the mansion the day after Anna's death to "secure" it. He claimed he was told items were being taken from the property by persons unknown.

Oh, yes, and while he was inside, Shelley said he looked into a refrigerator and saw a bottle of methadone, the substance that had been in Daniel's system. We have to believe it was a coincidence that photos of the refrigerator's contents showed up on the Internet. TMZ.com, the gossipy website that outed the transcripts of Mel Gibson's drunken, anti-Semitic diatribe, posted what looked like a prescription for methadone from a "Dr Kapoor, S." for a "Chase, Michelle," an alias that Anna Nicole was supposed to have used. As well as methadone, there were other injectable drugs, Slimfast shakes, and a box of Trimspa on the floor. Her Bahamian attorney, Wayne Munroe, said explicitly that the refrigerator photo was staged by people who broke in and took Anna Nicole's personal items.

The California Medical Board announced it would be looking into the matter since it frowns upon prescriptions being made out to fake names. The doctor in question, Sandeep Kapoor, firmly maintained his treatment of Anna Nicole was "'sound and appropriate," although he didn't say what he was treating her for.

TMZ.com, always on the ball, got a video of Anna and a bare-chested Kapoor kissing and hugging in a nightclub. And who were at the table observing? Howard K. and Larry Birkhead.

Back at Horizons, Howard did the only thing he could – he had the locks changed again and moved back in. The local gendarmes showed up at the mansion later in the week in a crime-scene unit van, presumably in response to Stern's burglary report. He claimed that items that included home videos and a computer had been taken in his absence.

By now, the mansion had become a tourist destination. According to the AP, "tour buses and taxis that rarely venture to the exclusive eastern corner of Nassau where Smith lived have been shuttling hundreds of tourists to the street outside the estate …"

As one Larry Paolini explained, "We were here on a cruise, and we were going to lunch. Since it was just a few miles up the road, we figured, 'Why not?'"

Why not, indeed?

The legality of Anna Nicole's Bahamian residency took another twist when a set of photographs emerged of Shane Gibson, the immigration minister whose mother was caring for Smith's baby. Embarrassingly, they showed him, fully clothed, embracing Anna Nicole in her bedroom at Horizons. Stern confirmed he'd taken the snaps, which had been stored on a laptop.

The question was inevitably asked: "Did Gibson fast-track Anna's application for residency in exchange for sexual favours?"

WITH ITS generous tax laws, residency in the sun-kissed islands is sought after by wealthy Americans and celebrities who are, more or less, left to their own devices. Johnny Depp bought a rugged private island ringed with white sand off Exuma; musician Lenny Kravitz snapped up a speck of land in the Eleuthera chain, among the archipelago's 700 islands in the western Atlantic. Explaining the lure of the Bahamas, the actor Nicolas Cage, another home owner there, said, "People are happy to meet you, but they don't want to exploit you or want anything from you. It's nice to be able to take a walk on the beach and not have to worry about having your picture taken."

Other stars who own Bahamas getaways include singer Shakira, former basketball great Michael Jordan, John Travolta, magician David Copperfield, singer Faith Hill and former tennis player Jim Courier.

Shane Gibson denied any wrongdoing, insisting he was simply a friend of the former Playmate but that had not influenced his decision. A political scandal, the like of which the islands had not seen for two decades, quickly engulfed him. He was forced to deny he had accepted the gift of a Rolex watch from Anna Nicole.

But on February 18, six days after the pictures were published in an island newspaper, he bowed to the inevitable. Gibson officially tendered his immediate resignation from Prime Minister Perry Christie's Cabinet shortly after 9 p.m. on Sunday. His nationally-televised resignation was followed immediately by a national address by Mr Christie, who announced that he had accepted Mr Gibson's resignation.

Political observers felt that Mr Gibson had jumped before he had been pushed. They said that the move to fall on his own sword had saved Mr Christie the unpleasant task of firing one of his key ministers only months away from a general election.

"This is a decision that I have arrived at after close consultation with my family and the Prime Minister," said Gibson, a former trade unionist. "I am convinced, however, that it is the right decision for the reasons I have given."

Gibson said he had been the target of relentless attacks, his good name had been besmirched, his integrity had been impugned, and his character had been assassinated.

"Never have so many lies and falsehoods been told," Mr Gibson said, adding that he would "set the record straight."

He concluded, "I flatly deny the scurrilous lie that I had a sexual relationship with the late Anna Nicole Smith. This is the dirtiest, most low-down lie of all. Not a shred of it is true. My friendship with Anna Nicole Smith was shared with my wife, my children and my parents. There was nothing that was in any way improper about this relationship.

"It can only get worse as long as I remain on the frontlines of the current controversy," he said. "I am not prepared to let them (my family) suffer any further. It is time for their anguish to end so that the wounds they have suffered already can begin to heal. Further, to the extent that my beloved country has in any way suffered from anything that I was perceived to have said or done, I want to apologize to the Bahamian people as a whole. It was never my intention to cause any damage, hurt or embarrassment to anyone."

If the episode with the government minister smacked of farce, it was nothing compared to the circus over Anna Nicole's burial.

Chapter 39

THE COMBATANTS DESCENDED on the courtroom of Broward County Circuit Judge Larry Seidlin, in Florida.

In one corner was Howard K. Stern, arguing that Anna Nicole wanted to be buried next to Daniel in Nassau, in the Bahamas, where she had spent most of her final months.

In the other was Virgie Arthur, petitioning that as her natural mother she had the right to decide that her Vickie Lynn be buried in Texas along with other family members. Initially siding with her was Larry Birkhead.

The issue before the court was simply: who would decide where Anna Nicole Smith would be buried? That single issue often got lost during the questioning about drugs and sex.

As NBC's chief legal correspondent Dan Abrams noted before the trial began, "You wondered, is this just a judge sitting with lawyers, just being a little bit casual, a little bit folksy? But once the witnesses come in he'll make sure that the decorum of the court-room is reestablished? No, didn't happen."

One problem was Anna's will. Stern was named as the executor of the estate. The will, written in 2001, was not updated after the birth of her daughter, Dannielynn Hope. In the aftermath of Daniel's death, arranging her financial affairs was far from Anna's mind.

The document said that Smith's estate should be held in trust for Daniel. The clause in the document which stated, "I have intentionally omitted to provide for my spouse, including any future spouses or children," seemed to exclude Dannielynn. Crucially, as far as the looming court battle over Anna's remains was concerned, she expressed no desire on a burial place for herself. The document, which gave no value of her worth, was signed by "Vickie Lynn Marshall" and gave Stern full authority to take care of assets and property.

Judge Seidlin cast doubt over the will's validity, stating that the document had "plenty of holes," taking particular exception to the way it seemed to exclude future children. "No way in America would a woman sign a clause like that," Seidlin said.

Apart from the confusion over the will and the row about to begin over her burial, there were also the issues of Dannielynn's parentage and custody still to be resolved. Yet again, the lawyers were ready for a feeding frenzy. And there were plenty of them. There was also something of a Hogan family reunion in the court room, as Anna's mother, Virgie, and father, Donald, sat a few yards apart without acknowledging one another. Birkhead, although due at another court in California to give evidence in the paternity battle, was also there, along with Stern.

No-one knew it then, but the unknown judge, Seidlin, was set to overshadow the main players, causing observers to ask: was he doing his job here, or auditioning for a TV show?

Seidlin, a New Yorker, had been on the bench for twenty-nine years. The balding, fifty-six-year-old Bronx-born judge first raised eyebrows before the main case began, when he referred to Smith's corpse as "that baby," and declared that her body "belongs to me now."

His courtroom demeanour was described as one part Bronx cowboy, one part preacher. "He is not as pretty as Judge Judy, but he is cut from the same tooth," said Vinnie Politan. "We here at Court TV love him. This is going to put him on the map, and he knows it." He would constantly refer to lawyers, not by their name, but their state of origin. He repeatedly mispronounced Birkhead's last name, until he was corrected by an attorney, and admitted he didn't really know much about Anna Nicole.

Seidlin's theatrics did not endear him to everyone. One lawyer, who spoke on the condition of anonymity, was mystified that Seidlin was getting national attention. "One of the worst judges in Broward County could wind up becoming a TV star," said the lawyer. In the 2004 Broward County Bar Poll, twenty-two percent of lawyers responding to the survey said Seidlin was not qualified, putting him near the bottom of the pack of judges.

But his supporters said that Seidlin, while controversial, had a no-nonsense approach that worked. Fort Lauderdale lawyer Bradford Cohen, who has had cases before Seidlin, has nothing but praise for him, describing the judge as fair and smart. "If judges don't have personalities, it would be a pretty boring world," Cohen said. "Critics think he is not taking the case seriously due to his demeanour, but look at how he controls the courtroom. Look at the decisions he has made. His skill speaks for itself."

His style certainly made for some comic moments in the case and, thanks to Court TV screening it live, he became an instant celebrity. The entertainment website TMZ.com reported that Seidlin wanted to become TV's next personality judge and was putting together a highlight reel as an audition tool. But some in the Broward legal world doubted that, pointing out that Seidlin wasn't acting any differently on Court TV than he did in lower-profile probate cases.

Some of his highlights:

To the roomful of lawyers: "Instead of fighting, you should join hands, join hands, because this is the only country where you can join hands."

Early in the week-long hearing, Seidlin told one high-strung blonde lawyer that she was beautiful, and took cell phone calls from his wife.

At another point, John O'Quinn, Virgie's attorney, collapsed, taking a lot of furniture with him as he went down. "Let's get him some water, (for) my Texas friend," Seidlin ordered. "I'm working them all too hard. Get him some food. He hasn't eaten. He's a diabetic. I can tell (from) his colour." Actually, Quinn said, he was fine. He had only tripped.

At the end of a hearing day: "It was delightful having everyone."

At one point he told John O'Quinn: "Texas, you can help me here. You're a bright guy. ... You're wonderful. I love you."

He suggested the courtroom proceedings stop to pay homage to US troops in Afghanistan and Iraq.

Referring to a dress being made for Smith's burial, Seidlin's face soured as he expressed his general discomfort over funeral details. "This is the one area I always ran away from – the death," Seidlin said. It prompted attorney Stephen Tunstall to note wryly, "But you're a probate judge," referring to the type of judge whose job is to deal with wills.

To an agitated attorney: "You were getting animated for no reason, my friend. You were getting stressed for no reason. Twice now we were on a different signal. I'm going to get you some juice."

To another agitated attorney: "I heard you, Texas. Let's move on. You're getting hungry for lunch."

In suggesting that the parties should try to reach a compromise: "We don't want to make each other (out) as evil. This would (happen) in a book (but) this is real life. We all come with some broken suitcases."

Court TV analysts said Seidlin got away with it because no jury was present. Throughout the hearing, Seidlin declined to speak to reporters, but his wife, Belinda, was less reticent. "People who know him, and people who meet him on the street, all say the same thing, 'You should have your own television show'. I don't think him to be crazy at all. I find him to be brilliant, and that's tough to say when you're married to someone for a long time."

UESDAY, FEBRUARY 20. Stern, who had been reluctant to attend court, was up first to make the case that Anna wanted to be buried in the Bahamas. Just before the hearing started, Virgie made a point of embracing Larry Birkhead in front of the cameras.

Stern told the court that he'd first met Anna Nicole in 1996, but they had not become lovers until 2000. Virgie's lawyer, Stephen Tunstall, one of eighteen attorneys in the courtroom, quizzed him about their relationship.

Tunstall: "Do you mean by lover that you got sexual relationship with her?"

Stern: "Yes."

He said Anna was estranged from her mother, with whom she only had occasional telephone contact. There had been attempts at reconciliation during her marriage to Marshall but none had lasted long. Howard then told the court how Anna never recovered from the death of her son. "Daniel was without question the most important person in Anna's life. From the time I met her, everything that she was doing was for Daniel. From the day Daniel died, Anna honestly was never the same. I would say that physically she died last week, but in a lot of ways, emotionally she died when Daniel died."

Howard admitted the Bahamas burial was a recent desire. "Anna in a lot of ways always thought she was going to die young, and she said that she thought she was going to be like Marilyn Monroe. Initially, Anna had always wanted to be buried near Marilyn Monroe." (Remember that Anna once told us she believed she was Marilyn Monroe's illegitimate child. We pointed out that Anna was born five years after Marilyn's death.)

According to Howard, Anna had decided to live out her days in the Bahamas with baby Dannielynn and wanted to be near her dead son. She had even bought some plots in the same cemetery, purportedly for her, Howard, and Dannielynn, costing $3,600 each.

Chapter 39

Anna's last bodyguard, Moe Brighthaupt, whose wife was the nurse who found Anna unconscious, and who administered CPR before the medical team arrived, told King that he was present during the purchase of the burial plots, giving credence to Stern's position.

Stern said his relationship with Anna "became intimate, but not exclusive."

"She was my best friend, my lover, mother of my daughter. She was everything to me. Literally, everything, my whole world."

LAWYERS FOR Larry Birkhead had fought to delay the embalming process on Anna's body until an additional DNA sample was taken from her body. It went ahead after the embalmers had promised not to discuss, write about, photograph or draw the body, which was now ready for the funeral. TV entertainment shows and tabloid publications were reportedly offering hundreds of thousands of dollars to anyone who could get them exclusive video footage of Smith's body as it lay in cold storage.

According to Joshua Perper, the Broward County, Florida, medical examiner: "They did an excellent job, and the body will be ready for viewing with no problem. In other words, she's basically looking like she looked in life or very, very close to that." The only difference was, she was now at peace.

Now, however, the court was told by Dr Perper that despite the embalming, despite the refrigeration, Anna's body was decomposing at a faster rate than expected and if action wasn't taken quickly, she would not be fit for an open-casket viewing. Here Anna had spent her adult life showing off her body, and it might not be fit to be seen in death.

Things got testy later in the day when Howard's team wanted to introduce a video of Anna railing against Virgie on *Entertainment Tonight*. Virgie's attorney argued for its exclusion saying it had been edited. An attorney for Birkhead said they had tapes, as well, and wanted to know if they be would be allowed to introduce them.

Debra Opri, speaking for Birkhead, said, "It's got to be all or nothing, your honour."

The chilling tape was shown to a spellbound courtroom and it did nothing to strengthen Virgie's case. There was complete silence as Anna spoke from beyond the grave about the interview Virgie had given to CNN in which she accused Anna of responsibility for Daniel's death.

Clearly sedated and occasionally slurring her words, Anna said, "I want to say to her, how dare you, how dare you. First of all, she's not my mother. She's my birth mother. Second of all, she doesn't know me. She doesn't know my son. I left home when I was fifteen years old, and, I mean, she, she hasn't seen my son since he was probably about five years old. And she doesn't even know who he is … Who does she think she is? She's just out there making money for herself.

"I saw how evil she looked [on CNN]. So bring it on, Mom. Mommie Dearest. Bring it on."

Anna said her mother would never know Dannielynn. "Are you kidding me? She won't touch my child. She may touch me, but she won't touch my child."

According to Anna, Virgie looked the other way when a male relative abused her as a child and ignored her when she hit the big time.

In another interview after seeing photos of her mother kiss the ground at Daniel's gravesite, Anna went ballistic. "I can't believe she had the nerve to come up here on my son's twenty-first birthday and lay her fat self on my son's grave."

WEDNESDAY, FEBRUARY 21. Judge Seidlin, as he did every day, opened with a long-winded discourse about how everyone present was in mourning. "It's a grieving process. All of us are suffering and feeling the weight of it."

Now it was Virgie's turn to speak her mind and explain Anna's rage. She gave her address in Montgomery, Texas, and told the court she was a former police officer, who'd been on jail duty for three years and patrolled the streets of Hosuton for the rest of her twenty-eight-year-career.

The judge wanted to know how she and Anna got along when she was a little girl.

"We had a good relationship," Virgie replied. "We, we went and had our hair done together. We went and got our nails and our toes done." She also cared for Daniel while Anna was away working as an "exotic dancer".

Virgie had no doubt why her daughter went off the rails. "She's been on drugs for the last ten years" and "had no mind of her own when she was on drugs." Virgie informed the court her daughter's drug of choice was Valium. "She liked downers. She didn't like uppers."

Virgie made no attempt to hide her distrust and dislike for Stern. She blamed him for keeping her apart from her daughter. When we were around Virgie and Anna in the early Nineties, they did everything together and got along great.

At one stage Virgie broke down and left the witness stand in tears. The emotional scene came as she testified that she was not allowed to go to her grandson Daniel's funeral. Glaring at Stern across court, she said she later travelled to the Bahamas to visit Daniel's grave on his birthday, but no one would tell her which grave was his. "I came all the way from Houston, Texas," she said. "I brought his little baby shoes."

Some diaries purportedly kept by Anna from 1992 to 1994 popped up. *New York Post* columnist Cindy Adams wrote that they showed Anna "was sure close with Virgie Arthur in those days, and mama was not what you'd call one of the all-time best role models in captivity. We're talking heavy-duty partying together. Drinking together."

In the same column, Adams did little to disguise her distaste for Virgie, questioning how Anna's mother was paying for the Everest of legal fees. "Mama Virgie can't even spring for her own bar tabs, so how's she flying to Florida and staying over and the Bahamas and staying over and packing along $500-an-hour attorneys who eat three meals a day?" But at least Adams added that the "whole cast of characters fighting for [Anna's] bones and her kid and her money, none – without Anna – have a buck and a half to rub together."

It's easy to understand why a lot of people don't take to Virgie. She was a deputy sheriff for almost thirty yeas, and she comes across tough and hard. But you know what? Inside she's a nice lady. There's been a lot of questioning of why she wants the burial in Texas. We think she truly loved her daughter and grandson and is afraid for Dannielynn's safety if the child is left with Stern. Throw in a little guilt for not trying harder to be with Anna over the past decade.

Not that Howard made it easy for her as he ran interference between Anna and her family. An example of this was on the day Daniel died. Anna called her mother to let her know. By the time Virgie got the message and called back, Howard had changed the phone number. Maybe Howard was only trying to protect Anna from the flood of press calls. Who, except Howard, knows?

On the stand, Virgie broke down when she said that after Daniel died, she knew Anna was next.

Virgie: "My grandson did not overdose. Howard was there when he died, and Howard was there when my daughter died. And he has my granddaughter now, and it is not even his child. I'm afraid for her life as well. Please help us."

Judge Seidlin, who at times sounded as if he was trying out as replacement for Dr Phil, asked Virgie if she had any regrets. "I wasn't able to get her away from drugs," was the answer.

In another bizarre turn, Virgie and Stern went for an open-casket viewing of Anna's corpse at the Broward County medical examiner's office. Medical Examiner Perper described the scene being like a funeral home with flower arrangements.

The scene outside the office was not so tranquil as media helicopters buzzed overhead. Dannielynn's guardian complained that the media had been notified about the viewing, which would have been in violation of a confidentiality agreement. What's more, whoever did the leaking may have done it for money.

Back in the courtroom, the lawyers went into a questioning frenzy over money. Had anyone been paid for interviews? Howard said he had got a free ride on a chartered plane provided by *Entertainment Tonight*. For Virgie, it was a free flight courtesy of *Splash* magazine. Birkhead said he received money for photos he had taken of Anna and Daniel.

Virgie took the opportunity to attack Howard again.

"The one who's ever, ever made money off of my daughter is that man sitting right over there," she said. " I heard that (*Entertainment Tonight*) is buying her death funeral. That's why he wants her body. For a million bucks."

Howard had to admit that since 2002, his only income came from his association with Anna, that she even paid his $950-a-month rent and that she gave him spending money for shoes and such. So who was paying the legal fees now? His parents, Stern answered. It was "a substantial amount, because we're expecting a substantial fight here."

Judge Seidlin had been roundly criticiced for his handling of the case up until this point, but his questioning of Larry Birkhead went off the charts. Suddenly, it was sex, more sex, with a good dose of drugs.

Seidlin wanted to know when Birkhead's relationship with Anna went from professional to personal. Birkhead answered in July and August 2004.

Seidlin: "Was your head on the pillow seven nights a week?"

Birkhead: "With Anna Nicole?"

Judge: "Yes."

Birkhead: "Um, most nights."

According to Birkhead, he and Smith lived together from August 2004 to April 2005 – and in January 2005 Smith told him she was pregnant, but a month later suffered a miscarriage.

"She thought I blamed her for the miscarriage so we had a little tension," said Birkhead, who claimed that Stern was actually the cause of the awkwardness. Stern, who often slept on the sofa in Smith's Studio City home, according to Birkhead, created "interference internally in the home."

After the miscarriage Birkhead says he and Smith separated, but reunited again on New Year's Eve 2005. Around Valentine's Day 2006, "Anna Nicole informed me that we were expecting another child," said Birkhead, who at first wasn't sure the baby was his. "We were trying to figure out the time frames, and she smacked me and said, 'I'm not a whore, you dummy.'"

Together, Smith and Birkhead planned for the impending birth – and even discussed getting married, he said. "We picked out baby names for the child…She said she didn't want to be a single mother, she had done that once before and didn't want to do it again…She said, let's talk about marriage."

Asked if they were planning to wed, Birkhead said, "I was considering it but I didn't want to do it for the wrong reasons."

He told how he and Anna looked at wedding rings. "She asked me to pick out a wedding ring for her…she got on the Tiffanys.com website and asked me to pick out a ring for her and I told her that we might need to go a different website. So…"

The judge couldn't resist another opportunity for humour: "You wanted more towards Target or K-Mart, right?"

Birkhead drew a different picture of the relationship between Anna and her mother to that seen in the video shown earlier in court. "I will say this and, and let me clarify. She, her mother, she, Anna Nicole always told me that she and her mother did not get along for the most part, and they had their differences, but one of the first people when Anna Nicole told me she was pregnant that she cried out for was her mother."

He revealed that doctors had tried to wean Anna off drugs by putting her on a drip while she was pregnant. "She was taking medications before and during pregnancy," said Birkhead. At one stage, Anna was on a suicide watch.

Birkhead argued with Stern over the drugs. "She was taking medication before and during her pregnancy," Birkhead testified. "I was very concerned…We had a couple of clashes in the hospital because she and Mr Stern brought in a duffle bag."

Birkhead also explained how Anna kept a baby book. "She maintained a baby book in the hospital where she wrote my name and it is the daddy, and I put my thumbprint. And she put her thumbprint as the, the mom, and I felt sorry for Mr Stern because he had no role. So at that time, I asked her, I said, you know, 'Howard's over here. I feel kind of bad for him.'

"And she said, 'Come here, Howard.' And she said, 'You put your thumbprint here,' and she wrote 'Uncle Howard' in the baby book."

Anna spoke to Birkhead about her death, too.

Judge Seidlin: "Did she ever talk about where she wanted to be buried?"

Birkhead: "Yes, sir."

Judge Seidlin: "Where?"

Birkhead: "She said in the same cemetery where Marilyn Monroe died."

*T*HE GOOD judge wanted to know from Birkhead where Howard stood with Anna in the summer of 2004.

Birkhead explained that Howard was her attorney, manager, friend, and errand boy. "He was kind of multitasking."

Then Seidlin turned even more tabloid interrogator.

"Did you know whether they had an intimate relationship?" he asked.

Birkhead sure did, and the answer was no.

Then it was Howard's turn again. He said Anna was taking prescription drugs for depression, which she got from various doctors. He believed, however, that "her doctors knew about each other." Howard said that after Daniel's death, he talked to Anna about her drug usage. "And she did cut down a lot on medication that she took. Can anybody stop someone else?"

He also revealed the various aliases used by Anna Nicole: Vickie Marshall, Vickie Hogan, Vickie Smith. Then doctors prescribed things to her in different names even though they knew it was for her. One of those names was Michelle Chase. Another one was Susie Wang. At hotels, she went by Mrs Flintstone.

And as long as drugs were fair game, why not address who's the daddy of Dannielynn? Birkhead's lawyer, Debra Opri, saw a jurisdictional issue.

Speaking of Stern, Opri said, "He testified yesterday under oath that he was the natural father of Dannielynn under the laws of the Bahamas. Bahamas does not recognize the biological father and the laws in this state [Florida] list the natural father as the biological father. Mr Stern, you can laugh at me all you want. Are you or are you not the biological father of Dannielynn?"

Now what all this had to do with burying Anna Nicole is anybody's guess. One lawyer had the temerity to liken the proceedings to a circus, much to the ire of Judge Seidlin. "Don't use that term," he said. "It turns me off. There is no circus here, my friend."

Many court watchers disagreed. Jeffrey Toobin, CNN legal analyst, commented that "this might be the most ridiculous legal proceedings I have ever watched. This judge is one of the least competent judges I have ever seen. He is letting this thing meander all over creation, mostly because he seems to enjoy being on television."

Yes, the judge had allowed cameras in the courtroom.

Court TV anchor Lisa Bloom likened Seidlin to "a combination of Jackie Mason and my yoga instructor. He wants to talk about the journey and everybody putting their arms around each other and singing 'Kumbaya.'" What do you want from a guy who drove a taxi in New York City while attending Hunter College? And if the *Miami Herald* reported that he was deemed "unqualified" by twenty-four percent of lawyers in poll conducted by the Broward County Bar Association, didn't that mean that seventy-six percent thought more highly of him? So what if he talked with Virgie about doughnuts and cops? Or that he asked one of the attorneys from California, "Do you remember the song 'California Dreaming'?"

Whatever anyone thought of him, Seidlin made it clear his decision would come the next day.

Chapter 40

THURSDAY, FEBRUARY 23. The judge started the day with more lengthy observations. That surprised no-one, but he caught everyone unawares when he began sobbing in the court room as he delivered his ruling. If this was an audition for a TV show, he had surely passed.

To begin, he allowed in a video of an eight-month-pregnant Anna at a party, appearing high. He heard testimony from Ford Shelley, who while he clearly disliked Howard, had to admit that Anna had indicated she wanted to be buried next to Daniel.

Then, just when observers thought events could not get more bizarre, for some reason, Seidlin found it necessary to get Anna's first husband, Billy Smith, on the phone.

Seidlin: Billy. How do I know who you are?
Billy: I'm Billy Smith believe me
Seidlin: Are you wearing boots today?

It was too much for one of the lawyers.

Seidlin: And you object to the identity of the father?
Lawyer: I object to everything on every possible grounds under the sun. That he's not here.
Seidlin: I'm with ya. *Then he overruled the objection, before continuing to interrogate Billy Smith.*

Seidlin: Billy do you know if your boy is presently buried in the country of the Bahamas?

Billy: Yes I do. I wish that he was buried in the Texas.

Seidlin: So what should I do with his body? If I was a judge who had jurisdiction over this over that boy's body.

Billy: I just wish they could be buried side by side.

Seidlin: The mother and the son.

Billy: Yes. Yes.

Finally, the judge said he was ready to rule that very day. But before he did, he had more to say.

"I feel for all parties here. I mean I suffer with this case day and night. When I pronounce the final resolution in this case, I want you to understand that I have reviewed absolutely everything. I have suffered with this, I have struggled with this, I have shed tears for your, your little girl. [At this point, if you can believe, Seidlin began crying. Anna's mother couldn't resist joining in.] But what worries me, and I'm not letting the cat out of the bag, but what worries me is the boy. Danny already is in the grave. He's in the Bahamas; it could have been San Francisco It could have been the Bronx. I'm trying to figure out how in a spiritual sense to bring it all together. Now the Supreme Court of Florida says justice in not perfect [the tears continue] it's … huh … [the judge takes his time before continuing] it's what is reasonable."

$\mathscr{A}$ND WHEN Judge Larry returned with his decision at 4 p.m., what did he do? He, as one observer said, fudged it.

Seidlin: "There is only one issue before this court to decide: who is entitled to custody of the remains of Anna Nicole Smith. [Some felt it was about time he realised that.] There can be only one proper and equitable answer to that question: Dannielynn, Anna Nicole's only child and heir and next of kin. Therefore the court orders as follows: Richard Milstein, esquire, as the guardian for Dannielynn Hope Marshall Stern is awarded custody of the remains of Anna Nicole Smith."

After all those days in court, he'd handed Anna over to another lawyer to make the decision. It was, one critic observed cruelly, "the moment of indecision."

But not without voicing his own feelings on the matter: "You'll read it, but I want her buried. I want her buried with her son. I want to, there's no, there's no shouting. This is not a, this is not a happy moment. I want her buried with her son in the Bahamas. I want them to be together. Oh! You know, she had to live all her years under this kind of exposure. I just get a week-and-a-half of it, and it's ready to flatten me down. She's going to be with her son. She's going to have her son next to her."

Darn, if he didn't cry some more. And some more as he expressed hope for Dannielynn's future.

Dan Abrams, NBC's legal correspondent, could hardly believe what he was witnessing. "I believe those tears were real. But it was almost as if it was the end of a show. And the judge had just seen the final chapter. And he became so emotional that he had to talk about it. It's not normal. And that's not the way most judges behave. It's human but bizarrely human."

With a final outburst from the judge, it was all over.

"Submit to DNA and find out who the father is," said Seidlin, raising his voice, then shouting, "'It's enough baloney!"

Milstein called all parties into the judge's chambers. He felt that Anna should be buried in the Bahamas, to which the warring factions agreed. The next thing you knew, there was a photo call of one-time combatants arm in arm on the courthouse steps.

Stern, Birkhead and Smith's mother, Virgie Arthur, seemed to have taken the message to heart, for the moment at least. All three, along with their attorneys, emerged from the courthouse with arms linked.

That harmony lasted all of a day. Virgie filed an appeal citing Seidlin's courtroom conduct and that under Florida law, the next of kin is given disposition of the body. In the court filing, her lawyer, Roberta G. Mandel, said Seidlin's ruling was an inconvenience because the mother "will have to have a passport and round-trip airplane tickets and several thousand dollars to even visit or put flowers on (Smith's) grave."

Outside court, Mandel said Arthur was willing to take the fight to the state Supreme Court, if necessary. "This mother is a mother who deserves the right to bury her child," Mandel said. "The trial court treated her as though she was nothing."

The Fourth District Court of Appeals disagreed. It was, the court ruled, that Anna's "last ascertainable wish" was for burial in the plot next to Daniel's.

Roberta Mandel, a lawyer for Virgie, said before the circuit court's ruling that they were prepared to take the case to the Florida Supreme Court. Then Virgie threw in the towel. She would not take her battle for her daughter's body any further.

Wayne Munroe, for one, applauded the outcome. The lawyer for Anna's estate said, "Everyone in this whole saga knows what her wishes were about every aspect of her affairs – custody, property, everything. But people are steadfastly trying to get their wishes met and not hers. Nobody seems to care about this woman's wishes."

On a brighter note, it was there that Larry Birkhead finally was able to hold the baby he felt was his. "She looks like me," he said.

And then it was Virgie's turn. It was not revealed who allowed her the visit, but at last she was with her grandchild.

Chapter 41

THE COURT CASE over the fate of her remains was described as a circus. Anna Nicole Smith's funeral on March 2, attended by 100 mourners, was pure pink pantomime.

The pearl white Lincoln hearse came to a halt within sight of the Mount Horeb Baptist church where the service was to take place. It stood there for twenty minutes.

Larry Birkhead, wearing a bright pink tie (Anna's favourite colour), arrived to a ripple of cheers from the throng of sightseers gathered along the road. There were both cheers and boos when Howard K. Stern arrived.

Meanwhile, Richard C. Milstein, the legal guardian of Anna Nicole's baby daughter, was in the motorcade pleading with Virgie Arthur to come to the church and allow the funeral to proceed. Even at the last minute she was still plotting a Texas burial, by seeking an emergency court hearing.

Virgie finally agreed and arrived thirty minutes late, mouthing "thank you" to people in the crowd who cheered her. But she, too, did not escape a chorus of boos. Everyone seemed to have an opinion on who was the villain.

Anna's mahogany casket was carried into the single-storey white chapel by six pallbearers, including former bodyguard Maurice "Big Moe" Brighthaupt and her Los Angeles attorney, Ron Rale. It was draped in a pink blanket with rhinestones spelling out her name. The casket had been moved at dawn from the Fort Lauderdale medical examiner's office and driven in a motorcade to Miami where it was loaded on a private plane. Inside the casket, Anna Nicole was wearing a pink gown with a heart shaped bodice, rhinestone sequins and lace appliqué, designed by her old favourite Pol Atteu. On her head was a rhinestone tiara. As flamoyant in death as she was in life.

During the ninety-minute service Anna Nicole's friend, country singer Joe Nichols, sang "I'll Wait For You" and Dolly Parton's "Wings of a Dove." Stern, dressed in black and wearing a white ribbon on his lapel, spoke forcefully from the podium of the church. Singling out Smith's "so-called family members" but without naming names, he vowed to continue to protect and fight for Smith in death.

After the ceremony, Smith's pink-draped coffin with flowing pink ribbons was loaded back into a white hearse and driven to Lakeview Memorial Gardens and Mausoleum, where a twenty-minute grave-side service attended by about thirty intimates preceded her burial alongside her son Daniel.

Each mourner was given two roses – one red, one pink – to lay on the coffin. The pink rose was supposed to represent Anna Nicole, and the red rose was to represent Daniel. Each guest was also given a pink, heart-shaped piece of paper and asked to write a message of love to Anna Nicole. The messages were then dropped on her coffin and a small flock of doves was released. *Entertainment Tonight* said she was buried with an urn containing some of the ashes of her late second husband, J. Howard Marshall II.

Milstein issued a statement. "This she chose as her final resting place. During her lifetime, Anna Nicole Smith became a larger than life persona. Her stars shown in the highest of zeniths, her pictures flashed, and her face was seen throughout the world. She luxuriated in that press, in that media, in that publicity.

"Unfortunately, at a time when life should have been reaching its highest peak for her, she received both a blessing and a curse. She joyously gave birth to her only daughter, Dannielynn, and devastatingly, three days later, she lost her only son, Danny. If one were to write a Greek tragedy, one could not write a script as sorrowful and as hurtful as this. How horrific is it for a mother to have to bury a son under twenty-one years?